KT-447-971

SCULPTURE

THE ADVENTURE OF MODERN SCULPTURE
IN THE NINETEENTH AND TWENTIETH CENTURIES

by

Antoinette Le Normand-Romain
Anne Pingeot
Reinhold Hohl
Jean-Luc Daval
Barbara Rose

SKIRA

RIZZOLI
NEW YORK

CONTENTS

© 1986 by Editions d'Art Albert Skira S.A., Geneva

Reproduction rights reserved by A.D.A.G.P. and
S.P.A.D.E.M., Paris, and Cosmopress, Geneva

Published in the United States of America in 1986 by

RIZZOLI INTERNATIONAL PUBLICATIONS, INC.
597 Fifth Avenue/New York 10017

All rights reserved. No part of this book may be
reproduced in any manner whatsoever without permission of
Editions d'Art Albert Skira S.A.
89 Route de Chêne, 1208 Geneva, Switzerland

Printed in Switzerland

Library of Congress Cataloging-in-Publication Data

Sculpture. English.
   Sculpture: the adventure of modern sculpture in the
nineteenth and twentieth centuries.

   Translation of: La Sculpture.

   Includes index.
   1. Sculpture, Modern—19th century. 2. Sculpture,
Modern—20th century. I. Le Normand Romain, Antoinette.
II. Title.
NB197.S3413 1986   735'.23   86-42718
ISBN 0-8478-0751-7

SCULPTURE

Nineteenth and
Twentieth Centuries

François Rude (1784–1855):
The Marseillaise: The Departure of the
Volunteers in 1792, 1833–1836.
High relief, limestone, c. 42′ high.
Arc de Triomphe de l'Etoile, Paris.

INTRODUCTION

Standing in real space, sculpture defies time. Many moving examples of it have come down to us from the past—moving, because this art always focuses directly on the image and work of man, who carved and modelled even before he took to building and painting. For many periods of history, statuary constitutes the sole remaining testimony of man's awareness of himself and his world.

Yet, of all forms of artistic expression, sculpture remains even today the least understood, the least appreciated. Often set in a public space, often of considerable size and weight, it does not stir the imagination as the other arts do. Nor can it arise and expand with the ease, independence and spontaneity of painting, for it is closely connected with architecture and needs a social setting in order to reach its full, monumental dimension.

In this survey of two centuries of sculpture, it has seemed right and necessary to pay particular attention to the most significant moments in the evolution of an art whose purposes are inseparable from the mind and its forms. The choice of main works has fallen on monuments which do not keep to recognized schemes of composition and serve to illustrate the innovations made at every stage. For at each turning point of history, renewal and innovation depended on the conditions attaching to the commission, on the prevailing image of man, on his awareness of space and his grasp of technical resources.

What functions were assigned to sculpture by a civilization which, from the nineteenth century on, freed itself from theological and metaphysical constraints, an age which no longer conceived of time as a synonym of eternity but as an instrument for measuring space? It was France that now asserted itself as the universal reference. The French spirit of democracy worked out the new functions of sculpture. Moving out of churches—and of cemeteries—it now became closely connected with the evolution of the urban space, it adorned and designated the new public buildings, it invented the commemorative and pedagogical monument.

By 1900 it was increasingly internationalized. Moving away from the social space, it was practised on the scale of the studio, of the private collection, of the museum. The appearance of some great personalities had an impact which entirely renewed man's awareness of reality; and sculpture reached out into new, unexpected, metaphorical domains, even achieving that fetishistic power peculiar to our modern age.

After the Second World War, in the devastated cities of Europe, sculpture progressively regained its monumental role and moved again into the urban space. And not only in Europe. For American sculptors too embarked on a venture as inventive, manysided and decisive as that of contemporary painting.

The result is that, today, sculpture is no longer an object to look at: it has become a space to live in. At a time when art forms are more and more overstepping their limits, overlapping each other and inventing the place where reality is staged and enacted, deeper reflection is called for if we are to understand the current interaction, so necessary and fruitful, between the space we live in and the art of our time.

Antonio Canova (1757-1822):
Venus and Mars, 1816-1822.
Marble, 82½″ high.

1 TRADITION AND RUPTURE

NEOCLASSICISM

SCULPTURE UNDER LOUIS-PHILIPPE

Antoinette Le Normand-Romain

THE SECOND EMPIRE

AFFIRMATION OF THE REPUBLICAN IDEA

Anne Pingeot

Antonio Canova (1757-1822):

Letizia Ramolino Bonaparte, 1804.
Clay, 12″ high.

Letizia Ramolino Bonaparte, 1804.
Terracotta, 11½″ high.

Letizia Ramolino Bonaparte, 1804-1805.
Plaster, 26⅜″ high.

NEOCLASSICISM
THE MAKING OF A SCULPTURE

Antonio Canova (1757-1822):

△ Draped Woman Seated.
  Pencil, 46½" × 37".

◁ Letizia Ramolino Bonaparte, 1804-1807.
  Marble, 57" high, 57" long.

▽ Letizia Ramolino Bonaparte, 1804.
  Terracotta, 11¼" high.

From rough sketch to finished marble or bronze, a sculpture goes through many stages. At each step moulders and assistants aid the artist. Canova, like Rodin towards the end of the century, was obliged by the sheer volume of his commissions to surround himself with assistants who, working under the supervision of his friend Antonio d'Este, freed him from mechanical tasks. Visitors flocked to the sculptor's studio on the Via San Giacomo, helping to propagate his working methods. Most of the nineteenth century sculptors were to adapt these methods to their own requirements.

Canova, though he had started his career as a stonemason and liked to make adjustments in person on his works as they were being carved in marble, was primarily a modeller. His main creative activity was shaping clay models. These had to be cast into plaster immediately, for they could not be preserved for long. It was the plaster mould that was considered the original work. The sculptor retouched the plaster (many of Canova's plaster figures at Possagno reveal traces of his hand), and his assistants then copied it accurately in marble with the aid of a pointing compass.

The marble was almost always finished by the artist himself. Canova, who attached a great deal of importance to surfaces, insisted on personally rendering flesh, hair, and folds of drapery. He did not hesitate to make subtle alterations in modelling or drapery, or to accentuate contrasts, in order to achieve the lifelike effect he admired in Greek sculpture.

Canova spent most of his time, however, drawing and dashing off vibrant sketches–his "*invenzioni*," as he called them–which were spontaneous expressions of his creative energy. These works, which he preserved carefully, were at once transcriptions of impressions captured on the spot and rough studies of volumes and forms. The clay and terracotta sketches of *Letizia Ramolino Bonaparte*, executed in 1804 during the Roman sojourn of Napoleon's mother, thus differ in posture and costume from the finished sculpture, which bears a far greater resemblance to the third sketch. Losing some of the spontaneity and naturalness of the preliminary sketches in his efforts to rival the classics (*Letizia Ramolino Bonaparte* is clearly derived from the famous pseudo-*Agrippina* of the Capitoline Museum, though Canova himself has denied any such influence), the sculptor, bringing a clearer focus to his idea, then executed a small, meticulously worked-out plaster model. This was followed by the marble version successfully exhibited at the Salon of 1808 in Paris and was later presented by Napoleon's mother to her imperial son.

Marble replicas (one of them now at Compiègne) were then made at Carrara, where the marble industry was being revived by Napoleon's sister, Elisa. Old quarries were being reopened and models were being carved on the spot and shipped throughout Europe. The Princess of Lucca (the title given to her by her brother) was soon reaping the benefits of a thriving business–with a shop on the Boulevard des Italiens in Paris–copying portraits of the emperor and his family.

THE MAKING OF A SCULPTOR

David d'Angers offers a classic example of the training undergone by young sculptors in the nineteenth century, following a well-defined curriculum. After showing a natural aptitude for art at Angers, he left for Paris against his father's will, but with the blessing of his local drawing master, in order to attend the classes of the Ecole des Beaux-Arts, which in 1816 had replaced the old Acadé-mie. But the teaching of the School of Fine Arts, like that of the Academy before it, was purely theoretical (and so remained until the reform of 1863), varied by competitions. So David had to gain admittance to a private studio, that of Roland, where he could learn the actual practice of his art.

In 1810 he was awarded second prize in the Prix de Rome competition, which earned him a grant from the municipality of Angers and set him free from money worries. In February 1811, with his *Sorrow*, he won the prize for an expressive head and in the autumn he was awarded the Prix de Rome.

This prize opened the doors of the Académie de France in Rome, housed since 1803 in the Villa Medici, and there he spent the next four years. The status of the inmates was that of pupils, subject to the authority of a director who represented the Académie des Beaux-Arts in Paris, and they were expected to divide their time between study and the execution of *envois*, compulsory works which had to be sent to Paris, and which pressed heavily on them.

"You have to try and imagine," he wrote to Roland in 1812, "how bewildered a young man may be (who, like me, is rather inexperienced) in a city full of the works of so many masters, a city then, where so many different roads meet that might be followed up... I think that the constant study of the antique and of nature may produce a strong effect."

On his arrival David was dazzled by antiquity as he discovered it in Rome, and also in Naples, where like his fellow students he made long stays, continually drawing from the ancient paintings. It was now, by a flash of intuition, that he felt the "inconceivable naturalism" of Greek sculpture, which struck him again so forcibly when he went to London in 1816 to see the Parthenon marbles

Pierre-Jean David d'Angers
(1788-1856):

Sorrow, 1811.
Plaster, 21½" high.

The Death of Epaminondas, 1811.
Plaster bas-relief, 43¼" × 58¼".

brought back by Lord Elgin. He responded at once to the artistic circles in Rome, then dominated by Canova, who exerted a strong influence on the French artists, and by Thorvaldsen, from whom the French held more aloof, while recognizing his unrivalled talent for relief carving.

But David was well aware too of the importance of studying nature and proved it with his *Young Shepherd*. It

Pierre-Jean David d'Angers (1788-1856):

△ Nereid Bringing the Helmet of Achilles, 1815.
Plaster bas-relief, 42″ × 72″.

▷ Young Shepherd, 1816.
Marble, 59″ high.

▽ Condé, 1817.
Plaster, 7′11″ high.

stands in striking contrast with his *Nereid*, which reflects both the French influences, from Jean Goujon to Girodet, which had marked his schooling, and his admiration for Canova. What had attracted him first of all in the latter was "the art of divinizing form and making one worship it." The deliberate opposition between the Nereid's smooth body, all in unnatural curves and torsions, and her pleated drapery suggestive of gushing water, gave rise to a mannerism further emphasized by the linearity of the relief. Not so with the *Young Shepherd* which, as we know from a sketch, had been originally intended to include a slaughtered kid at its feet–which motivated the earnest expression of the face. This figure is very much in the antique manner, as called for by the prevailing rules, but it was conceived with a fresh simplicity and naturalness (the hand stroking the ear).

He returned to France for good in July 1816 and was at once commissioned to do the statue of *Condé* for the Pont de la Concorde. It had been ordered originally from his master Roland who, before his death, had just had time to do the sketch. Executed rapidly, the model was exhibited at the 1817 Salon. The spirited, heroic attitude aroused the keenest admiration, also and above all the adoption of modern dress which David, breaking with tradition, had rendered with precision, without detracting from the overall effect. The *Condé*, soon followed by his statue of *Bonchamps*, brought David d'Angers into the limelight, making him one of the foremost sculptors of the Restoration and justifying in advance the pointed remark of Gustave Planche, who wrote in 1832 that for any artist who failed to win the Prix de Rome "the ceilings of the Louvre [i.e. commissions from the State] and the gallery of the Luxembourg [i.e. purchase for the Luxembourg Museum] would always be forbidden fruit."

THEMES AND STYLES

Bertel Thorvaldsen (1770-1844):

△ Ganymede Kneeling Before the Eagle, 1817.
  Marble, 36¾″ high.

▽ Hebe, 1806.
  Marble, 61½″ high.

Thorvaldsen was fond of saying that he was born on the day he arrived in Rome, 8 March 1797: "Up until then I didn't exist..." After first spending some time studying antiquities, he executed a *Jason* of colossal size, in keeping with the heroic character of the subject, which was immediately admired for its noble, perfect forms and for the balance of its masses undisturbed by any expression of passion. This was succeeded by a long series of works. The subjects of many of them had already been treated by Canova. Yet they are simpler and more natural, and closer to the classics, than the Italian sculptor's statues. Towards the end of his first stay in Rome, Thorvaldsen sculpted a *Ganymede Kneeling Before the Eagle*, treating it with originality almost as a bas-relief. Ganymede's limbs and, in fact, all the details of the group are conceived in relation to a single point of view. They are organized (much as the details in ancient metopes or Maillol's *Desire*) in such a way that none detracts from the others. Collectively they fill the sculptural field–a purely imaginary one here–to perfection.

Some thirteen years older than Thorvaldsen, Canova had been working in Rome since 1780. Trained in the

◁ Antonio Canova (1757–1822):
Hebe, 1796–1817.
Marble, 65½″ high.

Bertel Thorvaldsen (1770–1844):
Jason with the Golden Fleece, 1802–1828.
Marble, 7′11″ high.

Baroque atmosphere of Venice, he had only subsequently evolved toward Neoclassicism under the influence of archaeologists and theoreticians. Yet the "antique Bernini," as he was called, had lost none of his early brilliant technique, lively imagination, feeling for movement, and fascination with voluptuous graceful forms. These qualities were forever drawing him away from the classical models he admired essentially for their ability to suggest the breath of life: "*Tutto qui spira vita... I nudi sono vera e bellissima carne.*"

Though Canova got his inspiration from ancient sculpture, he created a type of female beauty which, precisely because it was derived somewhat freely from classical sources, was more in key with contemporary aspirations. This new style of beauty, which appeared in the *Psyche*, *Hebe*, *Dancers*, and *Venus* series, was admired by Stendhal; Flaubert and the poet Ugo Foscolo were entranced with it: "I kissed the swooning woman extending her long marble arms towards Eros... kissed her under the armpit, and felt I was kissing Beauty itself."

Canova and Thorvaldsen are considered the two foremost representatives of Neoclassicism, yet they interpreted it in very different ways. The Danish sculptor's *Hebe* is motionless, filled with a calm rhythm, and seems closer to the Greeks. Canova's buoyant figure appears, on the contrary, to be advancing towards us with a light, dancing step; the drapery, leaving the torso bare, tucked back in little waves above the belt, and billowing out in the back, suggests the refinement and preciousness of Hellenistic art, as do the gilded details which ornament the figure.

Protected by Napoleon, very much in favour with the Bonaparte family, Canova enjoyed a reputation that was almost unparalleled until his death in 1822. His influence on French sculpture was considerable. Thorvaldsen, on the other hand, was never popular in France, despite the fact that during his second stay in Rome (1820–1838) his preeminence went unchallenged. (The fall of the Empire prevented him from finishing Napoleon's commission for the Temple de la Gloire.) He was and is admired mainly in Germany, Scandinavia, England, and America.

FROM BONAPARTE TO NAPOLEON

Jean-Antoine Houdon
(1741-1828):
Bust of Napoleon, 1806.
Terracotta, 20″ high.

Napoleon was well aware of the power of the effigy, both as memorial and propaganda weapon, and exploited it to the full in painting and sculpture. As a result the plastic art produced a profusion of medals, statuettes (Moutony's *Napoleon Sitting at Work*, c. 1808, etc.), busts and statues.

From Corbet's bust (1798) with long hair recalling Gros' *Bonaparte on the Arcola Bridge* (although the thoughtful gaze and set face already foretell an uncommon destiny) to the heavier, fleshy, but very imperial *Napoleon* shown by Bosio at the 1810 Salon, we detect a general desire to heroize the subject intended to satisfy the neoclassical ideal. After the emperor's death, Thorvaldsen, Pradier and Cugnot, who combined his portrait with an eagle, the symbol of imperial majesty, with varying degrees of success, produced extreme examples of this tendency.

But French sculptors were still concerned with creating a good likeness, which is why Chaudet's bust (1805), which was equally satisfying from both points of view, was chosen as the official effigy. And with the skill and psychological acumen which put him in the front rank of portraitists, Houdon executed a masterpiece in 1806, the *Bust of Napoleon*. An excellent likeness, the face with the piercing look is endowed with a superhuman and dominating calm which confers on it the fascinating power of a divinity. For his part, Canova had modelled a bust (1802) which, although hair and costume were treated very freely in the plaster versions at Rome and Possagno, still produced an image of the First Consul very close to reality. When executing the marble, on the other hand, he accentuated the "Caesarean" character of the bust, thus realizing a moral portrait showing "that striking mixture of youthful force and... that will which seems to translate itself instantly into an almost feminine seduction" (Fernow, 1805), so characteristic of the physiognomy of his model.

Antonio Canova (1757-1822):
Napoleon as Peace-Bringing Mars, 1803-1809.
Bronze, 10′8″ high.

During his stay in Paris, Canova had persuaded Bonaparte to let himself be portrayed as the *Peace-Bringing Mars*. In 1806, the colossal marble (now in London) was successfully presented in Rome, but when it reached Paris–not until 1811, because of transport difficulties–Napoleon did not dare to show the public the statue, which was destined for the hall of famous men in the Louvre. Because its heroic nudity was clearly unacceptable in France, this major work by his favourite sculptor was immediately hidden behind a palisade. Nevertheless, it was defended by the theorists of Neoclassicism, the painter David, Visconti and Quatremère de Quincy, the writer, who recalled that the Ancients used the nude as "a poetic metaphor to assimilate famous men to divine personages." But, he went on, "there are no metaphors without metamorphoses," specifying that because the nude was destined to display the glory of the model beyond the limits of time or space, it ought to be stylized, not realistic (like Pigalle's *Voltaire*).

Although Canova's *Napoleon* is not the only example of heroic nudity in France (Dejoux's *Desaix*, 1807, intended for the Place des Victoires and given a hostile reception by the public, and Dupaty's *Leclerc*, 1812, were also nude), the other statues of the Emperor were more traditional. Roland at the Institute (1810), Ramey in the Senate and Cartellier at the Ecole de Droit (1805-1813) clothed Napoleon in his coronation costume, content to emphasize his majesty. Chaudet again drew his inspiration from Antiquity for the Corps Législatif (1805) and the Colonne Vendôme and heroized his model–as Napoleon in fact wanted–but without trying to deify him as Canova had attempted.

△ Claude Ramey (1754-1838):
Napoleon I in his Coronation Costume, 1813.
Marble, 6′11″ high.

▷ Bertel Thorvaldsen (1770-1844):
Napoleon I.
Marble of 1929 cut from
Thorvaldsen's model of c. 1830.
Height 39½″.

NAPOLEON'S FAMILY

Joseph Chinard (1756-1813):
Bust of the Empress Josephine, 1805-1806.
Marble, 26½" high.

▷ Lorenzo Bartolini (1777-1850):
Elisa and her Daughter Napoléonne, c. 1813.
Marble, 5'11" high.

Like the Emperor, the members of the imperial family liked sculpted effigies and under the Empire there were few Salons where the bust or statue of one of them was not on show, including the effigy of the King of Rome "executed from nature, a few days after his birth," in 1812. Solidly implanted in France, the tradition of the portrait was brilliantly represented by ageing sculptors such as Houdon, Chinard and Delaistre, who were soon joined by a newcomer, Bosio. In 1808 Bosio modelled a bust of the Empress which, together with the busts of Hortense and later the Duchess of Berry, is one of the artist's best works because of the daintiness of the model, the elegance of the pose and the refinement of the coiffure. This gracious bust contrasts sharply with Chinard's which presents a portrait of Josephine which is both more solemn–she is wearing court dress–and more moving, because it is a very good likeness and not made to look younger as Bosio's was owing to the neoclassical demand for idealization.

In 1810 Bosio was commissioned to execute a bust of Marie-Louise and produced an uncompromising portrait of his model, who was far less seductive than Josephine and her daughter. Delaistre was not overflattering either, but he did play down the new Empress's protruding eyes, Habsburg lip and chin by emphasizing the youthful bloom of her twenty years.

Italian sculptors were also employed. Napoleon's mother, Elisa, Caroline, Pauline, Murat, they all called in Canova, who executed the celebrated statue of Pauline as *Venus Victorious* and there is little doubt that the princess, who was proud of her body, actually posed for it in the flesh. Indeed, the folds in the flesh and the modelling betray an individualized study from nature contradicting the neoclassical aesthetic by its "earthy flavour." But the Olympian face is closer to that of the *Venus Italica* in Florence than to contemporary portraits of Pauline.

However, Bartolini, brought to Carrara by Elisa, executed there the first of those statues of women and children for which he was to be so much appreciated. The charming effigy of Elisa's little daughter Napoléonne holding a big dog by the muzzle (1810-1812), followed by the double portrait of mother and daughter, revealed the qualities which brought him success, a naturalism in rendering figures allied to classicizing idealism (mainly ornamental: coiffures, clothing).

△ Antonio Canova (1757–1822):
Pauline Borghese Bonaparte
as Venus Victorious, 1804–1808.
Marble.

◁ François-Joseph Bosio (1768–1845):
Bust of Josephine, c. 1810.
Plaster, 28½″ high.

▷ François-Nicolas Delaistre (1746–1832):
Bust of the Empress Marie-Louise, 1813.
Terracotta.

THE STATUE AND ITS POLITICAL IMPLICATIONS

Pierre Cartellier (1757-1831):
Glory on a Quadriga Distributing Wreaths
and Riding over a Field Covered with Trophies, 1807.
Hard limestone relief, 12'9" × 26'6".
East front, Palais du Louvre, Paris.

"O vengeful monument! Indelible trophy!
Bronze which, whirling on your motionless base,
Seems to raise up to heaven your glory and your noth-
ingness;
And, of all that a colossal hand has made,
Only a triumphal ruin of the giant's edifice
Is left standing."

Victor Hugo, 1827.

"After my death," Napoleon confided to General de Caulaincourt on his return from the Russian campaign, "they can do what they want. If France attains the degree of glory I want for her, they can honour me with a statue if they wish. If I fail in my enterprises, it would be better if they were not exposed to universal criticism. I don't want the homage of flattery, nor a statue exposed to public ridicule, as the effigy of Louis XIV was."

Although hostile in principle to the idea of appearing publicly as a conquering hero, Napoleon did want to stamp the imprint of his glory and that of his army on Paris and the towns he conquered (*Fountain of Victory*, Place du Châtelet; *Arches of Triumph* in Milan and in the Place du Carrousel and the Place de l'Etoile, Paris; *Columns of the Grande Armée* in Paris and Boulogne; *Temple of Glory*, present-day church of the Madeleine...).

Allegory is frequently given the responsibility for carrying the message. This happened to Cartellier's relief in the Louvre, whose unrealistic composition was criticized. But it was also the period when the narrative relief and the frieze developed. Bas-reliefs representing the principal victories and events of the reign were envisaged for the arches and in the same way that the great pictures of the *Coronation* and the *Distribution of the Eagles* were commissioned from David for Versailles, Spalla was called on to execute four reliefs, the *Coronation*, *Marengo*, *Jena* and *Austerlitz* for the great gallery of the Turin palace.

However, the most important realization in this field is the column first known as the *Austerlitz Column*, then the *Column of the Grande Armée* (after Napoleon had married an Austrian Archduchess) and today as the *Colonne Vendôme*. Indeed it was the day after Austerlitz when Vivant Denon managed to persuade Bonaparte to use the bronze from captured enemy cannon to erect a column to the glory of his army, modelled on *Trajan's Column*, on the site of the statue of Louis XIV demolished in 1792.

Seeking "an artist who would write to his dictation, so to speak," Denon commissioned the painter Bergeret to design the whole frieze. As a result, the 920-foot long frieze, divided into seventy-six sections executed by some thirty sculptors, became a homogeneous work and the

Antoine-Denis Chaudet (1763-1810): Colossal statue of Napoleon, 1810. Bronze, destroyed.

Emile Seurre (1798-1858): Napoleon as the "Little Corporal," 1833. Bronze. Hôtel des Invalides, Paris.

Augustin Dumont (1801-1884): Napoleon as a Roman Emperor, 1863. Bronze, 12'3" high. Photograph of 1875.

Giacomo Spalla (1775-1834):
Austerlitz, 1807-1810. Marble bas-relief, 57″ × 47″.

column (apart from the statue of Napoleon commissioned from Chaudet) a communal and anonymous creation which was to survive throughout the century for better or for worse; whereas the statue, which was too obviously associated with a political regime, had to undergo countless vicissitudes. Pulled down shortly after the entry of the Allies into Paris in 1814, it was used to cast Lemot's *Henry IV* and the top of the column stayed empty until 1833, when a new statue by Seurre depicting Napoleon as the "little corporal" was erected there. In 1863 it was replaced by Dumont's *Napoleon*, an approximate replica of Chaudet's work, conforming more closely to the Napoleonic myth in the form in which Napoleon III sought to propagate it.

Crystallizing the claims and hates of the Commune, the whole Vendôme column was overthrown in 1871, but restored in 1875. Then Paris rediscovered this "great mast all made of bronze, sculpted with Victories [with] Napoleon for lookout" (Balzac, *La Fille aux yeux d'or*), which was gradually to infiltrate into the imperial legend while the Arc de Triomphe was to take its own place as the symbol of military glory.

◁ The Colonne Vendôme, Place Vendôme, Paris, inaugurated on 15 August 1810. Height 144′.

Dumont's Napoleon thrown down during the Commune, 16 May 1871.

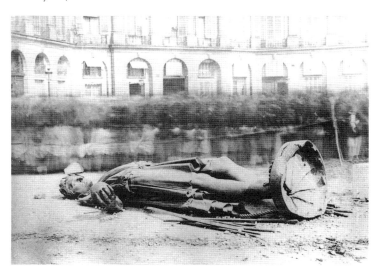

KINGS RESTORED BY KINGS

Pierre Cartellier (1757-1831):
Louis XIV on Horseback, 1814-1816.
Stone.
Doorway pediment, Hôtel des Invalides, Paris.

François-Frédéric Lemot (1772-1827):
Henri IV, 1816.
Bronze.
Pont-Neuf, Paris.

◁ Nicolas-Bernard Raggi (1790-1862):
Henri IV, 1819-1843.
Marble.
Place Royale, Pau (Basses-Pyrénées).

Pregnant with meaning, the statues of the monarchs which stood in the centre of Royal Squares in the seventeenth and eighteenth centuries appeared as the symbol of their power. The Revolution was quick to pull them down, thus demonstrating that royal authority had passed into the hands of those who had so long been subject to it. Yet, in the same way that he dated the beginning of his reign from the death of Louis XVI (1793), one of Louis XVIII's first acts was to order their replacement.

On 25 August 1818, the day of St Louis, a reconstruction of the popular effigy of Henri IV was erected on the Pont-Neuf. It was cast from the debris of the *Napoleons* on the Colonne Vendôme and the Column at Boulogne, and of Dejoux's *Desaix*. Victor Hugo, royalist poet at the time, hastened to celebrate this restoration:

"... The aspect of this august image

Will make our woes seem less, our happiness sweeter..."

Meanwhile Dupaty was commissioned to restore the *Louis XIII* in the Place des Vosges, Bosio was allotted the *Louis XIV* in the Place des Victoires (which he transformed into an equestrian statue by assimilating it to Girardon's statue, whose place in the Place Vendôme had been taken by the Column of the Grande Armée), and Cartellier the *Louis XIV* on the Invalides pediment and the *Louis XV* in the Place de la Concorde. Whereas the *Louis XIII*, executed in marble, evinces a faultless Neoclassicism, Bosio,

François-Joseph Bosio
(1768-1845):
Louis XIV, 1816-1822.
Bronze.
Place des Victoires, Paris.

like Cartellier in the maquette for *Louis XV*, tried to give more animation to the rearing horses. Nevertheless, in the case of Bosio, we should see if anything a reference to the antique *Dioscuri* rather than to Coustou's horses. Far from envisaging an accurate portrait of the Sun King, the only concession he made to the eighteenth century was the wig and a comparatively historical accuracy in the reliefs.

Completed before 1830, the *Louis XIII* and *Louis XIV* were erected as foreseen. The *Louis XV*, on the contrary, had varied experiences which must be recalled because they are significant of governmental recognition of the power of sculpture. In 1826 when Charles X decided to erect a statue of Louis XVI in the Place de la Concorde, where he had been guillotined, the *Louis XV* was destined for the Rond-Point des Champs-Elysées, but the project was abandoned in 1830 and the horse (the only feature cast) transported to Versailles, while a new rider, a Louis XIV this time, was commissioned from Petitot.

Provincial towns followed the example of Paris. The Salon of 1819 showed a *Henri IV* intended for Nérac, a modified replica of which was erected at Pau in 1843. Although the one commissioned from Raggi for Rennes was never completed, *Louis XIV*'s were replaced at Caen, Lyons and Montpellier. *Louis XV* was restored to his place at Reims on the pedestal spared by the Revolution.

The majority of royal statues recorded in the nineteenth century were equestrian statues. Nevertheless, even if their erection in France was the result of a specific political situation, we note too that their multiplication corresponds to a phenomenon which is referable to famous antique models and which also affected other countries (*Charles III* and *Ferdinand I* of Bourbon, 1807-1819 and 1820-1822, by Canova at Naples; *Emmanuel Philibert of Savoy*, 1836-1838, by Marochetti at Turin; *Maximilian I of Bavaria*, 1831-1839, by Thorvaldsen at Munich...) before experiencing a widespread development in the second half of the century.

NEOCLASSICAL VIOLENCE

To confute his reputation as a specialist in feminine grace, Canova frequently gave free rein to his impetuous temperament and represented massacres or battle scenes. An extraordinary example of the "heroic manner," the wax sketches for *Hercules Piercing his Children with Arrows* (c. 1799) equal the strength and beauty of the antique *Niobids*. The same violence recurs in the colossal groups of *Hercules and Lycas* (1795-1815), the *Pugilists* in the Vatican (1795-1806) and *Theseus and the Centaur*, commissioned in 1804 by Prince Eugène for a Milan square, finished in 1819 and offered to the Empress of Austria on the occasion of her fourth marriage.

A magnificent example of movement, inscribed in an almost perfect triangle, this group, executed after detailed studies of horses (a meticulousness uncommon with the Neoclassicists), whereas the head of the centaur is obviously inspired by *Laocoon*, became famous immediately. Thorvaldsen undertook to handle the same subject but soon gave it up, because by temperament he preferred to depict serene peaceful figures. Bosio, on the other hand, was the author of a *Hercules Fighting Acheloüs*. This was a virtual caricature of Canova's *Theseus* and was severely criticized, especially by David d'Angers: "He looks as if he was turning cartwheels. One does not fight one's enemy in profile... All the limbs seem to be made of wood."

Such groups did indeed proliferate around 1820. They all share a triangular composition conceived from a single point of view so that the forms stand out clearly, emphasizing a virile nude violently involved in a combat or heroic action. They all have their origin in the Roman environment. Although Dupaty's *Cadmus* was executed in France, it was the direct result of a stay of nearly ten years in Rome which made a profound impression on the artist. The *Nisus and Euryalus* by Roman and *Theseus Fighting the Minotaur* by Ramey were ambitious farewells to Rome which, incidentally were to guarantee their authors success. As for Schadow, a pupil of Thorvaldsen, and Alvarez, of Spanish origin, it was in Rome that the former produced *Achilles and Penthesilea* (1822) and the latter *Antilochus Protecting his Father Nestor*.

The violence that deforms–later a favourite theme of the Romantics–was rejected in principle by the Neoclassicists. However, although we must see at the origin of these groups a result of Canova's training in a Baroque environment, the neoclassical imprint marked them so strongly that Alvarez had to proceed by way of a subject drawn from the Homeric repertory to evoke a contemporary event, the defence of Saragossa! While attesting Canova's predominant position in Rome and the admiration aroused by what is indeed one of his masterpieces, these sculptors were visibly influenced, especially the later ones, by the celebrated Hellenistic groups, *The Dying Galatian and his Wife* in Rome and *Menelaus and Patroclus* in Florence.

Louis Dupaty (1771-1825):
Cadmus Fighting the Serpent
at the Spring of Dirce, 1819-1822.
Marble.
Jardin des Plantes, Orléans.

José Alvarez Cubero (1768-1827):
Antilochus Protecting his Father Nestor
or The Defence of Saragossa, 1823.
Marble.

Jean-Baptiste Roman (1792-1835):
Nisus and Euryalus, 1822-1827.
Marble, 65¾″ high.

Antonio Canova (1757–1822):
Theseus and the Centaur, 1805–1819.
Marble, 11′2″ high.

Charles Lebœuf-Nanteuil,
known as Nanteuil (1792–1865):
The Virgin and Child with
Adoring Angels.
Commissioned in 1830.
Stone, 9'10" × 39'4".
Pediment of the Church of
Notre-Dame-de-Lorette, Paris.

Charles Marochetti (1805–1867):
Mary Magdalen Exalted by Angels, 1841.
Marble, 14'9" high.
Church of the Madeleine, Paris.

SCULPTURE UNDER LOUIS-PHILIPPE
THE BIG COMMISSIONS

History Recording the Life of St Genevieve.
Dome of the Salon des Evêques executed under the Restoration.
Pantheon, Paris.

The July Monarchy initiated the period of large-scale sculpture commissions. In the religious sphere, however, it merely completed the work begun by the Restoration, which undertook the building of new Paris churches such as Notre-Dame-de-Lorette and Saint-Vincent-de-Paul, or returned previously secular buildings to religious uses. Thus the educational establishment of Mont Valérien was returned to the Abbé de Forbin-Janson and the Fathers of the Faith, who, unsuccessful in obtaining state aid, had to be satisfied with transforming the central part of the edifice built in 1812 into a chapel. The religious function of the Pantheon was confirmed and while Gros completed the fresco depicting the *Apotheosis of St Genevieve*, the bishops' salon was given an elegant dome culminating in a figure of *History* retracing the life of the saint.

Although Neo-Gothic was to predominate in the following period, all these churches with a porch sheltered by a portico, which were imitations of antique temples and Early Christian basilicas, required sculpted pediments. For Mont Valérien, the city of Paris commissioned Cortot to execute a *Resurrection of Christ* curiously composed on the basis of obliques running counter to the sloping elements. Nanteuil successively executed the pretty pediment of Notre-Dame-de-Lorette on which he sought to create an impression of depth and the pediment of Saint-Vincent-de-Paul (1846), composed more classically on a single plane. For the Madeleine, however, the artists took part in a competition which they all thought would be won by "the inevitable Pradier." It was actually won by Lemaire, whose *Last Judgment* contained references to Canova, Thorvaldsen and Antiquity, but which evinced a new interest, with a romantic tinge, when depicting the virtues and vices.

The Abbé de Forbin-Janson used features from the Musée des Monuments Français to decorate his chapel. On the other hand, Notre-Dame-de-Lorette, Saint-Vincent-de-Paul and the Madeleine provide excellent examples of religious decoration between 1830 and 1840. They combine mural painting, which they helped to restore to a place of honour, and sculpture which, while still contained in an architectural framework that it makes no attempt to hide, is used for holy-water vessels, pulpits, stalls, choir screens, and other features.

Even if painting has the primacy at Notre-Dame-de-Lorette and Saint-Vincent-de-Paul, although the altar of the latter is surmounted by a *Calvary* by Rude with Burgundian undertones, the Madeleine, with its forty-four sculptors, was one of the most important sculpture workshops of the 1830s. Thirty-four statues adorn the external peristyle, while in the interior altars surmounted by groups or statues replace the cenotaphs of the royal family originally envisaged by Louis XVIII and lead one's gaze towards the high altar crowned by a somewhat theatrical group: Mary Magdalen carried up to heaven by two angels whose wings frame the large curvilinear composition. However, Triqueti created one of the masterpieces of nineteenth-century religious sculpture for the door. While preserving the spirit of his model, the doors of the Baptistery in Florence, served by a remarkable feeling for relief, he interpreted the Ten Commandments by bringing out the curse which weighs on the guilty transgressors with a thoroughly romantic feeling.

Antonin Moine (1796-1849):
History and Fame, 1839-1844.
Marble.
Assemblée Nationale, Paris.

In the secular field, the stability ushered in by the July Monarchy finally made it possible to end the transformations that mirrored the fluctuations of politics. The Arc du Carrousel was given back the Empire reliefs which were previously due to be replaced by images of the Duke of Angoulême's Spanish campaign. As for the Pantheon, handed back for religious purposes in 1806, it was taken away from the church once again. The inscription of 1791 *To the Great Men from a Grateful Fatherland* was re-established on the façade and a new pediment was commissioned from David d'Angers, because the 1791 pediment executed by Moitte and dismantled on Charles X's orders was beyond restoration.

The new programmes were conceived to serve the policies of Louis-Philippe. They affirmed his desire for national reconciliation, but also showed him, the first constitutional monarch, as the defender of liberty. A sumptuous crypt was installed in the Invalides for Napoleon, whose ashes had been recovered from the English, but when it came to replacing a statue on top of the Colonne Vendôme, the conditions of the competition clearly stated that Napoleon was to be depicted as the "little corporal" and not as Emperor.

James Pradier (1790-1852):
Public Education, 1837-1839.
North front of the Assemblée Nationale, Paris.

Pierre-Jean David d'Angers (1788-1856):
"To the Great Men from a Grateful Fatherland," 1830-1837.
Stone, 19½' × 101'.
Pediment of the Pantheon, Paris.

James Pradier (1790-1852):
The City of Strasbourg, 1836-1838.
Plaster, 47" high.

Indeed, Louis-Philippe made skilful use of the hours of glory and did away with the bloodiest memories. The Arc de l'Etoile finally acquired its sculpted decoration exalting the Armies of the Revolution and the Empire. In the Place de la Concorde, on the other hand, which was still disfigured by the presence of the guillotine, the commission given to Cortot for a monument to Louis XVI in which the king was to appear holding the martyr's palm was cancelled and replaced by a safe programme. Two fountains framed the obelisk presented by the Viceroy of Egypt, while statues of *Towns*, including *Lille* and *Strasbourg*, by Pradier were placed on the pavilions built by Gabriel in the eighteenth century. They were appreciated immediately for their plasticity, elegance, the nonconformist look of coiffures (in coils on the ears) and the drapery, closer to a deshabillé than a classical tunic, and their attitude. Hand on hip, head proudly erect, Strasbourg seems to proclaim the spirit of revenge which was to animate France after the loss of Alsace-Lorraine to the point of becoming its symbol after 1871!

This message of reconciliation was duplicated by the promise of a development which would enable the new regime to establish liberty and public order. The decoration of the Palais Bourbon, while incorporating some older features (chimney piece by Moine, two of whose figures, *History* and *Fame*, successively framed the busts of the Duke of Berry, Louis-Philippe, Napoleon III and the Republic), forms one of the most important artistic ensembles in both painting and sculpture. This decoration first proclaims itself on the façade and is repeated in the meeting room in the decorative programme elaborated by Guizot and approved by Louis-Philippe from 1830 onwards. The large figures of *Liberty* and *Public Order* (Pradier, 1832) flank a relief by Roman depicting *France Distributing Crowns to the Arts and Industry*. Outside, the same ideas are developed on Cortot's pediment, *France between Liberty and Public Order Summoning up the Genii of Commerce, Agriculture, Peace, War and Eloquence* (1837-1841), and in the reliefs on the side walls, *Prometheus Awaking the Arts* by Rude (1835) and *Public Education* by Pradier (1839).

HONOURING PROMINENT MEN AND WOMEN

"What King Louis-Philippe did at Versailles," remarked Victor Hugo in *Choses vues*, "is good. His completion of this work... was like giving the magnificent binding we call Versailles to the magnificent book we call the history of France" (18 October 1837).

Decided on in 1833, inaugurated on 10 June 1837 and continually enriched throughout the century, the museum installed in the Palace of Versailles was dedicated "To all the glories of France." And although it originated at the express wish of Louis-Philippe, it was also the result of a general climate of feeling in which the interest in history which appeared at the end of the Ancien Régime with the commissions given by d'Angiviller, as from 1775, for historical pictures and statues of great men was combined with the conviction that objects placed on view played a vital role in keeping memories alive. On the pediment of the Pantheon and in the reliefs on the Gutenberg monu-

main courtyard. Meanwhile Guizot, Thiers, Michelet, Mignet, Augustin Thierry, etc., multiplied historical works, in addition to the publication of a quantity of *Memoirs*. These publications found their illustrations at Versailles in the historical pictures (the Galerie des Batailles has the most celebrated group), but also in countless portraits, because everyone who had any claim to fame was represented there. These portraits were both painted and carved. The sculptures, apart from old works collected at Versailles, were obtained either by casting (faithfulness to the original was unnecessary–the recumbent figures of Saint-Denis were presented standing!) or commissions. Commissions were given on the first floor of the north wing for the series of statues of monarchs, as well as personalities who played an important role in the history of France: Suger, Blanche de Castille, Joan of Arc and of course the regent, Philippe of Orléans.

Louis-Philippe commissioned a series comparable to that of Versailles for the Luxembourg Gardens, in memory of Marie de Médicis for whom the palace had been built or in homage to Madame de Genlis to whom he owed his education (but still in line with a more general

Augustin Dumont (1801-1884):
Francis I, 1837-1839.
Marble, 6′10″ high.
Château de Versailles.

Antoine Etex (1808-1888):
Blanche de Castille, 1837.
Marble, 5′2½″ high.
Château de Versailles.

Jehan Duseigneur (1806-1866):
Dagobert, 1836-1839.
Marble, 6′7½″ high.
Château de Versailles.

ment, David d'Angers evoked the famous men who were chosen by portraits, sometimes accompanied by inscriptions, but no longer by the indirect method of allegories.

Convinced that the study of past events made possible the understanding and orientation of future events, the nineteenth century was the century of history *par excellence*. In 1816, anxious to assert the continuity of the monarchy, Louis XVIII commissioned twelve statues of great men for the Concorde bridge in Paris. They included ministers such as *Suger* and generals such as *Condé*, and the latter commission was finally given to David d'Angers. Because of their excessive size, these statues were transported to Versailles from 1836 onwards and erected in the

trend, because the Queen's staircase in the Christiansburg Palace in Denmark was decorated with statues of famous Danish figures at the same time). Most of them are the queens of France, executed with a moving concern for historical accuracy, notably in the coiffures, clothing and sometimes, but more rarely, in attitudes suggesting character. There were, however, other famous women, including Joan of Arc by Rude straining to hear her voices and Clémence Isaure, the beautiful languid poetess, by Préault. This liking for historical series was to extend into the second half of the century. It also included contemporary figures and turned the façades and corridors of great institutions into veritable portrait galleries.

Auguste Préault (1809–1879):
Clémence Isaure, 1848.
Marble, 8′ high.
Jardin du Luxembourg, Paris.

FEMALE STATUARY

Georges Jacquot (1794-1874):
Paris and Helen, 1819.
Plaster bas-relief, 38″ × 49″.

(1817) and *The Nymph Salmacis* (1819-1824), and ill concealed by the title and the ankle bracelet, a modest concession to exoticism.

Pradier, in whom Gautier and Flaubert saw "the last of the Greeks," also took advantage of the orientalism then in fashion, but his *Odalisque* is mainly remarkable for the novelty and modernity of the pose, far from the affectedness of *Light Verse* (1846) or *Chloris Posing*, but close to *Women Bathing* and *Odalisques* by Ingres. In fact, Pradier here frees himself completely from the Antique, of which incidentally he always made a very personal use oriented towards an exaltation of female beauty in which he was served by a technical skill which makes his marbles incomparable.

In the 1845 Salon, Baudelaire preferred the *Young Indian Woman* to Bartolini's *Nymph with Scorpion* which, like the *Young Greek Girl* by David d'Angers, resumes the schema of the classical *Woman Playing at Knucklebones*, but testifies, like it too, to a closer study of the living model, to be noted also in Pradier's case. Had not the realism of the *Young Greek Girl* been criticized because "the soles of her feet are disgracefully furrowed like those of a shepherdess who goes barefoot"? David had sought in vain among his "al-

Neoclassical or Romantic? It is not always easy to make this distinction under the July Monarchy. A wind of modernity taking the form of a renewal of sources of inspiration penetrated the stricter Neoclassicism of the first quarter of the century. Of the latter, Jacquot's *Paris and Helen* (1819) provides an excellent example.

Bosio remained faithful to the Canovan aesthetic until its disappearance. In the Salon of 1845, the year of his death, he showed the *Young Indian Woman*, a "very pretty thing" according to Baudelaire, although he criticized it for lack of originality. Indeed in this figure, whose charm and natural quality made it one of the artist's most famous works, we recapture the smooth modelling, the penchant for youthful nudes and the reference to the Antique (here *The Thorn Remover*) already exhibited by his *Hyacinth*

Pierre-Jean David d'Angers
(1788-1856):
Young Greek Girl on the
Tomb of Marco Botzaris,
c. 1825.
Plaster, 31½″ high, 46½″ long.

James Pradier (1790-1852):
Seated Odalisque, 1841.
Marble, 41¼″ high.

legorical souvenirs," all of which seemed too emphatic to
him, for the idea of this figure intended for the tomb of
Botzaris, one of the heroes of Greek independence. He
found it when he saw "a little girl in a cemetery, kneeling
on a grave and spelling out with her finger the inscription
engraved on it." In contrast to Canova and the partisans of
a selected idealized nature, he sought to create stronger,
more moving works by basing himself on the observation
of nature. Bartolini, eleven years his senior, pursued a similar goal. After developing towards a pronounced naturalism, he finished a career that began very young with a
most charming work, *Innocence*, which we must compare
with Pradier's mythological figures to appreciate its apparent simplicity to the full.

François-Joseph Bosio (1768-1845):
Young Indian Woman Wrapping a Shell-Fringed
Band round her Leg, 1845.
Marble, 27½″ high, 42½″ long.

33

ROMANTICISM

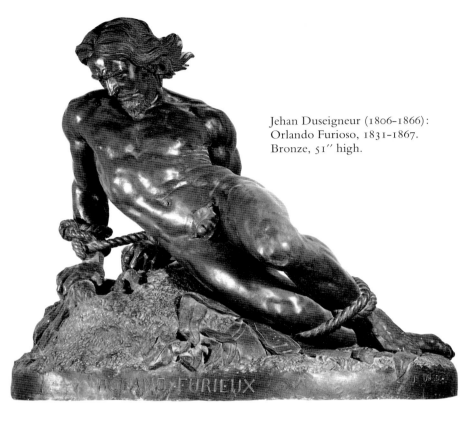

Jehan Duseigneur (1806-1866):
Orlando Furioso, 1831-1867.
Bronze, 51″ high.

Although Romanticism made its appearance in painting from 1820 onwards, there was a gap of ten years before it was expressed in sculpture at the Salon of 1831 by Duseigneur's *Orlando Furioso*, with its bulging muscles and twisted limbs (the figure described by Thoré as "a preface to *Cromwell* in sculpture"), and the *Tiger and Crocodile* by Barye. These works were soon followed by Etex's *Cain*, executed at Rome, as a bravado gesture because he did not win the Grand Prix, and by the creations of Préault. Pride of place in the latter should be given to *The Slaughter*, an unrealistic juxtaposition of screaming masks with gaping mouths, streaming or bristling hair and clenched hands, all depicted with unrivalled violence. Conceived as an "episodical fragment," it reminds us today of the technique of "assemblages." All these works, which are characterized by "a way of feeling" (Baudelaire), an "agitation of the soul" (Thoré), expressed by an inner dramatic tension, often called "savage," a search for movement, with expressiveness sometimes carried to extremes and not shrinking from any kind of deformation. "Shout louder," Rude said to his wife who posed for the *Spirit of the Motherland*, the "raging Megaera" as she was called! But Barye and Rude based themselves on a faithful and accurate analysis of nature. "Nature, then! Nature and truth," clamoured Victor Hugo in the preface to *Cromwell* (1827). Like Delacroix, Barye made a scientific study of the living and dead animals in the Jardin des Plantes. He was trying to work out an illusionist way of rendering skin and fur. He needed this for "the living matter" of the *Lion and Snake*, which could only be properly reproduced in bronze, the favourite material of Romantic sculptors, because it is more faithful to the modelling than marble, which nearly always entails a certain simplification and thus is more suitable for neoclassical abstraction.

Of all the works submitted by Préault to the 1834 Salon, only *The Slaughter* was accepted, as an example to frighten the young. Indeed, as from 1834, the Salon jury, a product of the Académie des Beaux-Arts, that bastion of classical tradition, became more and more conservative. To such an extent that from 1840 to 1848, when it was suppressed, only to be re-established the following year in a different form, the jury often rejected more sculptures than it accepted. Yet exhibition at the Salon was vital to nineteenth-century artists. It was the place where reputations were made and commissions obtained. And above all it was the place where the sculptor came into contact with the press (whose influence was growing) and with the buyer (the State or the private collector), who would enable him to translate the work shown in plaster for economy's sake into marble or bronze.

Faced with this situation, the artists reacted in different ways. Moitte committed suicide; Barye, commissioned by Louis-Philippe to cast the *Lion and Snake* after it was shown at the 1833 Salon, survived thanks to the bronze production of small models made possible by the mechanical reduction process perfected by Collas and Sauvage (1839-1844). It was not until the Second Empire that Romantic sculptors won official recognition. The State only acquired *The Slaughter* in 1859. It did not commission the casting of *Orlando Furioso* until 1867, while *Ophelia*, Préault's masterpiece, executed in plaster in 1842-1843, had to wait until 1876, although it had been shown at the Salon of 1850-1851. But when we take a look at these belated rehabilitations, we can only imagine how many works must have disappeared!

Antoine Etex (1808-1888):
Cain and his Children Accursed of God, 1832.
Plaster, 80½″ high.
Chapel of the Salpêtrière Hospital, Paris.

Auguste Préault (1809-1879):
The Slaughter, 1834-1850.
Bronze bas-relief, 43″ × 55″.

Antoine-Louis Barye (1796-1875):
Lion and Snake, 1832-1835.
Bronze, 53″ high, 70″ long.

LITERARY INSPIRATION

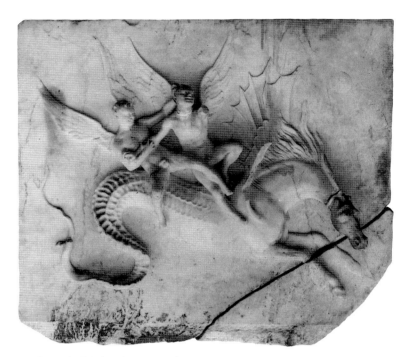

Antonin Moine (1796-1849):
The Goblins, 1831-1835.
Marble, damaged in 1940.

To differentiate themselves from Neoclassicism, Romantic artists sought new sources of inspiration in the literature and world of fantasy peculiar to each country. One of the first signs of this was Freund's *Loki*, executed at Rome, but drawing on the Scandinavian legends which this artist in particular made wide use of. In France, while Moine exploited dreams and the supernatural with the *Goblins*, which were akin to Victor Hugo's *Djinns*, Milton's *Paradise Lost* and Goethe's *Faust* helped to populate the Romantic Salons with demons and rebel angels, those accursed beings with whom several artists were happy to identify themselves. The most famous was undoubtedly Feuchère's *Satan* engrossed in thought, partly concealed by a large pair of enveloping wings. It paved the way for Carpeaux's *Ugolino* and Rodin's *Thinker*, thus attesting the persistence of the Romantic mood throughout the century.

Following the painters, Romantic sculptors drew on such sources as Dante, Shakespeare, Tasso and Ariosto, as well as contemporary novelists, which enabled them to transcend the boundaries of time and space, as is suggested by the fantastic career of the hippogryph which carries off Angelica and Roger, the heroes of *Orlando Furioso* by Ariosto. With *Atala* and *Les Martyrs*, Chateaubriand made

Ernst Freund (1786-1840):
Loki, 1822.
Bronze, 12¼″ high.

Antoine-Louis Barye (1796-1875):
Roger and Angelica, c. 1840.
Bronze, length 27¼″.

Auguste Préault (1809-1879):
Ophelia, 1842-1876.
Bronze bas-relief, 29½″ × 78¾″.

Francisque-Joseph Duret (1804-1865):
Chactas Meditating on Atala's Tomb, 1835.
Bronze, 53″ high.

Red Indians the fashion (*Chactas*, as pensive as Feuchère's *Satan*) and also the Druids (*Velléda*). With *Notre-Dame de Paris*, Victor Hugo made his own contribution to the fashionable cult of the Middle Ages.

That cult was primarily fostered by Dante's *Divina Commedia*. Following Delacroix, Préault depicted Dante and Virgil in Hell, a vision of Hell foretelling Rodin's. Around the two poets floats a tangle of bodies, nervously sketched on a base of columbines and small wax balls, among which it is possible to make out the shades of Paolo and Francesca caught up in the infernal whirlwind, as were later Rodin's couple known by the title *Fugit Amor*. Nevertheless, sculptors in the Romantic period preferred to make use of the medieval background in which the two lovers lived to realize picturesque groups. It was only in the second half of the century by a shift in romantic inspiration that they adopted their fatal destiny, as well as the torture of Ugolino.

"I am not for the finite, I am for the infinite," was how Préault inscribed his medallion of Delacroix. Instead of limiting himself to a historical evocation of the personages he represents, he allows himself to be carried away by a frenzied lyricism, the equivalent of which can only be found in poetry.

Préault's *Ophelia* with the body in disarray, the moving tortured face, floating in water which cannot be distinguished from her hair and the robes enveloping her, following a principle of equation which is already symbolist, is like a premonition of Rimbaud's lines:

"The wind kisses her breasts and shakes
Her long veils lying softly on the stream;
The shivering willows weep upon her cheeks;
Across her dreaming brows the rushes lean."

THE PICTURESQUE TREND

At the Salon of 1833, Rude's *Neapolitan Fisherman* playing with a turtle which he guides by a rush tied round its neck and Duret's *Neapolitan Fisherman Dancing the Tarantella* were exhibited side by side. They created a sensation by the freedom of their charming youthful attitudes and the picturesqueness of their costume. The Romantics congratulated their creators for their ability to rise against the "frozen dreams of the ideal."

They were certainly not the first sculptors to represent adolescents, but they rejected allegory, which Chaudet, Dumont and Bonnassieux used as a pretext to justify *Love with a Butterfly* (1802), *Love tormenting the Soul* (1827) and *Love clipping its Wings* (1841).

Winner of the Prix de Rome in 1823, Duret spent four years in Italy, during which time he stayed in Naples to draw antique works of art on several occasions. But he was also attracted by Neapolitan gaiety and animation, and once back in France he tried to reproduce them in his *Fisherman*, although its attitude was actually inspired by the famous classical *Dancing Faun*. Rude, however, had not yet made the obligatory journey to Italy and his *Fisherboy* was primarily a study of a young boy showing remarkable anatomical accuracy and naturalness, allied to the freshness and innocence of his expression.

Destined to have a great success, as evidenced by the large number of editions, the *Fisherman* initiated in sculpture the picturesque trend which was already firmly established in painting and literature. They were to be followed by a long line of adolescents (Duret himself was to supplement his *Fisherman* with the *Wine-Harvester* of 1849) which Carpeaux added to in homage to his two masters (he had been successively the pupil of Rude and Duret). Executed as an *envoi* from Rome–something Duret had not dared to do–his *Fisherboy Listening to a Seashell* combines the anatomical knowledge of Rude's *Fisherboy*, whose expression and smile are not very different, with the animation of Duret's version.

Francisque-Joseph Duret (1804-1865):
Neapolitan Fisherman Dancing the Tarantella,
1833. Bronze, 62¼″ high.

◁ Jean-Baptiste Carpeaux
(1827-1875):
Fisherboy Listening to a
Seashell, 1858.
Original plaster, 36″ high.

▷ François Rude (1784-1855):
Neapolitan Fisherboy Playing
with a Turtle, 1831-1833.
Marble, 30¼″ high.

PORTRAITURE

Napoleon and his family chose the Italian Canova as their favourite portraitist. Nevertheless, the art of the portrait was still very much alive in France. Its qualities of realism and life brought to a peak by Houdon did not leave Bosio or Bartolini indifferent. They recur in the animated physiognomy of the little *Elfride Clarke de Feltre* while the masterful handling of the marble recalls the influence of Canova on Ruxthiel.

Chaudet and Chinard were also to combine an "antiquizing" style and careful study of the model. A past master in the art of female portraiture, Chinard was distinguished by sensitive personal talent and an especially decorative elegance exhibited in the details of dresses, jewels, coiffures and in the skilful transition from bust to plinth. In the bust of Jeanne de l'Orme de l'Isle it is ensured by the

◁ Pierre-Jean David d'Angers (1788-1856):
Chateaubriand, 1830.
Plaster, 23½" high.

Joseph Chinard (1756-1813):
Jeanne de l'Orme de l'Isle, 1802.
Terracotta, 26" high.

Henri-Joseph Ruxthiel
(1775-1837):
Elfride Clarke de Feltre.
Bronze, 15¾" high.

Pierre-Jean David d'Angers (1788-1856):
Mademoiselle Mars, 1825.
Marble, 23¼" high.

Pierre-Jean David d'Angers (1788-1856):
François Arago, 1832.
Bronze medallion.

symmetrical and almost abstract fall of the dress held under the breast by an elaborately wrought marble plaque imitating goldwork.

The Romantic period saw a considerable development of the portrait. David d'Angers, who executed more than six hundred busts and medallions, was undoubtedly the artist with the biggest output. Around 1830 he made a series of colossal busts (the colossal is the natural dimension of sublimeness and genius as Victor Hugo said, referring to Michelangelo) in which he was mainly concerned with the moral character of his models, the great romantic figures, such as Chateaubriand, Lamartine, Goethe and Victor Hugo. The exaggeration of the forehead and the cranium in accordance with the theories of Gall and Lavater, the arrangement of the hair which nobly frames the face of Chateaubriand or radiates around Goethe's as if it were electrified, the contrasts created by accentuating the eye sockets and the wrinkles make these portraits symbols of the creative power of genius. David took care to use the moments when Chateaubriand was dictating to his secretary for his sittings. "In that way," he said, "the inner man is disclosed to me. The physical is illuminated by the moral."

He was not attracted to female models and although he makes a concession to the femininity of Mlle Mars by giving her an elegant coiffure, crowned with a wreath of everlasting flowers, he cuts off the bust like a herm (a harsh treatment usually reserved for men) to concentrate on the animated physiognomy with mouth open as if the actress was on the stage.

Carle Elschoecht (1797-1856):
Father and Son, 1846.
Bronze medallion.

Jean-Auguste Barre (1811-1896):
Maria Taglioni in *La Sylphide*, 1837.
Bronze, 17¾″ high.

Jean-Pierre Dantan (Dantan the Younger, 1800-1869):
Paganini, 1832.
Bronze, 12½″ high.

A very large part of David's production consisted of medallions. Sharing the taste for galleries of great men which originated the historical museum at Versailles in the same period, he modelled the effigies of his contemporaries over a lengthy period and in order to finish them he had no hesitation in leaving his position in Paris and undertaking a tour of Europe. There, too, he was mainly concerned with the character of his models, most of whom he showed in profile, a position enabling him to reproduce physical and moral characteristics more easily. "The face looks at you. The profile is in a relationship with other beings; it is going to escape you, it doesn't even see you. The face shows you several features and is more difficult to analyse. The profile is unity."

Meeting the public's growing interest in contemporary personalities, which was encouraged by the dealer-publishers of whom Susse was the most famous, medallions, as well as statuettes and caricatures, experienced from 1830 to 1840 an expansion which can only be compared with the progress of lithography. All the romantic sculptors executed medallions, a form of portrait that was quicker, less burdensome and cheaper than the bust. Many of them embarked on the portrait statuette connected with the contemporary world of politics and the theatre, unless it concerned the intimate effigy of the artist's wife and children. Distributed in series, it had a great success owing to its small-scale format which fitted easily into bourgeois apartments, but also to the fame of the model depicted

Honoré Daumier (1808-1879):
Ratapoil, c. 1850 (cast of 1891).
Bronze, 15″ high.

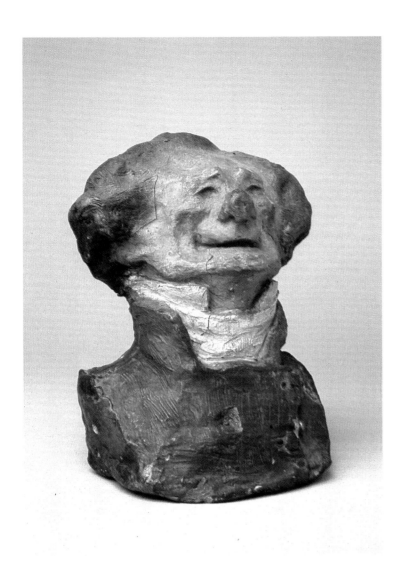

Honoré Daumier (1808-1879):
Charles Philipon or Toothless Man Laughing, 1832-1833.
Painted clay, 6⅛" high.

Honoré Daumier (1808-1879):
Guizot or the Bore.
Painted clay, 8¾" high.

with great accuracy of attitude and costume, whether it was Queen Marie Amélie, Rachel in the role of Hermione or Maria Taglioni in *La Sylphide* incarnating the ballet in its most aerial aspect, thanks to the recently invented technique of point work.

With the younger Dantan, the statuette shifts towards the burden, born of the excessive use of phrenology and physiognomy (Carle Vernet as a horse), of the accumulation of accessories. Forming the Musée Dantan or Dantanorama, this collection of caricatures which includes literary, political, artistic and scientific figures constitutes the satirical counterpart to David's medallions.

Daumier's sculptures evince the same liking for caricature, but he used it as a political weapon. The plaster of *Ratapoil*, "a synthesis of the shady agent, of the indefatigable auxiliary of Napoleonic propaganda," was hidden throughout the Second Empire and only reappeared in

1878. But, like the busts of the *Parliamentarians* commissioned in 1832 by Charles Philipon, the director of *La Caricature*, and executed during actual sittings of the Chambre des Députés if we are to believe contemporary evidence, it immediately served as point of departure for caricatures which appeared in the satirical journals of the period.

These busts mark a total break with the tradition of the neoclassical portrait. Helped by acute powers of observation and a remarkably expressive talent as draughtsman and modeller, Daumier tried to reveal the deep truth of his models through an uncompromising image enhanced by exaggeration and polychromy. Thus he opened the way to every kind of daring advance and whereas Dantan was gradually forgotten, his importance then began to grow as witnessed by the success of bronze editions of his sculpted work in the twentieth century.

PUBLIC MONUMENT OR FUNERARY MONUMENT?

GRACE AUX PRISONNIERS!

THOUARS   TORFOU   S·FLORENT

BONCHAMPS
MORT LE XVIII OCT. M.D.CC.LXXXXIII.

Pierre-Jean David d'Angers
(1788–1856):

◁ General Bonchamps,
1819–1825.
Marble, statue 51″ high.
Church of Saint-Florent-
le-Vieil in Anjou.

▽ Gutenberg, 1840.
Bronze, 10′10″ high.
Place Gutenberg, Strasbourg.

The monarchy was no sooner restored than the followers of General Bonchamps, heroes of the Vendean war, got
together and opened a subscription for a monument to the
memory of their leader. It was their wish that the monument should be put up on the esplanade in front of the
church of Saint-Florent-le-Vieil, where the republican
soldiers had been imprisoned for whose pardon the
General had pleaded as he died. King Louis XVIII, however, was afraid of provoking discontent among op-
ponents of the monarchy and the jealousy of supporters of
other Vendean leaders. He therefore stipulated that the
monument should be designed to stress the magnanimity
of Bonchamps—the base to be engraved with the words
Pardon the prisoners—and let it be understood that the monument should be placed inside the church rather than in a
public square.

Funerary monument or public monument? The question had arisen first at the beginning of the century when
Napoleon, to honour the memory of Desaix, killed at
Marengo, commissioned Moitte to make a funerary
monument for the chapel of the Grand-Saint-Bernard
hospice and Dejoux a public monument for the Place des
Victoires in Paris; but it did not become a live issue until
after 1830, or even 1840. It reappeared, for example in the
case of Cardinal de Cheverus, with the twin project for a
monument at Mayenne (1844) and a tomb at Bordeaux
(1850), and culminated at the end of the century in the case
of Alexandre Dumas junior with the almost simultaneous
orders from the same artist, Saint-Marceaux, for a tomb in

Montmartre cemetery (1897) and a public monument in the Place Malesherbes (1906).

Cemeteries, although enclosed, were semi-public places, and the demonstrations that had accompanied some funerals (for example that of General Foy in 1825, which rallied the liberal opposition) made governments defer as long as possible the erection of monuments liable to have similar repercussions. For example, the unveiling of the Cavaignac monument, completed in 1847, was only authorized in 1856, and then in strict privacy.

During the first half of the century, public monuments were chiefly reserved for famous historical figures (*Joan of Arc* at Orléans, 1803; *Racine* at La Ferté-Milon, 1819-1833; *Ambroise Paré* at Laval, 1840; *Monge* at Beaune, 1846-1849) and a few contemporaries noted for their scientific work (*Cuvier* at Montbéliard, 1835) or their virtues (*Cardinal de Cheverus* at Mayenne, 1844). These monuments were in reality the final product of the Enlightenment notion that sculpture could personify history and morality in the image of the individual "hero." David was profoundly convinced of this social and educational value of public sculpture and did his utmost to promote the erection of monuments to commemorate remarkable men. A typical example was the monument to Gutenberg. In 1839 a national subscription was opened for this in Strasbourg where the first sheet had been printed from movable type. The Gutenberg monument took what was almost a stock form, a statue in period dress representing a kindly humanist with a long beard and slender hands accompanied by reliefs illustrating his merits. In this case, the reliefs were designed to indicate the spread of culture and progress in the four continents as a result of the invention of printing. Evoking the pediment of the Pantheon, they grouped round a printing press writers, men of learning and statesmen from Europe, Asia, Africa and America.

Although monuments were usually financed by public subscription, the role of private initiative should not be overlooked. Captain Noisot, for example, who had commanded the grenadiers at Elba, commissioned Rude to make the famous monument *Napoleon Awaking to Immortality*. Placed on the isolated summit of a steep hill, it was unveiled in 1847 before several thousand veterans, in whom it stirred nostalgic memories of the imperial epic and roused the desire for change that was to lead to the 1848 revolution. Far more symbolic than historical, it was in marked contrast with contemporary monuments like Napoleon's tomb in the Invalides or the monument to King René at Angers (1846), comprising the statue of the king and twelve figures recalling the history of Anjou, which the Comte de Quatrebarbes commissioned from David with the proceeds obtained from the sale of the *Complete Works of King René*.

François Rude (1784-1855):
Napoleon Awaking to Immortality, 1845-1847.
Bronze, length 10′8″.
Parc Noisot, Fixin, near Dijon.

CEMETERIES BECOME MUSEUMS

The Père-Lachaise Cemetery in Paris, opened in 1804, was soon covered with monuments and these, together with the beauty of the site and the many plants and shrubs surrounding the tombs, made it during the romantic period a popular resort on half-days and holidays.

Under the Ancien Régime, people sought to ensure their salvation by endowing foundations; in the nineteenth century, their successors were anxious above all that their memory should not die, oblivion being in their eyes ultimate death. The decree law of 1804, followed by the creation of the big cemeteries outside the city walls, was an expression of this new materialistic form of respect for the dead and guaranteed the success of the sale of burial plots in perpetuity and monuments designed to preserve—and extol—the memory of the deceased.

In keeping with this trend, images depicting *Death*—apart from an exceptional example in the Bordeaux cemetery—were seldom placed in cemeteries. On the other hand, the representation of *Grief*, an indirect way of paying tribute to the dead, is a favourite theme very much in evidence in funerary sculpture, expressed sometimes in

Anonymous:
Death with a Scythe, tomb of Catherineau, c. 1874.
Chartreuse Cemetery, Bordeaux.

François Milhomme (1758-1823):
Grief, tomb of Pierre Gareau, c. 1816.
Marble, 53″ high.
Père-Lachaise Cemetery, Paris.

allegorical, sometimes in narrative form. As early as 1816 Milhomme created a fine figure expressing the sorrow of the widow and six children of Pierre Gareau, killed in an accident, and in the Salon Debay exhibited a low relief made for the tomb of Caroline Ternaux, showing the young woman in an antique setting, lying on her bed surrounded by her family.

The Milhomme figure begot many more of the same kind, but the scenes of affliction came to an end with the years 1820-1825. They were replaced either by recumbent effigies, after 1840, or by reliefs modifying the theme so as to bring out the idea of separation. In most of these, the survivor communes at the grave of the departed. In the Père-Lachaise Cemetery a fine example of this style, inspired by antique models and made fashionable by Houdon and Canova, is the tomb of the Comte de Bourcke; the inscription, taken from one of St Paul's Epistles, affirms

Jean-Joseph Debay (1779-1863):
Tomb Monument of Caroline-Blanche Ternaux, 1819.
Marble bas-relief, 39¼″ × 78¾″.
Crypt of Notre-Dame d'Auteuil, Paris.

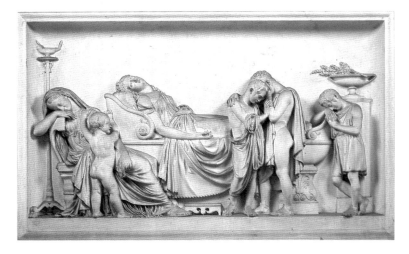

△ Antoine Etex (1808-1888):
Tomb of the Raspail Family, 1854.
Marble.
Père-Lachaise Cemetery, Paris.

Christian faith in the resurrection, *Expectantes beatam spem*, but in a widely disseminated engraving this was amended to read *Expecta me*, stressing the relations of the spouses. The contrary scene, the departure of the deceased, is more rare. It required the fertile imagination of Etex to conceive for the tomb of Madame Raspail, who died while her husband was a political prisoner at Doullens, a monumental figure wholly covered by a shroud, with arm outstretched towards a barred window and the legend: "Farewell, 8 March 1853, 12.30 p.m. Doullens."

The separation of the Bourcke husband and wife does not seem final, and for the Raspail monument Etex chose the narrative form. Préault alone succeeded in symbolizing the impassable frontier separating the world of the living from that of the dead. His monument *The Silence of Death* was described by Michelet as a "truly terrible work

△ Pierre-Jean David d'Angers (1788-1856):
Tomb of the Comte de Bourcke, 1826.
Marble.
Père-Lachaise Cemetery, Paris.

▷ Auguste Préault (1809-1879):
The Silence of Death, tomb
of Jacob Robles, 1849.
Marble.
Père-Lachaise Cemetery, Paris.

47

Antoine Laurent Dantan (1798–1878):
Tomb of Admiral Dumont d'Urville, after 1842.
Montparnasse Cemetery, Paris.

Pierre Cartellier (1757–1831):
Baron Vivant Denon, 1826.
Bronze, 61″ high.
Père-Lachaise Cemetery, Paris.

Auguste Bartholdi (1834–1904):
Tomb of the National Guardsmen
Voulminot and Wagner killed in 1870, 1872.
Stone and bronze.
Municipal Cemetery, Colmar.

creating an almost unbearable impression, as though it had been carved with the great chisel of death."

In most funerary monuments, however, the idea of death was rejected, and the defunct was recalled as he had been when he lived. The portrait became one of the most abiding elements of the work. One of the first life-size statues put up in a cemetery was the one made by Cartellier for Vivant Denon. Denon is portrayed in such a natural attitude, so supple and lifelike that he might seem almost to have been a visitor sketching a picturesque corner of the cemetery. Other portraits of this kind, frequent after 1850,

were the statue of Josephine in the church at Rueil–the Empress is kneeling, not in prayer but, as in the picture of the coronation, to receive the crown–and that of Armand Carrel at Saint-Mandé, drawing himself up to accuse his fellow peers in the Upper House of having "assassinated" Marshal Ney. Formerly, when it was intended to recall a typical attitude of a deceased person, or an episode in his life, this was done in a low relief: a sculptor was shown in his studio, a surgeon at the operating table, Count Lavalette disguised in his wife's clothes to escape from the Bastille. More succinctly, Dantan the elder–who always corresponded with his brother in riddles–surrounded the column on the tomb of Dumont d'Urville with outlines of the ships on which the admiral had made his voyages round the world, and of the *Venus of Milo* he brought back with him to France. This *strip cartoon* ends with a last relief in which the admiral, his wife and son, rise in a kind of apotheosis above a railway engine in flames, recalling their end in the railway accident at Versailles in 1842.

Allusion could hardly be more discreet. When the deceased had perished in tragic circumstances, these were evoked by funerary sculpture and a number of very powerful works, nearly always in narrative vein, were inspired by such events. David led the way with his statue of General Bonchamps; dispensing with the allegorical figures that traditionally accompanied the dying, he concentrated on gesture and expression. For General Gobert he composed an animated lifesize group showing the general falling from his horse, struck down by a guerrilla. The 1848 and 1851 risings, the wars of the Second Empire and above all the events of 1870-1871 provided ample

material for this kind of sculpture in which the high-minded aspirations of the defunct were emphasized, often by means of an inscription. For example, the words on the tomb of Kamienski (whose statue echoes the one of Bonchamps): "*I die calm, Polish and Christian. Magenta, 4 June 1859. Kamienski, foreign legion. Farewell to dreams, illusions, vanity!!! (his last words).*" This trend culminated in a hyper-realistic style with works whose impact forced the attention of the passer-by. Saint-Marceaux represented the Abbé Miroy lying face to the ground as he had fallen before the Prussian firing squad. On the other hand, Bartholdi chose a more indirect presentation for two National Guardsmen killed at Colmar in 1870. The former work highlighted the cruelty of the invader and the absurdity of such a death; the second created a symbol of the spirit of revenge that prevailed in France up till 1914.

For a century, funerary sculpture was inspired by praise of the deceased or the defence of a cause. Cemeteries were the "archives of mankind," as David d'Angers aptly put it. Nevertheless, the doubt and anguish of the symbolist generation were already germinating in the refusal to justify the death of the Abbé Miroy and preparing to undermine the prevailing style. In 1907 Saint-Marceaux would no longer create a figure of *Grief* for the family tomb at Reims, but a statue entitled *On the Road of Life* representing a "poor naked, blind woman, feeling her way forward, stumbling, her outstretched arms emerging from a shroud like a scarf of lead, weighing down her shoulders."

René de Saint-Marceaux (1845-1915):

◁ Tomb of Abbé Miroy, 1872.
Bronze.
North Cemetery, Reims.

▽ On the Road of Life, 1907.
Tomb of the Paul de Saint-Marceaux family.
Marble.
North Cemetery, Reims.

The Pavillon Richelieu, Nouveau Louvre, Paris.
Photograph of 1857 by Edouard Denis Baldus.

▷ Jean-Baptiste Carpeaux (1827-1875):
Imperial France Protecting Agriculture and the Sciences, 1863-1866.
Plaster model for the top of the pediment facing the Seine,
Pavillon de Flore, Louvre, Paris. Height 8½′.

SCULPTURE MINISTERING TO ARCHITECTURE

Pierre-Jules Cavelier (1814-1894):
Plaster model for the top of the pediment,
garden front, Pavillon de Flore, Louvre, Paris, 1864.

Elected on the strength of his name to a four-year term as president of the Republic in December 1848, Louis Napoleon Bonaparte seized power at the end of his mandate with the *coup d'état* of 2 December 1851. The Industrial Revolution, which had made a timid appearance under the First Empire and the two Restorations and had picked up under the July Monarchy, flourished under the favourable conditions of the new regime. Or perhaps Louis Bonaparte's authoritarian, highly centralized rule was itself the outcome of that industrial upsurge. In any event, a government programme of large-scale public works was a strong stimulant to the economy.

The most notable project during the first decade of Napoleon III's reign was the construction of connecting wings between the Tuileries and the Louvre. This ensemble of pavilions and galleries was completed in the short span of five years. The decorative motifs were "borrowed religiously from the Old Louvre," wrote the architect, Visconti, whose design was adopted in 1852. His successor, Hector Lefuel, a man of great energy and competence, modified the decoration at the regime's request. He added an attic and concealed it behind a balustrade ornamented with allegorical groups of children, as at Versailles. Eighty-six statues of famous men, originally destined to be placed under the arches along the ground floor, were instead set along the terrace balustrade, like Bernini's figures over St Peter's Square at the Vatican. The sculpted pediments; the paired caryatids reminiscent of the ones Sarazin designed in the seventeenth century; Barye's famous allegorical groups (*War* and *Peace* on the Pavillon Richelieu, *Order* and *Might* on the Pavillon Denon); the imperial coat of arms on the outspread court mantle sculpted by Gruyère; the circular openings with braid motifs like those Jean Goujon designed on the inner court: all this, executed by a team of 335 sculptors, was a stunning demonstration of the comprehensive genius of eclecticism.

It was decided to repeat this architectural tour de force when reconstructing the riverside gallery, badly in need of repair, without undue concern for preserving the original design by Henry IV's architect, Androuet Du Cerceau. The need for an apartment for the Prince Imperial in the Pavillon de Flore, and for a new Salle des Etats and visitors' apartments in the Grande Galerie, were added incentives for indulging the French predilection for symmetry. The sculptural motifs crowning the new Pavillon de Flore were executed by two Prix de Rome artists, forty-nine year old Cavelier and thirty-six year old Carpeaux. They represent the apogee of an architectural conception wherein sculpture plays a leading role. The pediments no longer contain the reliefs; the allegories, which are sculpted in the round, break out of the architectural frame and rest on top of it.

A SETTING FOR THE FESTIVITIES OF THE NEW SOCIETY

Charles Garnier (1825-1898):
The Paris Opera House, main front, 1860-1875.

Jacques-Léonard Maillet (1823-1895)
and a team of sculptors working on the attic decoration,
main front, Paris Opera House, c. 1869.

The reign's second great project marked the triumph of a new architect. A competition for a design for the Paris Opera was opened in 1860. Contrary to everyone's expectation, the winner was not Viollet-le-Duc but Charles Garnier. Garnier, who had been awarded the Prix de Rome in 1848 and had executed in his fourth year at the Beaux Arts a *Polychrome Restoration of the Panhellenic Temple of Jupiter on the Island of Aegina* (1852), chose to enhance Haussmann's grey, rectilinear centre of Paris with a vast, coloured, sound-filled jewel. The team of sculptors who had decorated the Louvre were put to work sculpting, once again, on an architectural scale. Winged allegorical figures (Millet's *Apollo*, Gumery's *Harmony and Poetry*, Lequesne's *Fame Restraining Pegasus*) gave buoyancy to the coping. The attic was lavishly ornamented—and somewhat too delicately, in the architect's opinion—by Maillet. Reliefs were crammed into the segmental pediments. Busts of composers were enshrined in the circular openings above the great windows. The piers at the base of the structure were embellished with enormous high reliefs by Guillaume, Jouffroy, Perraud and Carpeaux. The latter, a childhood friend of Garnier's, wrote in a burst of enthusiasm on receiving the commission, to his friend Dutouquet, on 25 December 1863: "I am filled with supreme joy, for I have just been chosen by Garnier to illustrate one of the most beautiful features of the Opera. I have been asked to design one of the great bas-reliefs of the façade, in the spirit of the Arc de Triomphe."

Here was a fine example of creativity, one that can readily be held up as a counter-example to the modernist dogma of the clean slate: the student's admiration for his master causes one masterpiece to be bred from another. The fruitfulness of such relationships was notable throughout the nineteenth century.

Jean-Baptiste Carpeaux (1827-1875): The Dance, 1865-1869. Stone group, 13′9″ high.

◁ Aimé Millet (1819-1891): Apollo between the Dance and Music, 1868-1869. Plaster model, 24½′ high.

GIVING AN OFFICIAL VENEER...

Upper front of the Gare du Nord, Paris, 1863–1869:
Above, Paris and Foreign Capitals by Jouffroy, Cavelier and Jaley.
Below, Cities of France by Nanteuil, Lequesne and Gruyère.

Elias Robert (1821–1874):
Allegory of
Industry, 1867.
Stone, 14½′ high.
Gare d'Austerlitz, Paris.

The State played a leading role in promoting large-scale sculpture. The new society followed its example. The product of economic upheavals, the new society of the Second Empire sought to affirm itself by giving an official veneer to its institutions. The power of the railways, for example, which had succeeded in unifying the country for the first time, was expressed in monumental stations with imposing stone walls watched over by goddesses. Elias Robert's *Allegory of Industry* at the Gare d'Orléans (as the Gare d'Austerlitz was called originally) still included such standard classical attributes as drapery, a diadem and an urn. But it also contained a locomotive, the very symbol of modernity. For the first time since the horse was domesticated, since the invention of the wheel and the sailing vessel, the fundamental concepts of space and time were undergoing a profound transformation.

The allegories of Cities at the Gare du Nord seemed more conventional. The Cities of France ornamented the great glass-and-steel ceiling at regular intervals, while the Foreign Capitals stood guard on the roof, holding shields and scanning the horizon. Like the Gare d'Orléans, the Gare du Nord was completed in 1867, the year of the second World's Fair in Paris, when the Empire invited the rest of Europe to measure its industrial wares against those manufactured in France.

The Bourse, or Stock Exchanges, celebrated a different type of exchange. As ornate as theatres, they were embellished with allegorical groups that gave ample scope for expressing the nude body (even when carved by a sculptor like Bonnassieux, the artist of the twelve statues of the Virgin, the tallest of which, *Notre Dame de France*, at Le Puy, measured 52 feet). Guillaume Bonnet, who made a name for himself sculpting in Lyons, specialized in sheathed caryatids, a characteristically Second Empire motif derived from the curious Renaissance and Baroque practice of turning human forms into architecture and architecture into human forms.

Not all of the Empire caryatids, however, were imprisoned in architectural forms. The ones supporting the dome of the Tribunal de Commerce in Paris are atlantes or slaves animating the drum. They connect the vertical dimension of the elliptical double stairs ascended by ordinary humanity to the dome which links, as have all domes since the beginning, earth with heaven.

Guillaume Bonnet (1820–1873): Telamon and Caryatid, 1859–1860. Painted and gilded wood. Bourse de Commerce, Lyons.

J.M.B. Bonnassieux (1810–1892): The Hours of Life, 1860–1863. Marble. Bourse de Commerce, Lyons.

René Dardel (1796–1871): Hall of the Stock Exchange, 1855–1862. Bourse de Commerce, Lyons.

New Tribunal de Commerce, Paris:

Hippolyte Maindron (1801–1884):
Maritime Commerce, 1865. Stone, 83″ high.

Didier Debut (1824–1893):
Caryatids, 1863–1865. Stone, 71″ high.

François Michel-Pascal (1810–1882)
Industrial Art, 1865. Stone, 83″ high.

Eugène Guillaume (1822-1905): Justice, 1862. Stone relief. Palais de Justice (Law Courts), Marseilles.

As for courts of law, their awesome function had to be clearly discernible from the street. They were the bourgeoisie's safeguard; their role was to preserve the new social order. Each institution tends to adopt the style which was in vogue at the height of its power. Justice generally favoured the neoclassical style. Rome, the cradle of law, had inspired a revival under Napoleon I, the promulgator of the Code Napoléon. So it was only appropriate that its stylistic canon should once again come into honour under his nephew's Empire. Moreover, the changelessness of neoclassical forms seemed especially well adapted to expressing the idea of infallibility.

The academic sculptor Eugène Guillaume understood this perfectly. The pediment he designed for the Palais de

Justice in Marseilles is a masterpiece of equilibrium. The seated allegory of Justice has all the time in the world; the scales she holds rests in undisturbed balance. Symmetrical allegories separate her from the Guilty and the Acquitted who crawl in the side angles of the pediment.

The façade of the Palais de Justice in Paris, remodelled by Joseph-Louis Duc between 1859 an 1868, was decorated by Augustin Dumont with allegorical figures of *Prudence* and *Truth* in high relief. With their vacant eyes, inexpressive mouths and square jaws, they are there to inspire awe. They do not animate the wall from which they detach themselves; they merely emphasize the pilaster crowned with a capital of Doric inspiration. Rigid and inaccessible, they simply communicate their message.

Eugène Guillaume (1822-1905):
The Spirit of Commerce, 1860. Stone high-relief.
Bourse du Commerce, Marseilles.

Augustin Dumont (1801-1884):
Prudence and Truth, 1865.
Palais de Justice (Law Courts), Paris.

NEO-GOTHIC

Madame Léon Bertaux (1825-1909): St Bartholomew and St James the Less, 1865-1868. Stone, 71″ high. Church of Saint-Laurent, Paris.

So far as the Church was concerned, the Golden Age was the age of the cathedrals. The alliance of throne and altar under the Second Empire benefited both the temporal monarch—his subjects were obedient—and the Sovereign of the Universe: urban development spurred the construction of churches. The style generally chosen by that

other *imperium*, the Church, was of course the Gothic style. Its advent had already been prepared in literature. In his *Mémoires d'outre-tombe*, Chateaubriand, the father of this return to the past, complains: "It is I who taught the young century to admire old temples. But am I to blame if my views have been carried to preposterous extremes and we are bored to death with the palaver about Gothic this and Gothic that?" (13 January 1832).

Victor Hugo (in *Notre-Dame de Paris*, 1831), the Romantic generation, and Viollet-le-Duc's scholarly *Dictionnaire raisonné de l'architecture française du XIe au XVIe siècle* (1854-1868, in ten volumes) contributed to popularizing the Gothic style to an unprecedented degree. So complete was this vogue that in 1868 the classical façade of Saint-Laurent was torn down and replaced by a "Gothic" façade. Here too the artists' imaginations were fed, if not always stimulated to great originality. The names of most of the neo-Gothic sculptors mean little to us today. Yet Madame Léon Bertaux, the artist of *St Bartholomew* and *St James the Less* at Saint-Laurent, was the founder (in 1881) and first president of the League of Women Painters and Sculptors.

At Notre-Dame Cathedral Geoffroy-Dechaume and his assistants were not always successful in their efforts to duplicate the freshness and strength of twelfth and thirteenth century popular imagery, traces of which are to be seen only on the Porte Saint-Louis, the Portail de la Vierge, the Porte Rouge, and the north and south transepts. Yet there is something genuinely original about Geoffroy-Dechaume's self-portrait among the apostles on one of the rampant arches supporting the flèche above the intersection of the nave and transepts. Its originality is further enhanced by the green tones of the oxidizing copper and its position between the sharp outlines of the ridge and the grimacing monsters so dear to the Romantics: "The modern muse... will soon imitate nature, blending within its creations... shadow and light, the grotesque and the sublime, the body and the soul, the beast and the spirit" (Victor Hugo's preface to *Cromwell*, 1827).

▷ Neo-Gothic façade of the Church of Saint-Laurent, Paris, in 1868. Print from *L'Illustration*, Paris, 1868.

▽ Classical façade of the Church of Saint-Laurent, Paris, in 1863. Print from *L'Illustration*, Paris, 1863.

Adolphe Geoffroy-Dechaume (1816-1892):
Apostles and Evangelist Symbols, installed 1861.
Copper, each 11 ½' high.
Cathedral of Notre-Dame, Paris.

Alexis Fromanger (1805-1892):
St John the Baptist, 1863.
Stone, 6'10" high.

Armand Toussaint (1806-1862):
St Stephen, 1862.
Stone, 6'10" high.

François Michel-Pascal (1810-1882):
St Genevieve, c. 1863.
Stone, 6'10" high.

Alexis Fromanger (1805-1892):
St Sylvester, 1863.
Stone, 6'10" high.

Portal of the Virgin, West Front,
Cathedral of Notre-Dame, Paris.

Charles Cordier (1827-1905):

△ Atlantes and Caryatids supporting the loggia in
the Grand Salon, 1861-1862.
Bronze, gilt bronze, marble, onyx, each 10′ high.

▷ Caryatid (Ethiopian Negress), 1861-1862.
Bronze, gilt bronze, marble, onyx, 10′ high.

Château de Ferrières (Seine-et-Marne), near Meaux.

SCULPTURE IN THE SERVICE OF APPEARANCES

Alfred Jacquemart (1824-1896) and Jules Dalou (1838-1902):
Fireplace in the main dining-room, 1866.
Hôtel de Païva, Paris.

The privileged few who could afford to have their homes lavishly decorated do not seem to have shared these preoccupations. The richest periods of art history offered a choice of pleasing models to choose from. What was wanted was rich material, gracious figures, a decorative abundance which drew from the freest Renaissance manner, the most opulent Baroque, the most whimsical Rococo. Sombre, glistening colours shimmered in the recesses and shadow-casting excrescences of their homes. Rumpled clothes, frothy drapery modelled in onyx and bronze, silver gleaming side by side with malachite. Their dwellings resembled Monte Cristo's cave. The importance of appearances was related to the credit system on which this new society, so accurately described by Zola in *La Curée*, *Pot-Bouille* and *L'Argent*, was founded–to credit and to such curious figures as the Marquise de Païva, *née* Theresa Lachmann, whose *hôtel particulier* on the Champs-Elysées was frequented by the politicians, writers and artists of the day.

Exiled in 1871 after she married Henckel von Donnersmarck, the German governor of Alsace-Lorraine recently annexed by Germany, she imported a team of Parisian artists–being above nationalistic considerations–to Neudeck in Silesia, where she wished to have a new castle built. Lefuel was the architect. The garden was ornamented with statues by Fremiet.

The Rothschild family, around the same time, commissioned Joseph Paxton, the architect of the Crystal Palace, to design the Château de Ferrières. Napoleon III visited it in pomp and style in 1862 and again in 1863. Charles Cordier, who inspired the revival of polychromy under the Second Empire (and one of whose future assistants was to be the young Rodin), composed for the great Italian salon at Ferrières a magnificent loggia admired by Charles Garnier.

Albert-Ernest Carrier-Belleuse (1824-1887):
Fireplace with two nymphs, 1865.
Gilt and silver-gilt bronze. Hôtel de Païva, Paris.

FOUNTAINS

Pierre-Jules Cavelier (1814-1894):
The River Durance between allegories of Wheat and the Grapevine, 1869.
Calissane stone, 32′10″ high. Palais de Longchamp, Marseilles.

Charles-Alphonse Gumery (1827–1871):
Fountain of the Three Graces, 1865.
Place de la Bourse, Bordeaux.

Jean-Baptiste Carpeaux (1827–1875):
The Four Continents Upholding the Celestial Sphere, 1872.
Bronze, 9′ high without the sphere.
Jardin de l'Observatoire, Paris.

Such retrograde lavishness was by no means confined to interior decoration. Elected municipal officials were anxious to enrich public thoroughfares. Along with sewers, city water supply is one of the modern era's proudest achievements. Remember the cholera epidemics which ravaged towns under the Second Empire. The public fountain had a utilitarian function. It was also to become a prop for art.

Germain Pilon's monument to Henry II's heart at the Louvre inspired Gumery's *Fountain of the Three Graces* on the Place de la Bourse in Bordeaux, a site formerly occupied by a statue of Louis XV which was destroyed in the French Revolution.

In Marseilles, the great river that brings its running water to the city was deified. Cavelier's triumphant Durance, flanked by the allegories of Wheat and the Grapevine, stands on a cart drawn by the oxen of fertility, surrounded by Lequesne's tritons blowing into conch shells (shades of Rome and Versailles). The group is placed in the centre of a combined triumphal arch and grotto above a frothing cascade, a rather Baroque setting for Cavelier's pure classical lines. This fountain, clasped by the curved wings of the buildings, inspired Davioud's design for the Palais du Trocadéro in Paris in 1878.

It was Davioud, the city architect of Paris, who commissioned Carpeaux to design a fountain for the Observatoire gardens. The sculptor, a master of movement, seized this opportunity to indulge, to a degree of complication as yet undreamt of, his love for twisting gestures. The allegorical figures representing the four parts of the world stand on a base ornamented with shells and festoons (carved by Villeminot) and surrounded by sea horses (by Fremiet) spewing water into the basin.

MONUMENTS TO FAMOUS MEN
THE POLITICAL MESSAGE

Albert-Ernest Carrier-Belleuse (1824–1887):
Inauguration of his Monument to the Painter A.G. Decamps
at Fontainebleau, Place Decamps, 31 August 1862.
Print from *Le Monde Illustré*, Paris, 1862.

Monuments to famous men designed for public squares are commissioned as a rule by left-wing governments, as the historian Maurice Agulhon has demonstrated—with the exception of the Second Empire, when the vogue for public statues, begun under Louis-Philippe, continued unabated.

At Fontainebleau a bust of the painter Decamps was placed in the middle of a fountain (decidedly a privileged spot for sculptures). At Agen the florally-named poet Jasmin was honoured with a full-length statue over six feet high. (It is still in existence, though the taps on the base have dried up.) At Grignan Madame de Sévigné, her pen poised in mid-sentence, cast a thoughtful eye on housewives coming to fill water jugs and cattle quenching their thirst. At Valenciennes the chronicler Jehan Froissart sat meditating above a circular bench flanked by reliefs of the two rivers, the Scheldt and the Rhonelle. Here the monument served as an open-air salon, its benches inviting pleasant conversation. Art combined with the useful. Art by itself was still too daring an idea, except when the utilitarian was contained within the statue, as it were, in the form of a political message.

Napoleon III, who wrote a book on Julius Caesar, as a way of defending the principle of authoritarian government, remarks: "What greater error can there be than in not acknowledging the superiority of those privileged beings who appear in history from time to time like beacons? When providence creates men like Caesar, Charlemagne and Napoleon, it is for the purpose of showing the peoples of the world the path they must follow... Neither Caesar's assassination, nor the years of captivity at St Helena succeeded in destroying irrevocably a popular cause overthrown by a political faction concealing itself behind the mask of liberty."

One can hardly be clearer. Inevitably Napoleon III extended his interest to the Roman conqueror's opponent, Vercingetorix. In 1865 Aimé Millet's gigantic statue 22 feet high, on a base 23 feet high designed by Viollet-le-Duc, was unveiled on the plateau of Alésia in Burgundy. It represented the Arverni chief who had succeeded in uniting the undisciplined Gaulish tribes. This was France's answer to Ernst von Bandel's *Arminius* in the Teutoburger Wald in Westphalia. Begun in 1819, the German statue had been reproduced in *Le Magasin pittoresque* in 1843; it was completed in 1875. Millet's work was funded from Napoleon III's personal fortune. The Emperor himself composed the inscription on the base: "United Gaul, forming a single nation, inspired by a single spirit, can defy the universe. Vercingetorix to the assembled Gauls." Unfortunately, the tribes are soon divided again and Vercingetorix, defeated, is plunged deep in thought. He surrenders to Caesar on the next day in order to save his own troops. This figure in embossed copper was exhibited at the fourth Salon of the liberal Empire before being erected at Alésia.

Vital Dubray (1813–1892):
Monument to the Languedoc Poet Jasmin, 1867.
Bronze, 7½' high.
Place Jasmin, Agen (Lot-et-Garonne).

Louis Rochet (1813–1878):
Monument to Madame de Sévigné, 1857–1859.
Bronze.
Place du Château, Grignan (Drôme).

Henri Lemaire (1789–1880):
Monument to Jehan Froissart, 1856.
Marble, 7′2″ high.
Jardin Froissart, Valenciennes (Nord).

Bartholdi, on the other hand, chose to portray Vercingetorix in a warlike pose in a monument for Gergovie in Auvergne, the site of the Gauls' victory over the Romans. The monument was to measure 115 feet in length. A model was displayed at the 1870 Salon, a few months before the outbreak of the Franco-Prussian war. It was only in 1903 that a considerably reduced version was erected on the Place de Jaude at Clermont-Ferrand.

Emperors have their own lineage, as Napoleon III observed. It was by virtue of this principle, no doubt, that Clesinger was commissioned to do an equestrian statue of Charlemagne for the Cour Napoléon at the Louvre. The work was not completed in time, however, and has been preserved only in photographs. A monument on the same theme, by the brothers Rochet, after having been displayed in plaster at the 1867 World's Fair and in bronze at the 1878 Fair, was finally erected, after numerous vicissitude, on the square in front of Notre-Dame.

Like Charlemagne's faithful companions Roland and Oliver, Napoleon I's four brothers stand guard at the four corners of the emperor's monument at Ajaccio. Much importance was attached to fraternal descent under the Second Empire. Napoleon III was the son of Napoleon I's brother Louis, the king of Holland, and Josephine's daughter, Hortense de Beauharnais. Barye's monument is a masterpiece of concentration on simple volumes. "Barye approaches form by way of the cube and the square. His concern with line is not as great as Clesinger's," wrote Marcello (Adèle d'Affry, Duchess Castiglione Colonna) after visiting Barbedienne on 12 September 1864.

The monument's other sculptors, Millet for *Joseph*, G.J. Thomas for *Lucien*, Petit for *Louis* and Maillet for *Jerome*, all pay homage to the classical tradition of the toga.

Aimé Millet (1819-1891):
Vercingetorix, 1865.
Beaten copper on stone base designed
by Viollet-le-Duc, overall height 46'.
Alise-Sainte-Reine, near Dijon.

Auguste Bartholdi (1834-1904):
Vercingetorix, 1866-1870.
Plaster, 75" high.

Louis Rochet (1813–1878):
Charlemagne with Roland and Oliver, 1867–1878.
Bronze.
Place du Parvis Notre-Dame, Paris.

Antoine-Louis Barye (1796–1875):
Napoleon I and his Brothers, 1865.
Bronze.
Place Charles-de-Gaulle, Ajaccio,
Corsica.

Sir Thomas Brock (1847–1922):
The Victoria Memorial, 1901–1911.
Mall in front of Buckingham Palace, London.

Sir George Gilbert Scott (1811–1878):
The Albert Memorial, 1864–1876.
Hyde Park, London.

Four examples of the statues and busts commissioned
by Kaiser Wilhelm II for the Tiergarten, Berlin, 1895-1901.
Destroyed or damaged.

Fritz Schaper (1841-1919):
Frederick William of Brandenburg, the Great Elector.

Rudolf Siemering (1835-1905):
King Frederick William I of Prussia.

Adolf Brütt (1855-1940):
King Frederick William II of Prussia.

Karl Begas (1845-1916):
King Frederick William IV of Prussia.

Georg Reichsfrhr. von Derfflinger.   Otto Frhr. von Schwerin.
Friedrich Wilhelm, der Grosse Kurfürst, 1640—1688. Von Fritz Schaper.

Fürst Leopold von Anhalt-Dessau.   Heinrich Rüdiger von Ilgen.
König Friedrich Wilhelm I., 1713—1740. Von Rudolf Siemering.

Graf Kasimir von Carmer.   Immanuel Kant.
König Friedrich Wilhelm II., 1786—1797. Von Adolf Brütt.

Alexander von Humboldt.   Christian Rauch.
König Friedrich Wilhelm IV., 1840—1861. Von Karl Begas.

England is rich in political monuments, richer than most countries, as is demonstrated by Benedict Read's fine book on *Victorian Sculpture* (1982). Unlike France, it does not destroy them. Nor does it change its system of government.

The Albert Memorial in London, raised by Queen Victoria to commemorate her husband, who died on 14 December 1861, is a mausoleum of Gothic structure designed by Sir George Gilbert Scott. It offered British sculptors a fine opportunity of showing their mettle. Begun in 1864 and completed in 1876, its programme was on the scale of the British Empire. At the corners, *America* by John Bell, *Africa* by William Theed, *Asia* by J.H. Foley and *Europe* by MacDowell. Beneath the famous frieze of painters, sculptors, architects and musicians studied by Francis Haskell in 1975, are *Trade*, *Techniques*, *Industry*, *Agriculture*, allegories of the Arts and Sciences, the virtues of a Prince Consort, with *Prudence*, *Humanity*, *Temperance*, *Faith*, *Justice*, *Hope*, *Courage* and *Charity*, the virtues reserved to woman in general. Beneath the angels crowning the shrine is the pensive figure of Prince Albert, seated like the *Ludovisi Ares*; commissioned from Marochetti, then from Foley, the statue was completed by Teniswood.

The memorial to the dead queen, forty years after her husband, and after a reign of sixty-four years, stands in front of Buckingham Palace. The initial designs were ordered from a sculptor, Thomas Brock, described by Susan Beattie (*The New Sculpture,* 1983) as "the great plagiarist of the New Sculpture"; the competition between architects came later. The models were presented to the king in 1904; the monument was completed in 1911, then added to in 1914 and 1924. The queen is enthroned against a background of Renaissance architecture, surrounded by allegories, *Truth* on the left, *Justice* on the right, *Motherhood* at the back. In the latter group, as in the accompanying putti, Dalou's influence makes itself felt; that of Gilbert is tangible in the Victory at the top, and that of Stevens in the two figures crouching at its feet. The decoration later invaded the Mall, each decade adding to it through public subscriptions from an Empire grateful to their sovereign.

In Berlin the impressive series of the Tiergarten is known now only from photographs. The full-length kings accompanied by bust figures, with arms, of their best servants adorned the exedrae of this historic promenade.

OFFICIAL PORTRAITS

▷ Alfred-Emilien Nieuwerkerke (1811-1892):
Eugénie de Montijo, 1852.
Marble, 26″ high.

▽ Jean-Auguste Barre (1811-1896):
The Empress Eugénie, 1861.
Marble, 30¼″ high.

▽ ▷ Paul Gayrard (1807-1855):
Emilie MacDonald, Marquise de Las Marismas,
Vicomtesse Aguado, 1852.
Marble, 23″ high.

Emmanuel Fremiet (1824–1910):

△ Napoleon III on Horseback, 1860.
Model rejected by the Empress.
Silver-gilt bronze, 17¼″ × 16″.

△▷ Napoleon III on Horseback, 1860.
Final version.
Silver-gilt bronze, 14″ × 12¼″.

Henri-Frédéric Iselin (1825–1905):
The Duc de Morny, 1861.
Marble, 33″ high.

"Painters wind up doing portraits the way poets wind up doing journalism," wrote Robert de La Sizeranne in 1902. The same might be said of sculptors. The need to capture his own likeness in a durable material has haunted man since Antiquity. Rome gave us the heritage of the bust portrait, and it was this tradition the nineteenth century used to great advantage. More than a third of the sculptures on exhibit at the Salons were busts.

"One day Monsieur Reiset entered his office thoroughly stunned and amazed," relates Philippe de Chennevières. "'Where the devil did that fellow Nieuwerkerke meet the splendid woman whose bust he is working on in his studio? A delightful head, features of an ideal refinement and distinction... I've never seen anything like it in my life.' Not long afterwards, we discovered that the bust being modelled by the director of museums was the portrait of Mademoiselle de Montijo, and that this same Mademoiselle de Montijo, whom the Emperor made no secret of being in love with, was shortly to become the Empress of France... When the bust was brought to the Tuileries—only a day or two, a few days at the most, before the wedding at Notre-Dame—the Emperor, like a child in love, was unable to stop himself from kissing the marble."

This was for some time the "only official bust" of the Empress, but Nieuwerkerke was supplanted by Barre. Replacing the antique drapery, a court dress in the pleasantly rumpled eighteenth-century style failed to warm up the model's elegant coldness. Paul Gayrard's portrait of the Vicomtesse Aguado is a livelier work: the model looks down with a half smile at her sheer, Ingres-like shoulders (which seem to defy anatomy, but as everyone knows, the latter should not always be slavishly respected...).

In order to complete the Emperor's small army of miniature soldiers, Fremiet was commissioned to sculpt the equestrian statue of the Emperor. When Napoleon III posed coming out of Mass at the Tuileries, the sculptor was given permission to take measurements. Nieuwerkerke brought the finished statuette to the monarchs. The Empress found the thighs too short and the model was rejected. Fremiet then carved a second, more imperial-looking, though less realistic version. Yet realism was the path of the future. Iselin had already paved the way with his busts. Zola saw this clearly. In L'Evénement illustré (16 June 1868), he wrote: "The naturalist sculptors will be the masters of tomorrow."

THE COMMERCIAL CIRCUIT

Jean-Baptiste Carpeaux (1827-1875):
Count Ugolino and his Sons, 1867,
at the Paris World's Fair of 1867.
Marble, 76½″ high.

Distribution of prizes, Palais de l'Industrie, Paris, 1 July 1867.
Print from *L'Illustration*, Paris, 1867.

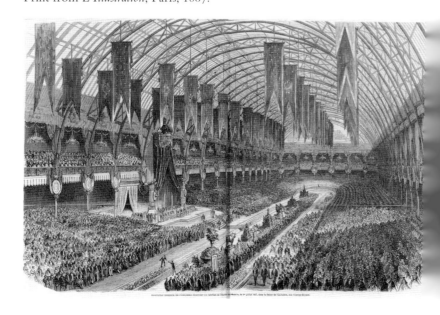

How did these sculptors live? From commissions. The raw material was too costly, the work too slow and laborious, for an artist to undertake a personal creation of any scope unless he was sure of an outlet for it. Where did he find purchasers? At the Salons organized by the State up to 1880, by the artists themselves thereafter, and at the Expositions Universelles, the Paris World's Fairs, where the French public was swelled by an influx of visitors from all over Europe and the New World.

The first great International Exhibition was held in London in 1851. It was the only one to show a profit; the surplus went to build the Victoria and Albert Museum. Two others followed in France under the Second Empire (1855 and 1867), three more under the Third Republic (1878, 1889 and 1900), so that the country was said to be "governed with a volley of world's fairs." Others (to men-

But the sculptors did not confront alone the millions of potential buyers among the visitors. Between sculptors and public, publishers acted as middlemen.

Achille Collas, Frédéric Sauvage and several others arrived independently at a mathematical means of reducing large-sized sculptures to the scale of modern apartments. Collas presented his invention in 1839, the very year when photography was invented.

Other techniques helped to lower the cost price of a sculpture: sand casting, from a master model in well-chiselled metal cut into several parts to simplify the making of the casting-moulds, the patina-coating and mounting of the pieces, the division of labour between each operation, the unlimited run of casts–advertised in the papers and sales catalogue or sold by correspondence.

The ornamental bronze thus became accessible to a new clientele. The less well-to-do contented themselves with plaster casts, hawked by street vendors to passers-by. In 1848 Alexandre Dumas *fils* placed the first meeting of Marguerite Gautier and Armand Duval, the two leading characters of *La Dame aux Camélias*, at the door of the bronze-caster and publisher Susse, in the Place de la Bourse in Paris. Such business houses, intent on combining art and industry, were awarded medals at the international exhibitions; for example, the French firm of Victor Thiébaut, in London in 1862.

Another of these businessmen was Ferdinand Barbedienne, in partnership with Achille Collas. After difficult beginnings his firm rose to a high pitch of prosperity. He signed contracts with living artists, while selling reductions of famous statues from antiquity onwards. Little by little the notion of author's rights took form in this new field. As for ethical rights, these were finally taken into account in the French law of 11 March 1957.

tion only the biggest) were held in Vienna in 1873, Philadelphia in 1876, Chicago in 1893, and there, as in London and Paris, sculptors played a leading part. It fell to them to assert the glory and wealth of the competing countries by decorating, and overdecorating, the large temporary buildings erected to house the exhibits; and they themselves figured among the exhibitors. Such was Marcello, a Swiss lady living in France, widow of a Roman nobleman, and symbolizing the international society of the Second Empire.

△ Sculpture studio of Dantan the Younger,
Cité d'Orléans, Paris.
Print from *L'Illustration*, Paris, 1857.

▷ Adèle d'Affry, Duchess Castiglione Colonna,
known as Marcello (1836-1879):
Marbles exhibited at the
Paris World's Fair of 1867.

STYLE: REVERENCE FOR THE PAST

Aimé Millet (1819-1891):

Phidias, 1887.
Stone, 8' high. Jardin du Luxembourg, Paris.

Cassandra Appealing for Protection to Athena, 1877.
Marble, 6½' high. Jardin des Tuileries, Paris.

While artists were not always contractors, they were always cultivated men, for in the nineteenth century reverence for the past was intact and unchallenged. Archaeologists, when necessary, came to the rescue. Such was the Duc de Luynes, who ordered from Simart a copy, reduced to one quarter, of the *Minerva* of Phidias on the Parthenon. Ivory, bronze, silver, gold and lapis lazuli fail, however, to recreate the splendour known to us now only from ancient copies and medals.

Millet prolonged this echo late in the century. His *Cassandra* (1877) in the garden of the Tuileries places herself under the protection of Pallas Athene. The impassive statue did not prevent Ajax from seizing and ravishing the fleeing prophetess. Millet's *Phidias* (1887) in the Luxembourg gardens stands, mallet in hand, at the foot of his masterpiece in reduced size. Even Renan is seen inspired by a sort of Minerva on his monument at Tréguier, executed by Jean Boucher in 1903.

Michelangelo was the other source of inspiration of this century of "neo" styles. The San Lorenzo chapel with the Medici tombs was the grammar consulted by sculptors. For the crowning of the Pavillon de Flore the debt is obvious, but Carpeaux's handling of it is more baroque. Perraud, an artist from Franche-Comté, invoked the *Moses* in his *Adam after the Fall*. It was the creation of man painted on the walls of the Sistine Chapel that Horace Daillion referred back to in his awaking *Adam*, a work which has since disappeared.

Horace Daillion (1854–after 1937):
The Awakening of Adam, 1885.
Marble.

André-César Vermare (1869-1949):
Monument to the War Dead of 1870, 1898. Stone and bronze.
Square Jovin-Boucharel, Saint-Etienne.

Henri Allouard (1844-1929):
Monument to the War Dead of 1870-1871.
Inaugurated 27 October 1901. Chartres.

Frederick MacMonnies (1863-1937):
The Army, 1901.
Bronze high-relief on the Soldier and Sailors' Arch,
Grand Army Plaza, Brooklyn, New York.

REALISM AND THE TABLEAU VIVANT

The 1880s saw the rise of realism. A powerful new social force made its appearance in art: the working class. The first sculptures to depict humble working men and women engaged in their daily tasks and to give them a heroic dimension appeared in Belgium and Italy. Painters and mainly writers, more attuned than sculptors to the political evolution of their age, had paved the way. Their realism was contemporary with the new social legislation.

Did realism reflect a new social awareness or the emergence of a new social force? Achille d'Orsi's *Proximus Tuus* (Thy Neighbour) inaugurated the new trend towards the reality of the soil. It was life-size. Moreover, the scope of its inscription was clearly not just biblical. In all the works illustrated on this page, the models look downwards. In the work of earlier centuries, dominated by religion, the privileged motif in art–the saint or martyr–always looked up towards Heaven. But now all hope of alleviating life's hardships has vanished. Vincenzo Vela's *Victims of Labour*, which commemorates one of the great achievements of the age, the building of the St Gotthard tunnel, renews the traditional motif of the procession. So does the *Quarry*, executed some twenty years later. Weight is now the subject. The dead weigh heavily on the living. So heavily that the female figure in the *Mine Explosion* is literally unable to bear the burden. A modern Pietà or rather a modern Stabat Mater, she is bowed down over the eternally set features of her lifeless companion. The epic of industrial-

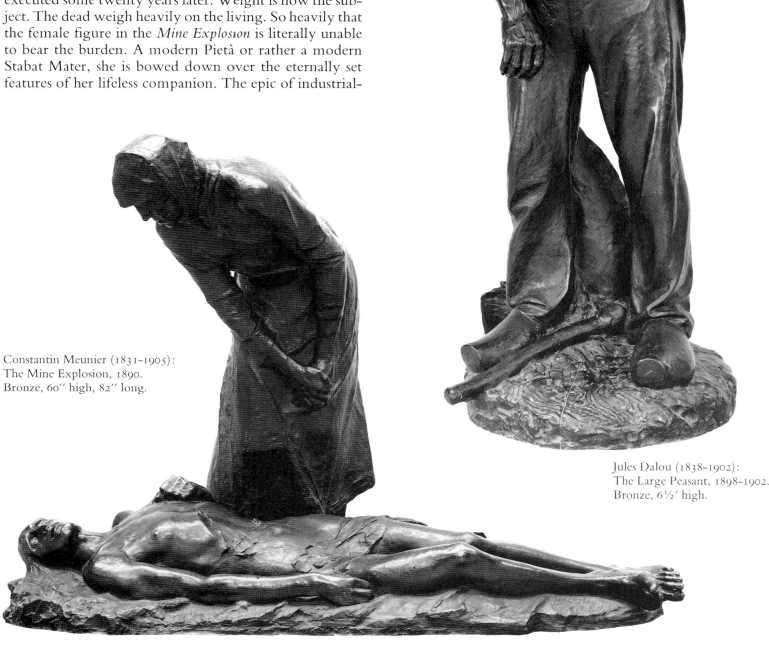

Constantin Meunier (1831-1905):
The Mine Explosion, 1890.
Bronze, 60″ high, 82″ long.

Jules Dalou (1838-1902):
The Large Peasant, 1898-1902.
Bronze, 6½′ high.

Henri Bouchard (1875-1960):
The Quarry, 1906.
Stone.
Parc Montsouris, Paris.

ization exacted a heavy price at times, but some paid more than others. Hoetger's *Human Machine* is a stirring defence of the oppressed. Reproduced on the cover of *L'Assiette au Beurre* in October 1903, this powerful image seems both a dramatic overstatement and a weak understatement compared to Dalou's *Large Peasant*. The latter gazes down at the ground, his feet seem planted in the earth, he is rolling up his shirt sleeves and is about to start work. His lowered head might belong to a labouring ox.

This realistic and universally understandable style was to become the vocabulary of public monuments. The exact depiction of the toiling man in his characteristic pose offered a convenient means of communication, one resting entirely on verifiable appearances. It was not a style that

Bernhard Hoetger (1874-1949):
The Human Machine, 1902.
Bronze bas-relief, 17¼″ × 14½″.

Vincenzo Vela (1820-1891):
The Victims of Labour (to the workmen killed
in building the St Gotthard railway tunnel), 1882.
Bronze bas-relief (cast in 1932), 10′8″ high.
Airolo railway station, Ticino, Switzerland.

Eugène-Jean Boverie (1869-1910):
Camille Desmoulins, 1905.
Formerly Jardin du Palais-Royal, Paris.
Bronze melted down under the Occupation.

allowed for much depth, but there was no misinterpreting it. Consider the young revolutionary, Camille Desmoulins, who climbs onto a chair at the Palais Royal to harangue his fellow citizens. This popular image of the French Revolution was cast in bronze in 1905 and installed on the very site where the event took place. It clearly expresses the determination with which left-wing governments under the Third Republic went about creating a modern iconography. If a comparison is needed, one might recall that creation of the Revolution, the wax museum of Madame Tussaud, a niece of the revolutionary

Curtius, who collected the heads of guillotined counter-revolutionaries and had them cast in wax, thus perpetuating, as it were, her uncle's "royal banquets," a favourite Parisian spectacle at the end of the eighteenth century. Like the Musée Grévin wax figures, the statue of Camille Desmoulins seeks to re-enact a moment of history.

A chair can serve as a prie-dieu as well as an orator's platform. Madame Grand-Guillaume was able to meditate in comfort on the grave of her husband, the inventor of the glass photographic plate. Her position may remind us of the interminable posing sessions of pioneering photography.

On yet another monument, Victor Noir's striking figure appears "taller in death than in life," as Henry III is reported to have said of the Duke of Guise whom he had assassinated in 1588. Noir, a young journalist, was shot dead by Pierre Bonaparte in the latter's drawing room. This scandal, which occurred in 1870, ended with the prince's acquittal. But after the collapse of the Second Empire, public opinion vented its anger in a national subscription towards a monument for Victor Noir. And Dalou, a staunch republican, was at last able to express his sentiments publicly. More than a manifesto, the monument was a successful work of art, adding its own artistic energy to the political aims of those who commissioned it. The realistic corpse in frock coat and ankle-boots, his top hat resting by his feet, is an effective political image of an unarmed victim. It also has a life of its own, apart from political connotations. In the cemetery of Père-Lachaise where the monument stands over the young journalist's grave, strange happenings recalling the rites of spring are said to take place. They have nothing to do with republican feelings about the imperial family.

Anonymous:
Grand-Guillaume Tomb, after 1848.
Cemetery, Arras (Pas-de-Calais).

Jules Dalou (1838-1902):
Tomb of Victor Noir, 1890.
Bronze.
Père-Lachaise Cemetery, Paris.

PORTRAITURE IN THE LATE NINETEENTH CENTURY

Eugène Guillaume (1822-1905): Henri Germain, 1882.
Marble. Salle du Conseil, Crédit Lyonnais, Paris.

Eugène Guillaume (1822-1905): Marc Seguin, 1881.
Marble. Salle des Séances, Chamber of Commerce, Saint-Etienne.

The portrait busts of the last quarter of the nineteenth century reflect the prevailing stylistic trends. Realism naturally dominates, being well suited to this class of sculpture.

Marc Seguin, the inventor of the suspended bridge, the tubular boiler, the iron rail laid on wooden ties, and Henri Germain, the founder of the Crédit Lyonnais, both commissioned portraits from Eugène Guillaume. Guillaume was the sculptor with the most laurels and consequently, from the social point of view, the best. He had spent five years in Rome after getting the Grand Prix de Rome in 1845, and he admired all things Roman. He was someone you could trust. He modelled Germain's bust with an almost scientific precision just barely idealized by the antique nakedness of the neck and shoulders. At Saint-Etienne as in Paris, the founder's bust was installed on a mantelpiece, which served as a pediment and setting.

Hildebrand, a sculptor situated somewhere between Rauch and Lehmbruck, drew on Florentine art to create his portrait of Julia Brewster. In Verrocchio's *Lady with Bouquet* at the Bargello Museum, the model's hands resting on her bosom seem more interesting and beautiful than her face. Hildebrand, a citizen of Florence by virtue of the fact that he had bought the cloisters of San Francesco di Paolo, succeeded in catching the marvellous equilibrium of the fifteenth-century bust in his portrait of the daughter of the last ambassador of the court of Hanover to Paris. "The

Jean-Léon Gérôme (1824-1904):
Sarah Bernhardt, c. 1890.
Coloured marble, 27″ high.

◁ Adolf von Hildebrand (1847-1921):
Julia Brewster, 1881.
Marble, 27″ high.

incomparable Julia has just arrived. What a pure spirit!"
wrote Irene Hildebrand. It was with the same respect that
her husband rendered the trim hands and clean-cut, severe
features of the well-read and musical young lady who had
taken her first piano lessons from Chopin.

The painter Gérôme was a late-comer to sculpture. In
1878 he first exhibited the *Gladiators* (the same group as in
one of his paintings), now in Phoenix, Arizona. Trying his
hand at the genre of historical reconstruction (the speciality of his friend Fremiet), he assembled pieces of Roman
armour, or rather plaster copies of Roman armour which
Colonel de Reffye had brought back from Naples. His
fascination with the trompe-l'œil interplay between painting and reality, sculpture and antiquity, led him further
and further off the beaten track. Using coloured waxes to
tint marble, he created strange and ambiguous effects.
Long banished from French museums, these works were
bought mostly by North Americans. Gérôme's bust of

Sarah Bernhardt at the Musée du Luxembourg was exiled to Lunéville in 1922 and remained there until 1981. The great actress has now been moved to the Musée d'Orsay in Paris, but the colour has faded from her cheeks. To show her in the Louvre would have been unthinkable earlier.

Rodin's busts started out as graceful portraits in the manner of Carrier-Belleuse and gradually acquired symbolic weight. The sculptor's student and mid-life passion, Camille Claudel, is depicted in a series of busts after 1892, sometimes under an allegorical title: *St George* (before 1889), *Dawn* (1890), *The Convalescing Woman* (1892), *The Parting* (1892), *The Byzantine Princess*, later rebaptized *The Byzantine Empress*, and, finally, *La France* (1911). In *La Pensée*, shown here, she is the symbol of Thought. Barely emerging from the stone, her hair coiffed by a small bonnet, she does not appear to float in mid-air like one of Odilon Redon's severed heads, but seems watchful, as though she were the marble block's conscience.

The other woman in Rodin's life, his first and last companion, Rose Beuret (whom he married a few days before his death in 1917), lent her lovely features to *Mignon* (1870), *The Alsacienne* (1871), and the *Bust of Bellona* (1881). The 1880 mask, with its inward-looking eyes, might be a plaster mould. The seams are left to show and the model's face is caught in a network of lines which break it up into fragments. The effect reminds one of the leading in a stained-glass window or the arabesques of a painted face. It suggests a subtle interplay of meanings.

As for Camille Claudel herself, when it came to modelling a private portrait, she was no less inhibited than her master and lover to express her most intimate feelings. Her bust of Rodin, which is far above being merely one artist's tribute to another, was unveiled at the Salon of the Société Nationale des Beaux-Arts in 1892.

Auguste Rodin (1840-1917):

Rose Beuret, 1880.
Plaster, 8″ high.

◁ Thought (Camille Claudel), 1886-1889.
Marble, 29″ high.

▷ Camille Claudel (1864-1943):
Rodin, 1888.
Coloured plaster.

RODIN

Auguste Rodin (1840-1917):
The Bronze Age, 1875-1876, three views.
Plaster.

At the beginning of the last quarter of the nineteenth century, the creative genius who was to change the history of sculpture was as yet only an assistant working for other sculptors. He was thirty-seven years old. He had failed the entrance examination at the Ecole des Beaux-Arts. He was employed in the studios of Charles Cordier and Carrier-Belleuse. After the Franco-Prussian War, he was associated with Van Rasbourg in Brussels. It was there that he modelled a large standing nude, posed for by a Belgian soldier named Auguste Neyt. Exhibited at the Cercle Artistique in Brussels in January 1877 under the title *The Vanquished*, it was a bold work in at least two respects. First because it dispensed with the motif's traditional attribute, the lance, that standard academic prop. Second because Rodin changed the title when he exhibited the plaster version at the 1877 Salon in Paris. Neither the new title, *The Bronze Age*, nor any of those subsequently given to it–*Awakening Nature*, *Primitive Man*, *The Golden Age* –helped much to explain the symbolism of the standing male figure with his perfect anatomy, simplified features, and oddly extended left arm, its gesture rendered incomprehensible by the suppression of the lance.

The scandal provoked by this work established Rodin's name. Some critics accused the sculptor of having moulded the statue on a living model. Opinions were sharply divided. Paul Dubois, Chapu, Falguière, Carrier-Belleuse, Eugène Delaplanche, Chaplain. Gabriel-Jules Thomas

came to Rodin's defence. The sculptor's own answer to the critics was a larger-than-life *St John the Baptist*, executed three years later. Rodin was now forty-one. His work had been in gestation for many years. Now it surged forth in a continuous outpouring, if one can use that word in connection with an artist who was extremely slow to develop the forms and ideas of his art. His *St John the Baptist* strides forward preaching. He strides forward, yet his two feet rest squarely on the ground like those of an Egyptian statue. The rear heel is not raised; both legs bear the figure's weight equally. Thus the two stages of walking are concentrated in a single pose. The cross on the shoulder has been suppressed. Rodin's *Striding Man* clearly developed from this statue, though there is some debate among experts as to its exact origins. Is *St John the Baptist* a preliminary sketch? Is it a model Rodin abandoned and took up later, fascinated by the expressive power of the mutilations? In any event, the figure strides into the twentieth century like the figurehead of the avant-garde. Yet (such is the nature of sculpture) it is also a recapitulation of all the mutilated statues of antiquity. The realist treatment of the legs, the torso which seems to have been wrested from an archaeological dig, the eloquent lacunae, would seem to indicate a late date of composition, perhaps 1900.

To compensate the artist for the critical attack mounted against the *Bronze Age*, Rodin was commissioned in 1880 to design a portal for the as yet unbuilt Musée des Arts

Auguste Rodin (1840–1917):
Striding Man, 1877–1900.
Plaster, 34″ high.

THE GATES OF HELL

Auguste Rodin (1840-1917):

△ The Gates of Hell. 1880.
Plaster, 44″ × 29⅜″. Third model.

◁ The Gates of Hell, 1880.
Plaster, 6¾″ × 5½″. Second model with figures.

Décoratifs. The museum was to be erected on the site formerly occupied by the Cour des Comptes which had been burned down in 1871 during the Paris Commune. The new project aborted, however, and the museum was not built. Instead the site was eventually occupied by the Gare d'Orsay. When the present Musée d'Orsay replaced the trains and travellers long after the station was closed, it inherited the plaster version of the *Gates of Hell*, which had been kept in storage at the Musée Rodin in Meudon. Thus, in 1986, some 106 years late, the relief was finally installed in the site to which it had originally been destined. A veritable summation of the artist's life, the work emerges from a powerfully kneaded mass. Its plastic rhythms and highlights are distributed over a number of panels, following the principle Ghiberti adopted in his portal for the Florence Baptistery. Rodin streamlined his initial design, dividing it into three principal areas: the two gates and the lintel. Over a span of eight years, the sculptor built up a teeming universe which clings to the Renaissance structure like seaweed to rocks exposed at low tide. The completed work was assembled partly in 1908-1910, partly after 1917, by Léonce Benedite, the curator of the Musée du Luxembourg, assisted by Rodin himself. The frame was to be sculpted in marble, the gates and the *Three Shades* were to be cast in bronze and gilded. But the First World War and Rodin's death (1917) prevented this plan from being executed. The first two bronze versions were commissioned in 1928 by Jules E. Matsbaum for the Rodin museums in Paris and Philadelphia.

The *Three Shades* topping the gates are in fact three representations of Adam. Rodin, an artist who worked his

terms into multiple versions, offers the viewer a triple view of the same figure executed in the round. The joined left hands point down towards the *Thinker* seated on the lintel. This figure with his caveman's skull is Dante–as well as Rodin himself. The enlarged statue placed at the entrance of quite a few Swiss, American, and Japanese museums (twenty-one copies have been catalogued, though only twelve were authorized to be cast) also broods over Rodin's grave in the garden of his house at Meudon.

Of the preliminary sketches for the *Gates of Hell*, the third maquette is specially interesting for the symmetrical treatment of the reliefs. The *Kiss*, the main group on the left door, echoes *Ugolino*, the main group on the right. Each scene develops its own communion in horror. In the *Kiss*, Paolo Malatesta and Francesca da Rimini are joined eternally in hell, despatched thither by her jealous husband's sword. This group was to undergo a number of changes, though Rodin executed his initial idea on a monumental scale. This was the famous marble statue exhibited at the Salon de la Société Nationale des Beaux-Arts in 1898. It was commissioned by the state on 31 January 1888 and was installed in the Musée du Luxembourg in 1901 after being exhibited at the 1900 World's Fair. When the Musée Rodin opened, it was transferred to the Hôtel Biron. (The sculptor bequeathed his works to the nation in 1916 on condition that the Hôtel Biron be turned into a museum.) It seemed only right at the time to move all of Rodin's sculptures–and there was already a large number of them–in the Musée du Luxembourg (which was the museum of modern art of the period) to the graceful town house where the sculptor had spent his last years.

Auguste Rodin (1840–1917):
The Gates of Hell, 1880–1917.
Bronze, 20′ × 13′.

NEO-BAROQUE

Jules-Félix Coutan (1848-1939):
Luminous fountain at the foot of the Eiffel Tower.
Paris World's Fair of 1889.

Symbolism was reserved for literary and musical sensibilities attuned to the hidden connections between things. Elected officials preferred works of a more explicit nature. They wanted art that the man in the street could understand. They clung to the belief, though obscure allegories were still in fashion (more so than ever, in fact), that a work of art must deliver its meaning at first glance.

The neo-Baroque style blossomed in Paris with the World's Fairs. Identical causes produce identical results. The Counter Reformation had sought to gain back its recalcitrant faithful by turning its churches into brilliant theatres. The Third Republic hoped to dazzle its European neighbours and the nations of the New World with its own lavish ornamentation. Moreover, the swirls and scrolls of the neo-Baroque had definite ideological connotations. The dynamic forms of the illuminated fountain at the 1889 World's Fair and Recipon's quadrigas (1900) poised above the cornices of the Grand Palais in Paris

Auguste Bartholdi (1834-1904):
The River Saône and its Tributaries, 1887-1889.
Hammered lead.
Place des Terreaux, Lyons.

Achille Dumilâtre (1844-?) and
Gustave Debrie (1842-1924):
Monument to the Girondins, 1894-1902.
Bronze.
Place des Quinconces, Bordeaux.

seemed to proclaim: Long live movement, long live progress, long live the future!

In spite of a new and threatening rival, the automobile, the horse remained a favourite motif for expressing movement. The *Monument to the Girondins* in Bordeaux, whose fifty-two tons of bronze were reinstalled on the original site in 1984, and the Lyons fountain both make ample use of blowing manes, bared teeth, arched necks and menacing hoofs. With their wave-like silhouettes, these fiery steeds seem emanations of the tangled shadows and misty light at their feet.

Dumilâtre called on Debrie to design the horses, the only composition of any aesthetic interest in the *Monument to the Girondins*. Bartholdi changed the title of his group which was originally conceived for Bordeaux. In 1857, tired of waiting, he sold it to the City of Lyons, merely changing the names of the river and its affluents. Both compositions draw on the same model, the horses skimming over the surface of Tuby's *Bassin d'Apollon* at Versailles, itself derived from Guido's *Aurora* at the Casino Rospigliosi. The nineteenth century absorbed the artistic traditions of earlier ages and restated them with a magnificent lack of restraint. Therein lies its greatness.

Georges Recipon (1860-1920):
Harmony Triumphing over Discord, 1900.
Beaten copper.
Seine side, Grand Palais, Paris.

TEXTBOOKS IN STONE

The vogue for public monuments took on such proportions under the Third Republic that it resulted in the near extinction of the genre. Among other things, the public statue became a pedagogical instrument. The worthy citizen set the example. Raised on a pedestal, his effigy looked down on the passing crowd. The altar on which this god was placed was usually ornamented with reliefs depicting his achievements. He was often surrounded by figures of secondary rank to offset his own importance. But inevitably, once each public square had been provided with its monument and each personage of first and even second magnitude had been honoured, there came a time when public monuments seemed to have degenerated into an industry. And since it was essentially an industry of the left, right-wing governments were quick to put an end to it. The monuments of the Third Republic were conceived as a way of "writing history in capital letters"; to us they are merely forgotten landmarks.

The *Monument to Victor Hugo* seemed doomed from the start. Hugo's literary executor, Paul Meurice, was obliged to donate his share of the royalties from Hugo's posthumous œuvre to the fund for the monument, for the public subscription had failed to bring in the required amount. (This gesture was perhaps not entirely dictated by unselfish motives: the pedestal was to be adorned with medallion portraits of Meurice and Auguste Vacquerie.) The Place Victor-Hugo in Paris is no longer graced with the bronze figure of the poet meditating on a rock at Guernsey, surrounded by the Four Winds of the Spirit (each standing some ten feet high): the lyric and epic muses beating their wings, like great birds on a reef, the muse of satire with her whip, the muse of drama with her mask. They were among the first bronze statues to be sent to the foundry by the Vichy government in November 1941. One relief alone has survived.

Louis-Ernest Barrias (1841-1905):
Monument to Victor Hugo, 1902.
Bronze, melted down under the Occupation.
Formerly Place Victor-Hugo, Paris.

Alexandre Falguière (1831-1900):
Monument to Louis Pasteur,
1896-1904, completed
by Victor Peter.
Detail of the base.
Place de Breteuil, Paris.

Gustave Doré (1833-1883):
Monument to Alexandre Dumas the Elder, 1883.
Bronze and stone. Place Malesherbes, Paris.

during a grape harvest. These scenes have a common theme: the peace of health restored, death recedes.

Yet another means of giving one a new lease of life—or at least of reliving the past–is reading. Writers let us experience other lives, visit other worlds. They were favourite subjects for monuments. Alexandre Dumas, who had helped generations to dream, was considered important enough to merit a particularly large monument on the Place Malesherbes. Actually the three Dumas are celebrated, each on his own pedestal. Alexandre Dumas *père* is graced with four secondary figures; a seated bronze d'Artagnan wearing a magnificent plumed hat, and three attentive readers, or rather two readers and an illiterate worker who is obviously listening intently to one of the master's tales. The group's role is to make it clear that the personage towering above is a writer (as though the quill in the statue's hand were not a sufficient clue). Thanks to this device, we learn something about the public Dumas was addressing.

The position of the secondary figures enhancing the principal personage was by no means insignificant. The monument to Guy de Maupassant, installed in 1897 in the Parc Monceau, Paris, includes a female reader of novels or stories reclining at the writer's feet.

Raoul Verlet (1857-1923):
Monument to Guy de Maupassant, 1897.
Marble.
Parc Monceau, Paris.

One of the personages most frequently honoured with a public monument was Louis Pasteur, the scientist whose discoveries relating to microbes, fermentation, rabies, and so forth, earned him statues in Alès (1896), Lille and Melun (1897), Arbois and the Paris Sorbonne (1901), Dôle and Chartres (1902). The Pasteur monument on the lawn of the Avenue de Breteuil in Paris is the last of the series. Despite the fact that the governing board of the Institut Pasteur named a committee to erect a monument to the scientist as early as 1895, it was only in 1904 that the indelibly white pyramid was unveiled. Designed by Falguière, who died before completing it, the monument was finished by the sculptor's student Victor Peter. An anecdotal frieze of life-size figures runs along the base. It shows a mother holding out her child to the scientist who will save it, a shepherd playing his pipes while watching over his flock, an oxherd driving his oxen, a young woman resting

FIN-DE-SIÈCLE STATUETTES

Agathon Léonard (1841-1923):
The Swirling Scarf, 1900.
Sèvres biscuit ware,
height 15½" and 16½".

▽ Raoul Larche (1860-1912):
Loie Fuller Dancing, c. 1900.
Gilt bronze lamp, 13" high.

▷ Pierre Roche (1855-1922):
Loie Fuller Dancing, c. 1900.
Bronze, 21½" high.

Only a few monumental sculptures reflect the stylistic influence of Art Nouveau. The most noteworthy examples are Pierre Roche's *Fleur de Lys Tomb* (1902), now in the gardens of the Ecole de Nancy museum, and some of Gaudí's structures in Barcelona. In England, Alfred Gilbert's masterpieces are a blend of flamboyant Gothic and Art Nouveau. Meissonier's Renaissance armour and his gold and silver work tend towards the slender sinuous lines which characterized the new art around the turn of the century. His *St George* (1895), an Apollo in classical contrapposto, seems draped in wing sheaths and glittering seashells. The outer forms reveal the languid ambiguities of the soul.

Agathon Léonard's *Swirling Scarf* (1900) is an expression of pure movement in the manner dear to the neo-Baroque artists of the dawning 1900s. It was issued in biscuit ware by the Sèvres porcelain works, and figured in an elaborate centrepiece which was presented to the Czarina when the Russian monarchs visited Paris. In spite of its technical brilliance, its graceful forms can hardly compare to the artistry of Loie Fuller's sweeping veils. The American dancer offered sculptors new forms, which enthralled them, much as the "dance" of jellyfish captivated Paul Valéry: "The freest, most flexible, most voluptuous dance there is is that of the giant medusae... madly susceptible flesh of glass, domes of waving silk, hyaline crowns, alert elongated ribbons swept by rapid tremors, fringes, wrinkles and creases they draw in and out... Nothing is solid in their elastic crystal bodies, no bones, no joints, no fixed ligaments, no discernible segments..."

Air and light completely revolutionized classical academicism. Yet Art Nouveau statuettes were often merely decorative adjuncts. More often than not they served as lamps, vases, epergnes. This is not to say that Art Nouveau was confined to the minor arts; even the most purely artistic creators of the period succumbed to its enchantments.

Alfred Gilbert (1854-1934):
St George, detail of the Tomb of the Duke of Clarence,
c. 1894-1896.
Aluminium and ivory, 18″ high.

FUGIT AMOR

Ernest Damé (1845-1920):
Fugit Amor, 1877.
Plaster, 8'10" high.

René de Saint-Marceaux (1845-1915):
Our Destinies, 1898 (destroyed).
Plaster, 59" high.

The railways, steamships, and the telegraph brought about great changes in human habits and customs. Even feelings seemed to be speeding up. Modern lovers were in too much of a hurry to respect the slow stages of seventeenth-century courtship plotted out in Mademoiselle de Scudery's *Carte du tendre*. Thanks to the speed of modern transportation–a speed never previously attained by man–everybody dreamed of catching up with happiness. After the seething forms of neo-Rococo made fashionable by the Goncourt brothers under Napoleon III, the fleeing movements of Baroque art were back in style and becoming increasingly fluid under the influence of Art Nouveau.

At the Salon of 1875, Jean-Paul Aubé exhibited a smiling *Siren* leading away her victim. In 1877, Ernest Damé created a sculptural equivalent of the following lines from Victor Hugo's *Chants du Crépuscule*:

Do not flee from me!
Ah, how different are our destinies: I linger,
While you fly away!

Shown under the title *Fugit Amor*, the model of this sculpture was acquired by the City of Paris, cast in bronze in 1879, and installed on the Square Ranelagh. (It was removed under the German occupation during World War II.) Its theme recalled the flirting eighteenth-century cupids and Psyches.

Jean Hugues, who was awarded the Grand Prix de Rome in 1875, modelled, for his second submission from the Villa Medici, a group depicting the *Shades of Francesca da Rimini and Paolo Malatesta*. It was displayed at the Salon of 1879. There is nothing gay or light about the sketch at the Musée d'Orsay. The interplay of parallel oblique lines creates an effect of speed which is counterbalanced by the tragic weight of the figure of Francesca. Perhaps Rodin, who exhibited two bust-portraits at the same Salon, understood the true originality of this amorous pursuit. After sculpting his own version of the famous Dantean episode (*The Kiss*), he was to go even further in the tragic exploration of this theme. His lovers lie entangled on the ground, their forms swelling confusedly like magma. Then he turned them around. A new group emerged, *Fugit Amor*, described by Paul Bourget in his book *Mensonges* in 1887. Rodin's creative energy flowed from form to form, title to title. *Fugit Amor* was initially called *Headlong Towards the Abyss*, then *Night*, then *Dawn*, then *Voici Venir* (the first words of Baudelaire's poem "Harmonie du soir"), and lastly *La Sphinge* (the female sphinx). The group's forms underwent change too. The male figure kneels and stretches his arms skywards in the *Prodigal Child*. The female sphinx became a female *Centaur*.

The forms and title of Camille Claudel's masterpiece changed too. The *Vanished God* she exhibited at the 1894 Salon was called *L'Age mûr* (Middle Age) a year later, when it was viewed by Inspector Armand Silvestre in the artist's studio. The first version, a plaster copy of which survives in the Musée Rodin, depicts the male figure hesitating, leaning back towards the young woman clasping him with both her hands. In the definitive version exhibited at the 1903 Salon the group has crossed the great divide and is drawn forward towards the yawning abyss. The old woman in her heavy drapery is a dead weight. She firmly grips the hands of the man journeying along the crest of the wave. The young woman leans forward, imploring him to turn back. She has lost. The gap is widen-

Camille Claudel (1864-1943):
Middle Age, 1894-1903.
Bronze, 45″ high, 64″ long.

ing. This was in fact the sculptor's own drama, and it led her to the asylum where she was to die thirty years later. Even in the age of speed, heartbreak was slow to heal–as slow as it had always been in the past.

Saint-Marceaux gave the angst at the passing of time a particularly dynamic expression. Watching clouds scudding in an autumn sky, he got the idea of his group, *Our Destinies* which was exhibited at the Salon de la Société Nationale des Beaux-Arts in 1898 under the title, *Towards the Unknown*. The three figures rest for a moment on the ruins of a Greek temple before resuming their horizontal flight. They were never cast or carved in a durable material. The model donated to the Reims museum in 1931 was destroyed. Man's life is but a moment, happiness is elusive, sorrow is eternal. Sculpture is ill equipped to express such sentiments, which are the true territory of poetry and music. Yet by giving movement an allegorical role, it created a new language in the age of Symbolism.

Auguste Rodin (1840-1917):
Fugit Amor, before 1887.
Bronze, 11¾″ high, 20″ long.

THE LIVING MOMENT

Catching movement on the wing had its polar opposite: a preoccupation with the significant instant. A number of sculptors labelled Impressionists found their inspiration in scenes of everyday life. Some sought to capture a particular atmosphere, for example Medardo Rosso in his *Omnibus Impressions* (accidentally destroyed in 1887), *The Bookmaker* (1894), *Boulevard Impression, Paris at Night* (about 1895, no longer extant), and *Conversation in the Garden* (1896). Others, like Degas, sought to seize the fugitive moment. It was in London that Rosso composed the three figures conversing in a garden. They can be viewed only from a single point of view, an intentional limitation. Although they form a mass with the ground, they interrelate within the atmosphere recreated by the sculptor. Yet each figure rises to a solitary apex, creating an impression of individual reserve.

With Degas there is nothing imprecise. The viewer's imagination is never left to its own devices. A master draughtsman, the artist created clear-cut unambiguous forms, and willed himself to become a master of modelling. The statuettes he kneaded, then flattened, were never shown to the public. The only work of Degas's exhibited at the Salon of 1881 is the *Fourteen Year Old Dancer* with real ballet slippers, a tulle tutu, and strands of horsehair glued to her head, tied together with a real ribbon. Its impact was considerable. Yet hundreds of maquettes were found in the artist's studio after his death. The fragile nature of these wax figures (only 73 of the 150 discovered have survived) made it imperative to cast them into metal. This was done from 1921 to 1932. Twenty series were inscribed A to T. To these were added two further series not for sale. One, inscribed MODELE, was exported from France in 1976. The other, reserved for Degas's heirs, was marked HER. One more series, bought back by Hebrard and completed by him, is sometimes marked HER.D. The foundry of A.A. Hebrard, directed by Palazzolo, where they were cast, was then the best in France for its lost wax casting and patina work. The subtlest details of the modelling are reproduced in the bronze statuettes, whose spirited lines are as fresh and vigorous as in the original wax models.

Modernity oscillated between these two poles: the everyday impression, the fleeting instant. History and Knowledge were temporarily forgotten, abandoned for the delights of sense perceptions and rapid glimpses. Yet modernity also meant speed, a spark jumping between the artist and viewer. The artist, having swept away allegory, opened his eyes on a realm hitherto ignored: the quotidian. Thus each generation discovers its own New World.

Medardo Rosso (1858-1928):
Conversation in the Garden, 1896.
Wax over plaster, 29½″ × 19″.

Edgar Degas (1834-1917):
Woman Caught Unawares, between 1896 and 1911.
Bronze, 16½'' high.

SYMBOLISM

Nor was the inner dimension limited merely to the mind and the body. Matter itself was searched. This was one of the reasons why sculptors began to work again directly in wood. What interested them now was the grain, the resistence of the material they chipped at, its nodes, and the inner life of the structures that would eventually determine the finished work of art.

Maillol began his career working in tapestry, but suffered from poor eyesight and took up carving wood with a knife. His *Dancer* (1895) is a hymn to the rings in sapwood. It is a fine piece of Art Nouveau and an exemplary demonstration of respect for the inner properties of the material being carved.

Jean-Joseph Carriès experimented with ceramics. To gain a better understanding of the way clay and enamels fuse under the action of fire he settled near the porcelain and faience manufactories of the Nièvre.

The Princess of Scey-Montbéliard, née Winnaretta Singer (and later to become the Princesse de Polignac), commissioned a reliquary to house the original manuscript of Wagner's *Parsifal*, which she owned. She asked Carriès to create a monumental door in enamelled earthenware. The gates' underlying design (by Grasset) is inspired, like Rodin's *Gates of Hell*, by Renaissance portals, but the masks ornamenting it are an eclectic combination of the

Aristide Maillol (1861-1944):
Dancer, 1895.
Wood bas-relief, 8¾″ × 9½″.

It was an inner world the Symbolists explored. At about the same time psychoanalysis began probing the subconscious. To describe the mind's twilight zones, artists concentrated on the interplay of "correspondences," those secret connections Baudelaire had been the first to celebrate in verse.

Jean-Joseph Carriès (1855-1894):
Doorway (for the room where the
Parsifal manuscript was kept), 1889-1894.
Plaster model, 53¾″ × 70¾″.

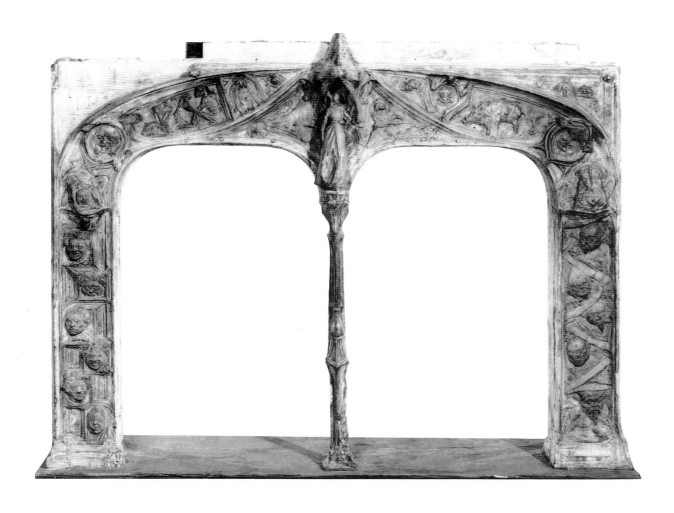

Paul Gauguin (1848–1903):
"Soyez mystérieuses"
(Be mysterious women), 1890.
Painted limewood relief,
28¾″ × 37½″.

medieval, the Chinese and the Symbolist. The animals (frogs and toads) and vegetables (pumpkins, aubergines, colocynths) from which Carriès drew his inspiration create strange teeming forms. The door was moulded in 1890. But the princess and the artist had a falling-out and it was never completed. The original model in plaster was given to a museum. It was destroyed in 1936 to make room for an exhibition. Only a maquette remains, depicting a serene "damsel" surrounded by monsters.

One of the most beautiful backs in all sculpture is that of Gauguin's Tahitian woman in the relief *Soyez mystérieuses*. The figure's forms wed the colour of the wood, to suggest the coppery skin of the climate-blessed inhabitants of the South Seas. Gauguin carved the relief prior to his first stay on Tahiti. The influence he was soon to come under was already present in his imagination. The moon and its Egyptian eye, viewed frontally, in the upper

right corner, and the face derived from a Breton calvary on the lower left, counteract the diagonal composition, which leaves half the surface (the lower right corner) empty or rather defenceless before the assault of Art Nouveau wavelets.

In Lacombe's relief, on the other hand, the entire rectangle is filled with convolutions recalling eternity's circle. For the Nabis' atelier in Versailles, Lacombe carved four bed panels in 1892. *Love* and *Death*, their realistic treatment simplified to the verge of abstraction, ornament the sides, while *Birth* and *Existence* (or *Dream*, as it was called for a long time) adorn the head and foot.

Nabi means prophet in Hebrew. The name was chosen by several painters towards 1888 as an apt label for their spiritual quest for the original sources of art, an inner quest conducted in reaction to the Impressionists' predominant sensitivity to surfaces. Lacombe was the "Nabi sculptor."

Georges Lacombe (1868–1916):
Existence (Two Lovers Merging),
1892.
Wood relief, length 55″.

RODIN'S BALZAC

In 1851, a year after Balzac's death, the sculptor Etex proposed to raise a monument to him and received the backing of Alexandre Dumas *père*; but Balzac's widow, Countess Hanska, vetoed the idea. In 1883, the day after the Dumas monument had been inaugurated, the Société des Gens de Lettres (the French writers' association), decided to follow up the idea of a Balzac monument. It opened a subscription and in 1888 the commission was given to Henri Chapu. He set to work and made many sketches for it; over seventy of them are extant. Some represent Balzac standing in his famous "monk's robe," with arms folded. In the terracotta sketch in the Musée d'Orsay, Paris, the writer still has his robe on, but the legs of his trousers are visible and he has a pen in his hand. The feminine allegory of *La Comédie Humaine* leans on the edge of the plinth, gazing up at her creator and disclosing to the world his glorious name, engraved on the plinth. Chapu died in 1891, the year when Zola was elected president of the Société des Gens de Lettres, and with Zola's support Rodin was asked to take over the work.

At that point it would have been possible to carry out Chapu's project under the direction of colleagues sympathetic to him, like Dubois, Falguière and Mercié. Or the choice might have fallen on Marquet de Vasselot, who had produced Balzac busts in plaster (1868), in bronze (1870) and in marble for the Comédie-Française (1875); he duly solicited the committee and, at the Salon of the Société Nationale des Beaux-Arts in 1896, he exhibited a Balzac-Winged-Sphinx for the centenary monument. But two men of genius had recognized each other. Just as history,

great history, is written out of the impact of an event on a dedicated mind, so Rodin, thanks to Zola, proceeded to conceive his most amazing masterpiece.

Rodin's friends, Léon Cladel and Gustave Geffroy, both fervent admirers of Balzac, came forward with advice. Like Zola himself, who carried out his own investigation, Rodin studied the portrait by Boulenger, the daguerreotype of 1842, the one of 1850 by Bisson (Balzac on his deathbed) and of course the famous bust by David d'Angers. Then he left Paris for Touraine, where he sought out local people who seemed to bear some resemblance to his subject and had them pose for him. This procedure of Rodin's was not unlike that of Charles Cordier who, for his ethnographic portraits, specifically chose what he considered to be "local types." Rodin even approached Balzac's former tailor and ordered a suit made to the writer's size; and he tried on Balzac's dressing gown, the "monk's robe." His sketch model was approved by the committee in January 1892.

The nude studies he made at the same time (as good academicians were wont to do) were done in modern attitudes, with arms folded, "defying the world." The legs, wider apart than those of his *John the Baptist*, seemed rooted in the ground.

To Marquet de Vasselot, for his *Balzac-Sphinx*, the vice-president of the Société des Gens de Lettres paid his compliments in 1896 in a letter which, in effect, "released" Rodin: "The stoutness, the stunted figure and ugly profile of the inspired writer could on no account be observable and reproducible realities. The only thing that can possibly interest us is the representation of his mind by way of the general design of his attitude, the accenting of his features, the deep and arresting flash of his eye. The physical difficulties are transient contingencies that need not be recorded in marble and bronze. These noble materials can

Auguste Rodin (1840-1917): Balzac with Dressing Gown, 1891-1892. Balzac Standing, 1891-1895.
Plaster, 42½" high. Plaster sketch, 10" high.

Balzac, nude study, 1892-1893. Balzac, nude study, 1896.
Plaster, 52¾" high. Plaster, 37" high.

Auguste Rodin (1840–1917): Balzac, 1898.
Bronze, 9′2″ high. Boulevard Raspail, Paris.

only transmit to future ages the imperishable, the permanent and the immanent, the outline of the abiding spirit, with none of the fleeting qualifications that time sweeps away to eternal oblivion."

Rodin took these pointers to heart and concentrated on the head; in other words, on the mind. Through the mane of hair and the protruding eyebrows, he conveyed an intimation of genius by exaggeration. The shapelessness of the body may owe something to Medardo Rosso, whose influence seems perceptible in the third reproduction.

The plaster, exhibited in 1898 at the Salon of the Société Nationale des Beaux-Arts, created a scandal and the *Balzac* was rejected. "The committee of the Société des Gens de Lettres feels bound, with all due regret, to protest against the rough model which Monsieur Rodin is exhibiting at the Salon and in which it declines to recognize the statue of Balzac." Rodin's friend Mathias Morhardt got up a petition in its favour and a subscription very soon covered the purchasing price of the model. Several collectors offered to buy it. Rodin turned them down: "It is my positive desire to remain the sole owner of this work of mine." The commission for the Balzac monument then fell to Falguière, the third artist called upon since 1883. The seated statue which he modelled seemed a sorry commentary on this long-drawn-out affair. Falguière had already died when, in 1902, his monument was inaugurated in the Carrefour de Friedland, in Paris. Rodin never saw his *Balzac* cast in bronze. The first casting dates from 1930 (Antwerp Museum). It was not until 1939 that Maillol and Despiau unveiled Rodin's bronze statue at the Raspail-Montparnasse intersection in Paris.

Auguste Rodin (1840-1917):
The Gates of Hell, 1880. Second sketch.
Pen and ink, 7⅞″ × 6″.

TWENTIETH CENTURY

2 THE ADVENTURE OF MODERN SCULPTURE

PERMANENCE AND AVANT-GARDE

A NEW TECHNIQUE: THE ASSEMBLAGE

SCULPTURE CONQUERS SPACE

REALISM AND SURREALISM

ABSTRACTION AND FIGURATION

Reinhold Hohl

MONUMENTALITY AND NEW TECHNIQUES

THE SPACE OF REPRESENTATION

Jean-Luc Daval

THE REDEFINITION OF AMERICAN SCULPTURE: FROM MINIMALISM TO EARTHWORKS

Barbara Rose

THE AFFIRMATION OF SCULPTURE

Jean-Luc Daval

PERMANENCE AND AVANT-GARDE

The term "modern" has been applied since late antiquity to every cultural movement which, of set purpose, has broken away from traditional forms and content and opened a new era. The transition from the nineteenth to the twentieth century was, however, more consciously felt than other such turning points as the end of an age, a *fin de siècle*, and the dawn of a new one, that of Art Nouveau and Modern Style. The economic justification for the optimistic view of the new century lay in the powerful development of science, industry and trade which had led to the prosperity of the Belle Epoque and a growing taste for art among the middle-class *nouveaux riches*, in Europe, Russia and North America. And the fruits of the colonization of India, East Asia and Africa were reaped by the commercial firms and museums of Europe.

The series of Paris World's Fairs or Expositions Universelles came as an organized manifestation of the new period consciousness in Europe. The 1889 Fair had left behind a memorial in the shape of the Eiffel Tower. That of 1900 centred on two palatial exhibition halls, the Grand Palais and the Petit Palais, where the fine arts were given pride of place, and by now they also figured prominently on the public promenades.

Paris, in 1900, stood out as the centre of the civilized world and the showplace of modern art, owing in part to the native development of French art but even more to the innovations made by the young, ambitious artists who flocked to Paris from all over Europe and from America as well. For in Paris alone, in contrast to Berlin, St Petersburg, Milan, Madrid or London, prevailed a climate favourable to modernity. The stubborn opposition to earlier innovations, those of Courbet, Manet and the Impressionists, was giving way to curiosity and interest, stimulated by further outbreaks of novelty, and collectors eager to buy were being attracted to Paris from Central Europe, Russia and the United States. Subversion paid off, in gold franks, and the artist who could administer a shock made his name overnight.

In the field of sculpture, it was Rodin who drew artists and purchasers to Paris. During the 1900 World's Fair he exhibited bronzes and marbles, produced with the help of many studio assistants, in a pavilion of his own erected in the Place de l'Alma at the expense of wealthy friends; it cost 160,000 francs, and there he sold works to the value of 200,000 francs. By now Rodin's achievement had placed him in the forefront of the progressive movement. It was searchingly studied by the young moderns, who some five years later were ready to go beyond it and develop new concepts. Independent Paris exhibitions, like the Salon des Indépendants (from 1884) and the Salon d'Automne (from 1903) offered the avant-garde a forum where its researches were publicly documented every year, and where, in separate rooms, retrospectives were held; those, for example, of Medardo Rosso's impressionist modellings or Gauguin's South Sea pictures. So 1905 is a reasonable starting point for what is here called modern sculpture, while 1950 marks the transition from modern to contemporary sculpture after the Second World War.

◁ A turn of the century Sculpture Salon
in the Grand Palais, Paris, 1900.

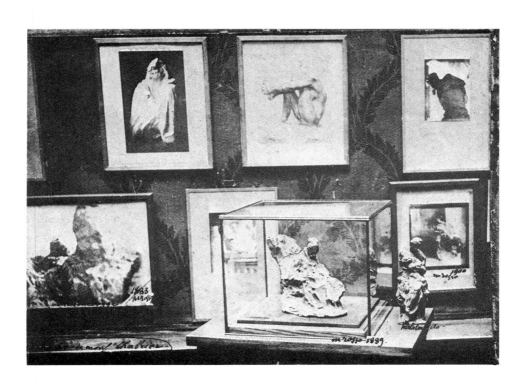

The Salon d'Automne, Paris, 1904:
View of the Medardo Rosso exhibition, with
a photograph of Rodin's *Balzac*, upper left.

Henri Matisse (1869-1954): Madeleine I, 1901.
Bronze, 23¼″ high.

THE SITUATION BETWEEN 1900 AND 1905

Pablo Picasso (1881-1973):
Mask of a Picador with Broken Nose, 1903.
Bronze, 7¼" high.

While Rodin was still rising to the heights of justly lasting fame, a number of progressive younger artists were already calling his art in question. Drawn to Paris by the reputation of the master, provincials and foreigners–like Constantin Brancusi coming from his native Rumania in 1904–no sooner felt the winds of change blowing over Paris than they made a clean sweep of all their previous standards and dubbed traditional works from Michelangelo to Rodin "beefsteak sculpture."

It is true that the academic and official style of sculpture, to which Rodin's works still belonged, was so firmly entrenched in middle-class taste and the criteria of selection committees for public monuments that renovation from new sources was an artistic necessity. It is also true that the pathos of Rodin's style, the literary nature of his compositions and the predominance of bronze and marble (commercialized as forms for modelled wares) were making way for other and newer principles better suited to the expression of a "modern" mentality. Recently acquired knowledge of the sculpture of earlier epochs and other continents obtained from archeological excavations and overseas colonial empires had significantly changed and widened the horizons of European culture.

Before considering the various modern tendencies critical of Rodin, it is necessary to establish clearly what permanent innovations Rodin contributed to modern sculpture. The first of these was the artistic use of the torso and in general of fragments as a definitive art form. The Rodin

exhibitions of 1898 and 1900 contained anatomically incomplete figures, lacking a head, arm, leg or even all their limbs. These were not conceived as *bozzetti* or studies, but as complete works of art and were at once taken as models by some young painters and sculptors. In 1901 Matisse's armless statuette *Madeleine I* was a lyrical version of Rodin's likewise armless *Meditation* (1897). Picasso's *Mask of a Picador with Broken Nose* (1903), not solid but made as a thin mask, reflects Rodin's *Mask of a Man with Broken Nose* (1864). This latter piece, which was only hollow owing to an accident in the studio, recalls the busts of Michelangelo by Daniele da Volterra (1565). Following Rodin's example, many later sculptors have regarded the head as valid treatment of an initially entire figure (Bourdelle's *Head of Eloquence* for the General Alvear monument, 1914-1917). Other separate parts of the body were likewise considered complete sculptures. The finest examples are undoubtedly Giacometti's *Arm* (1947) and *Leg* (1956). In each case, as in Rodin, the fragment is more expressive than the representation of the whole body. This effect had already been noted by Rainer Maria Rilke in an essay on Rodin (1903) and in a poem on an ancient torso of Apollo (1906).

The speed with which the torso in the narrowest sense of the term (without head or limbs) became a theme, and a fashionable one, was quite remarkable. The best example of this vogue is Maillol's torso of *Action in Chains* (1906). Its plastic force far exceeds that of the original allegory of the woman with her hands tied behind her back, which

111

Wilhelm Lehmbruck (1881-1919):
Woman's Torso, 1910.
Artificial cement, 46″ high.

Maillol had conceived for the monument at Puget-Théniers commemorating the often imprisoned socialist agitator Auguste Blanqui. As in Maillol's later bronze figures of nude women personifying *Spring* or *L'Ile de France*, the body alone has imposing plastic presence, whereas complete with head and treated as a stylized portrait, the effect would be a lasting calamity.

Typical of the transition from Rodin to the younger generation is the Elberfeld Torso by Bernhard Hoetger, who had come to Paris in 1900 and exhibited it at the Salon d'Automne five years later. Rodin commented on this work in a letter he wrote to Louis Vauxcelles, art critic of *Gil Blas*: "Hoetger has found the way I was seeking, the only right way to the monumental, and if I were not an old man, I would follow it."

In 1910 Hoetger's neighbour in Paris, Wilhelm Lehmbruck, produced his well-known, basically still symbolist torso of a woman, which won him in Germany the reputation of a "modern" sculptor, a reputation he strangely enough still enjoys.

The victory over symbolism, which in Rodin's art was more striking in his subjects than in his style, was one of the tasks that fell to the younger generation of modern sculptors. A fine work, typical of this symbolism in sculpture,

which was particularly flourishing in Belgium, is George Minne's *Fountain with Five Kneeling Boys* in Ghent (1898) and in the new museum built in Essen by Henry van de Velde (1905). It is not apparent at once that the figure, repeated five times kneeling on the rim of the basin, like Narcissus looking at his reflection in the water, is one and the same youth. Minne had been in Paris in 1891 and worked for a while with Rodin, and this fountain was a most successful application of another part of Rodin's heritage, namely the principle of the incorporation of a figure or fragment, repeated in many different or varied postures, in a work of many parts. Rodin's most effective composition of this kind is the group *The Three Shades* (1880) which crowned the project for the *Gates of Hell* (1880-1887) with the same figure (originally a Michelangelesque Adam) cast three times. This permutation principle created by Rodin was to be taken up again much later by contemporary American sculptors.

Aristide Maillol (1861-1944):
Torso known as Action in Chains, 1906.
Bronze, 47¼″ high.

George Minne (1866-1941):
Fountain with Five Kneeling Boys, 1898.
Marble, height of figures 30¾″.

Joseph Bernard (1866-1931):
Striving After Nature, 1906.
Stone, c. 16″ high.

Regarded by the ageing Rodin as "the only right way to monumentality," this renovation and at the same time authentic victory over Salon sculpture and symbolism, though still neoclassical in Germany with Adolf von Hildebrand and in France with Maillol, was none the less officially recognized as "modern sculpture" in both countries until the Second World War. The principles of this style were set forth by Hildebrand in 1893 in his influential book *Das Problem der Form in der bildenden Kunst* and the monumental Wittelsbach Fountain in Munich (1894-1901). In his view, the massive art of the Egyptians under the Pharaohs was the only pure sculpture. The technical requirements for this "pure" sculpture, the means of superseding Rodin's neo-Baroque modelling, were, he maintained, to be found in the direct cutting technique, by which the master, hammer and chisel in his own hands, carves his figure, removing layer by layer from the block of stone but leaving both the original block and the marks of his chisel still visible. In France this technique was introduced by Joseph Bernard, who was inspired by medieval French cathedral sculpture (another favourite subject of the ageing Rodin); the first example was probably his neoclassical head of a woman, *Striving After Nature* (1906). Direct cutting was the watchword of the school

that held the field until after the First World War, and even later with Henry Moore, who kept to it in his imitations of Aztec ritual figures. Another lesser master, Brancusi, claimed to continue the tradition of the peasant art of his native Transylvania by means of this "true," as opposed to Rodin's "beefsteak" sculpture. In reality, he had taken it over from Joseph Bernard in 1907, and from 1908 onwards, indirectly, at first through André Derain and possibly also Modigliani, and later directly from African tribal art in the Ethnographical Museum in Paris.

The finest achievement of neoclassical monumental sculpture was, however, the *Mediterranean* by Aristide Maillol, shown in plaster at the 1905 Salon d'Automne, and also executed in stone and bronze. Its cubic stability of form harks back neither to Egyptian art nor to the ordinary square hewn stone, but rather to early Greek classical art. After 1881, illustrated reports of the excavation campaigns made known the metopes and reliefs of the Temple of Zeus at Olympia. Maillol modelled his work on the figure of the youth, in the group of athletes on the east pediment, seated on the ground with one leg raised and the other tucked under him.

It is perhaps significant that this masterpiece of "pure" sculpture was not the work of an artist trained as a sculptor, above all not by Rodin, but on the contrary of a symbolist painter and tapestry weaver who was already past forty when he took up sculpture. In the nineteenth century, painters like Daumier, Degas and Bonnard sculpted in private and in the European tradition; shortly before and above all during the first decade after 1900, however, painters like Gauguin, Matisse, Derain, Picasso, Kirchner and Boccioni, shattered all the rules of sculpture and introduced innovations that had a decisive influence on the development of modern sculpture.

Aristide Maillol (1861-1944): The Mediterranean, 1901. Bronze, 40½″ high.

THE SHOCK OF THE PRIMITIVE ARTS

What led modern sculptors (and modern painters) to break with the rules of the Western art tradition was the discovery that the images of the "primitive" peoples in the colonial empires of Oceania and Africa were not merely exotic curiosities, ethnological specimens, examples of art in its infancy, or barbaric fetishes, but creative works with the same title to consideration as the Venus of Milo. This reappraisal was brought about by avant-garde artists in Paris and Germany (Dresden, Berlin and Munich) after 1905.

The products of primitive art had, it is true, been known in Europe for a long time. Since the middle of the nineteenth century, they had been seriously studied by scholars hoping to find the origins of art in the works of children and primitive races. In the second volume of his *Réflexions et menus propos d'un peintre genevois* (1848), Rodolphe Toepffer had affirmed that a monumental stone head from Easter Island was as much a work of art as Michelangelo's *Moses*. In the last third of the century, examples of Oceanian and African primitive art obtained the entry to public collections, world's fairs and popular magazines, and also—although mainly as curios—to some artists' studios. It was only after 1900, however, that we hear of artists visiting ethnological collections (1902, Jacob Epstein, the Trocadero Museum in Paris; 1903, and more knowledgeably after 1906, Ernst Ludwig Kirchner, the ethnographical collection in Dresden; 1904-1905, Vlaminck and Derain, the Trocadero Museum, Paris; early 1906, André Derain, the British Museum, London; early summer 1907, Picasso the Trocadero Museum, Paris; in 1907, Kandinsky, the Berlin ethnographical collection, which was also visited several times after 1911 by Schmidt-Rottluff, Franz Marc and other German artists). From 1906 onwards, artists began to buy Oceanian and African figures and masks (first Matisse and in the same year Derain; in 1907 Picasso and a little later Braque). After another two years, there were already collectors and dealers who specialized in these works and knew how to appreciate their artistic value; one of the first of these was the Hungarian, Joseph Brummer, who had worked as a sculptor with Rodin. The influence of "Negro art" on modern sculpture and painting began to be noticeable in Paris from 1907 on, and in Dresden, Berlin and London after 1911-1912. By 1920 it had become almost universal, and it held its own without any decline until the thirties, when Oceanian, Indian and Eskimo art became a main source of inspiration of the Surrealists and their followers.

Paul Gauguin (1848-1903):
Oviri (The Savage Woman), 1891-1893.
Sandstone, 29″ high.

André Derain in his Paris studio, winter 1908-1909.
Beside him, his *Standing Female Nude*;
beneath it, his *Crouching Figure* of 1907.

The most oppressive yoke of the European past was the *contrapposto* principle, the difference in a figure between the "supporting leg" and the "free leg," according to which if one arm is relaxed, the other will be tensed in compensation. This rule was discovered about 480 B.C. by Greek sculptors (according to some, by Kritios) as a means of giving a stone statue the lifelike appearance of a body of flesh and blood. In reality, counterpoise is the natural position of the body, as can be seen, for example, in the attitude taken up by a person waiting for a bus. The principle was no longer known to the "primitives" of the Middle Ages, but from the early Renaissance until Rodin and Maillol hardly a figure was created in which it was not applied. From 1907 onwards, on the other hand, following the lesson of Gauguin, it disappeared from modern sculpture except when it was deliberately retained in reactionary protest against "primitivism" in modern art.

Nearly all ethnographical photographs show negroes in the same *contrapposto* position. Tribal art, however, could not use such natural positions because it was supernaturally oriented. The necessary resemblance for supernatural efficacy was the reason for the predominant align-

Standing Songwe Figure from the Congo (Zaïre).
Wood, metal, feathers, 41¼" high.

The Gauguin retrospective at the 1906 Salon d'Automne in Paris, which included his *Oviri* (1891-1893), showed that the primitive races as well as the ancient and non-European cultures afforded an alternative to the academic canons of sculpture. In 1901, in Paco Durrio's Paris studio, Picasso had already seen some of Gauguin's "exotic" works and also pieces from the South Seas (in particular, Tiki statues); and in 1906 Picasso himself made good use of Iberian sculpture (that is, the pre-Roman carvings of Spain). How he and other artists integrated primitive art in their works will be considered in the next chapter.

It is necessary now to identify the specific features of this art. Picasso described it as "reasonable"; Matisse said that, unlike European sculpture always rooted in the representation of a given body and muscular structure, it was based in the first place on the material and on invented forms and proportions. In the objects created by primitive peoples, both Picasso and Matisse saw an art (in reality many different arts) whose inexhaustible power of invention was aimed at the production of highly expressive images embodying an independent lifelike personality. That this was a liberation was recognized by even the archclassicist Maillol, although he himself did not have recourse to it: "Negro art contains more ideas than Greek art. We no longer know how to take such liberties. We are too much tied to the past."

ment of the body, torso and limbs on the same axis. The size of the various parts of the body was made proportionate to the magic informing them. "Too short" legs were only a plinth with the knees bent half-way between the sitting and standing positions. The volume given to the torso, hands and genitals was an expression of their supernatural force. The primitive artist did not copy a face, he

Grebo Mask from the Ivory Coast or Liberia.
Wood and fibres, 25¼" high.

Colossal Stone Head on Easter Island.

Bangwa Mask from Cameroon.
Wood, 8" high.

created a physiognomy; he did not portray eyes but the power in their gaze; he did not set out from a comprehensive synthetic "head" or "body" but rather put together their most active component parts. Altogether, he had the difficult task of embodying something invisible and wholly secret in images and masks resembling real bodies and faces only by approximate analogy. The presence of these creations among men was a matter of ritual, often only a momentary appearance in conjunction with costume and rhythmic dances. The examples reproduced here show how deeply their appearance is marked by the materials and methods used in making them as well as the painting and other material adjuncts, and how much of their strength stems directly from their "primitive" technique. They have been chosen with a view to comparison with the corresponding European works considered in the following chapters.

ADAPTATION AND IMITATION OF TRIBAL ART

Derain's first sculpture was probably the *Standing Female Nude*, after Gauguin's *Oviri* which he had seen at the 1906 Salon d'Automne. The stance of the figure, however, is still strongly marked by the European counterpoise principle. The *Twins*, in the Wilhelm Lehmbruck Museum at Duisburg, recall archaic terracotta statues from Mali. In their crudity, they might almost be forerunners of the *Crouching Figure* in Vienna, exhibited by the dealer Kahnweiler in the autumn of 1907. This compact cubic figure has a significant place in modern sculpture. Its square form and stumpy feet bring to mind the Aztec stone statue of the god Xochipilli, which Derain could have seen in the British Museum in 1906. In the photograph of Derain in his studio taken by the American Gelett Burgess in the winter of 1908-1909, this *Crouching Figure* serves as a plinth for the *Standing Female Nude*. In the lower right-hand corner, the photograph includes the frontal view of ·

◁ André Derain (1880-1954):
Crouching Figure, 1907.
Stone, 13″ high.

▽ Pablo Picasso (1881-1973):
Figure, 1907.
Painted oakwood, 32″ high.

The first European artists to study Oceanian and African objects as instructive works of art were not trained sculptors but painters: Matisse, Picasso, Derain, Kirchner and Schmidt-Rottluff. The conclusions they reached were therefore concerned with their painting. For the French, the qualities of "Negro art" confirmed the autonomy of the picture, a concept which they had learnt from Cézanne. Picasso went still further, seeing art not as a reproduction or decoration but as a magical counter-force independent of reality. The young German artists who had founded the Brücke group in Dresden in 1905, a year later adopted a programme to free themselves from traditional standards, and from 1910-1911 onwards joined up with other "Expressionists" in Berlin. For these artists, the art forms of primitive peoples were the expression of a sensually attractive and frankly voluptuous Eden-like existence.

The influence of tribal art was manifested in different ways and differing degrees, ranging from barely noticeable adaptation to open imitation. Its impact on modern sculpture was clearly indicated by the presence of "African proportions," short legs, thick thighs, a long torso and an even bigger head (or a very small one). From the autumn of 1906 to the winter of 1908 André Derain, teaching himself, produced half a dozen sculptures which he cut directly in limestone from the staircase of his parents' home at Châtou. These works have an important place in the history of art, because they were examples of the stage reached by European sculpture at the time when Gauguin was opening up a new world, and extra-European and primitive sculpture although not yet fully differentiated, together with the direct cutting principle, were pointing the way to a new aesthetic.

a stone head, after a Peruvian model. In his arms, Derain is holding perhaps his latest work, a *Cat* carved from a cylindrical piece of wood and painted green with red spots. The reproduction of Cézanne's *Five Bathers* (Kunstmuseum, Basel) was a help to Derain in painting his big picture, *Bathers*, in 1908 (National Gallery, Prague).

Picasso's "Negro period" (summer 1907 to autumn 1908) was preceded by a longer preliminary trend also affecting his sculpture. This period, after his "Iberian" phase (1906-1907), was at first strongly marked by the influence of Gauguin's relief carvings, then with the production of many drawings after partly identifiable tribal works it became finally more specifically "African." The only exception was the statue of a man with features and form recalling New Hebridean fernwood carvings. No other artist mastered the stylistic rules and spirit of Negro art so completely as Picasso, or created in keeping with them such characteristic and significant sculptures. Indeed, in 1907 he worked as though he had been the artist of an African tribe of which he was the only member. *Figure (Caryatid)* is one of four carvings of women made by Picasso in columnar form, 32 inches high and express-

Karl Schmidt-Rottluff (1884-1976):
Red and Blue Head (Anguish), 1917.
Painted wood, 11¾" high.

Ernst Ludwig Kirchner (1880-1938):
Woman Dancing, 1908-1912.
Wood painted yellow and black, 34¼" high.

ing monumental strength and size. According to the preliminary sketches, they should have supported a bowl on their heads and the palms of their upturned hands, in the same way that figures of African women carry a throne or a drum. The orange drawing on the wood and the rough marks of the axe still on the surface show that Picasso had not finished the work.

The difference between French and German adaptations of tribal art is brought out clearly by a comparison of Picasso's *Figure (Caryatid)* with Kirchner's *Woman Dancing*. Kirchner poses a European model in a lascivious, barbaric dance. In this work, he created the style and substance of German Expressionism, to which Schmitt-Rottluff, Max Pechstein and, a generation later, Hermann Scherer, contributed typical works.

The German Expressionists were fascinated by the art of the South Seas. In 1914 Emil Nolde and Max Pechstein went out to New Guinea. After the First World War, Kirchner fell ill and had to spend some time in Davos. There, in the Alpine heights of eastern Switzerland, he led a Gauguin-like existence. Like Gauguin, he carved his own furniture, half-African, half-Oceanian, akin to folk art and in any case drawing only on exotic reminiscences. For his *Red and Blue Head (Anguish)* (1917), Schmitt-Rottluff was inspired by the reproductions in Carl Einstein's book *Negerplastik* (1915). He combined the favourite bright colours of the expressionist painters with various African tribal styles including the concave facial forms characteristic of the inventive capacity of primitive peoples.

In 1912-1913, almost at the same time as in Berlin, the study of tribal art bore fruit in London in the work of Jacob Epstein and Henri Gaudier-Brzeska. In Paris, between 1902 and 1905, Epstein had studied the ethnological

Henri Gaudier-Brzeska (1891-1915):
Hieratic Head of Ezra Pound, 1914.
Marble, 36″ high.

Sir Jacob Epstein (1880-1959):
The Rock Drill, 1913-1914.
Bronze, 27¾″ high.

Amedeo Modigliani (1884-1920):
Head, 1911-1912.
Stone, 19¾″ high.

collection in the Trocadero, after which he was better able to appreciate the wealth of material in the British Museum. Before adopting the subjects and forms of African sculpture, he passed, however, through an Assyrian phase, of which the last and finest example was, in 1912, his Oscar Wilde memorial in the Père Lachaise cemetery in Paris. This evolution and attitude were not exclusive to Epstein; from then on, spreading from Paris, the "Negro style" became fashionable, the hallmark of an artist's modernity. Epstein was thus led to change his style by his second stay in Paris and his close contact with Modigliani. From 1912 to 1915, he made his decorative stone imitations of tribal art and South American sculpture by direct cutting. Ten years later, Henry Moore followed his lead. Epstein's most original work of this period was the *Rock Drill*—remarkable, however, not on account of the "African" presentation of the worker, almost wholly integrated with his pneumatic drill and the protective mask covering his face, but rather because his body (first cast in plaster, then in bronze) was mounted on a real tool.

In 1913, in Epstein's studio, Gaudier learnt not only the technique of direct cutting, which he made his guiding principle, but also the trend of the modern exotic style. He went to the British Museum to choose his models, particularly among the monumental stone busts from Easter Island. These were the inspiration for his *Hieratic Head of Ezra Pound*, which it took him months of work to cut out of a huge block of stone.

In Paris, the difference between adaptation and imitation of tribal art can be clearly seen in the works of Modigliani and Brancusi. In the winter of 1905-1906,

Constantin Brancusi (1876-1957):
Head of The First Step, 1913.
Wood, 10¼″ high.

Amedeo Modigliani came from Leghorn to Paris where, in 1909, he had Brancusi for a neighbour. The latter taught him the merits of direct cutting and also helped him to appreciate the plastic strength of extra-European sculpture. On that basis, between 1909 and 1915-1916, Modigliani produced only a limited number of works, but they were all purely sculptural. Constantin Brancusi, on the other hand, from 1907 to 1912 took up every stylistic novelty. From 1913 to 1918 he imitated above all works of tribal art and Rumanian folk art combining both with cubist stylization and an almost machine-tooled finish.

The aesthetic of Modigliani was an esoteric temple. His heads of women inspired by an elegant refinement of African and Buddhist art were in a style very much his own. Cut from ashlar stones stolen by night from Parisian building sites, they should all be regarded as sculptured fragments of architecture. His output totalled only twenty-three pillar-like heads, one kneeling caryatid and a standing nude woman; the last, one of his early sculptures, shows that he must have known Picasso's work in the years 1907-1908.

Brancusi did not manage to make so personal an adaptation as Modigliani. Since he did not want to imitate certain African figures too openly, he split them into fragments. He changed the title of his severed head (reminiscent of Rodin) from the *First Step* to the *First Cry*; then, placing it horizontally on an African style sculptured plinth he developed it, in polished metal, into the *Newborn* or a smooth, shining egg entitled *The Beginning of the World*. That was his way of adapting "primitive" modernity to the modernity of the technical era.

Constantin Brancusi (1876-1957):
The First Step, 1913.
Wood, 43¾″ high.

MATISSE AS SCULPTOR

Recent publications and exhibitions have given an appropriate prominence to Matisse's sculpture, which illustrates the change in character that marked the transition from nineteenth century to modern sculpture. The creations of modern sculptors were neither public monuments nor pieces for glass cases but rather personal and monumental works for private dwellings. All of them, apart from big reliefs, were made to human measure. Their subjects were busts, or heads, but not portraits, and also nude women, although not designed as reproductions of the female body. In 1900-1918, 1925-1932 and 1949-1950, Matisse produced seventy bronzes in all. Many of them evoked the problems of composition that were faced by painters of the same period. Several called forth an answer from Picasso, and some even from Giacometti. Once only, in a cylindrical relief in wood inspired by a Gauguin model, Matisse used direct cutting. Generally he modelled in clay, like Rodin, even when he also, particularly in 1913, worked with knife-blade and wire. In their final form, his sculptures were cast in bronze.

The *Recumbent Nude* (1907) can be said to have developed from the painting *Blue Nude, Souvenir of Biskra* (Baltimore Museum). Its rhythmic power springs from the torsion between the upper and lower parts of the body. Matisse had freed himself from the sculptural styles of Degas and Rodin; there was no precedent for such a distribution of volumes. Apart from the aspect shown in the reproduction, the view from the feet is particularly rich in exciting initiatives. After Picasso had seen the work, he made a number of bold experiments (1907-1908), transposing the subject in two dimensions in drawings and paintings. The simultaneous view of the back and front of a body in Matisse's *Two Negresses* (1908) prompted Picasso, in his cubist paintings of 1909, to still more daring combinations with a single figure. In the long-standing conflict between painting and sculpture as to which of the two can more completely reproduce reality, both Matisse and Picasso proved that for the intelligent artist everything is possible and the need for him to spend his time on academic instruction is a popular myth. Matisse's *Two Negresses* were his faithful reproduction of a photograph in an erotic "ethnological" magazine. The question at once arises: counterpoised or not? In the photo they are, but not in Matisse's bronze, or barely, and the reason has been given already. It is only necessary to turn to the illustration of a Cameroon carving to understand the change in the form of the busts from *Jeannette II* (1910) to *Jeannette V* (1916). This series, which began with a head even closer to a portrait, *Jeannette I*, shows how decreasing naturalism was more than offset by increasing strength in pure, plastic values. Following the rules of tribal art, the parts are treated separately, the forms are stressed and the sculpture is presented in absolute terms. In 1931 Picasso was to go even further than Matisse in this direction.

Henri Matisse (1869-1954):

◁ Recumbent Nude, 1907.
Bronze, 13½″ × 19¾″ × 11″.

▷ Two Negresses, 1908.
Bronze, 18½″ high.

Henri Matisse (1869–1954):

1. Jeannette I (Jeanne Vaderin), 1910–1913.
    Bronze, 13″ high.
2. Jeannette II, 1910–1913.
    Bronze, 10¼″ high.
3. Jeannette III, 1910–1913.
    Bronze, 23¾″ high.
4. Jeannette IV, 1910–1913.
    Bronze, 24⅛″ high.
5. Jeannette V, 1916.
    Bronze, 22⅞″ high.

Henri Matisse (1869-1954):
Woman in Back View I, 1909.
Bronze, 74¾" high.

Woman in Back View II, 1913.
Bronze, 74¾" high.

From this most instructive series, it can be seen that the sytlistic development of modern sculpture obeys an almost scientific law. It goes without saying that this is no genetic necessity; it is much more an expression of the plastic genius of Matisse, for whom each new situation was already an aim in itself before he discovered whether or how he could go still further. This point must be stressed, lest consideration of Matisse's other series, the reliefs *Woman in Back View O-IV*, should create the impression that it had been conceived as a demonstration. (The first of the series, since lost, was designated "O" because it only became known after the other four had been numbered.) The subject is a monumental woman bather seen from behind, her feet invisible under the water. The bare (feminine) back is an old theme. It was favoured in the nineteenth century not only by painters (Courbet in 1833; Chassériau, 1842; Cézanne, *Three Bathers*, 1882, bought by Matisse in 1898; Burne-Jones, 1885; Hermann Pleuer, 1888; Gauguin, 1892; Rouault, 1905), but also by sculptors (Dalou, 1889; Rodin, 1890; Bartholomé, 1901). It combined a traditional studio pose with the sensual attraction of an imagin-

ary bathing scene. In his pen and ink studies, Matisse drew the model true to nature and in the counterpoise position. In the relief, on the other hand, the figure stands in false counterpoise, exactly like the standing figure seen from behind in Gauguin's *Bathers in Tahiti*, 1892 (Metropolitan Museum, New York), with the supporting leg and the outstretched arm both on the left side. This is already an artistic programme. In any case, in *Woman in Back View O* and *I* the diagonal lines of shoulders and hips are reversed; the diagonal of the buttocks is even more strongly marked in relief *I*. From *II* onwards, the shoulder line becomes horizontal and in *IV* the hip line also. The radical change from *I* (1909-1910) to *II* (1913) was due to the use of different tools. Initially, Matisse had preferred to cut rather than model clay. The differences between *II* and *III* are still more significant. Much more of the relief space, reduced by 4 inches, is taken up by the figure, and the top of the head rises above the upper edge of the relief. The forms, even more sketchy, are twin vaults with an angular groin in the middle. The hair, as in Cézanne's *Three Bathers*, is a long tress, a half-pillar set in the hollow middle line of the

Henri Matisse (1869-1954):
Woman in Back View III, 1916-1917.
Bronze, 74¾'' high.

Woman in Back View IV, 1930.
Bronze, 74¾'' high.

back. For fifteen years, Matisse kept to this as his definitive formula.

The version *Woman in Back View IV* was made in 1930 in connection with an order for a mural piece. The artist took an old studio subject in order to try out his new conception of art, aimed at the integration of painting and architecture. The supporting and the idle limbs are no longer distinguishable. The composition, with one exception, is based on a rectilinear arrangement of vertical and horizontal lines, including now the borders of the relief (formerly, these were simply the necessary limits of the work). The figure in relief becomes itself a piece of architecture. The "error" (as Gauguin said) of the Greek sculptors from 480 B.C. on was undone! What the art of sculpture lost in "fleshly" realism was regained a hundredfold in sculptural reality.

Henri Matisse (1869-1954):
Woman in Back View O, c. 1909.
First version in clay.

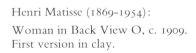

125

THE BEGINNINGS OF CUBISM

Pablo Picasso (1881–1973):
Head of Woman (Fernande), 1906.
Bronze, 14″ high.

limit: see page 166). Basically, however, the second *Fernande* is altogether different. The surface is buckled and scored with angular cavities; the several parts, head, face and neck, stand out sharply separated, a bit like a skinned animal. It might be thought that in the three years' interval Fernande's features had been disfigured by some terrible illness. The idea would be as absurd as the widely held view that the different angles of the surface parts with regard to each other were a last manifestation of "Rodin's impressionism" and served to intensify the multiple broken gleams of light on the bronze. It would be no less mistaken to think that here (and in Analytical Cubism generally) Picasso broke down the human face in order to analyze it in its different parts. In fact, the contrary is true, already for early Cubism, which had begun in the summer of 1909. In drawings and paintings, as in this sculpture, Picasso composed his objective themes out of non-objective forms. To do this, he brought together segments of surface squared off to each other and lit sometimes from the right, sometimes from the left, creating now a concave, now a convex effect. In the 1909 sculpture, he also gave his sculpture in the round the character of a relief by bringing forward, to right and left, parts of the neck that are not in real life visible from the front.

Before considering this work further, mention should be made of a story told by some historians which involves Elie Nadelmann and credits him with the invention of Cubism. Nadelmann came to Paris from Poland in 1904. After 1914 he made his career in New York, altering his

Elie Nadelman (1882–1946):
Head, c. 1906.
Pen and ink, $7\frac{1}{8}″ \times 5\frac{1}{2}″$.

At three years' interval, Picasso twice modelled the head of his companion Fernande Olivier, but the *Head of a Woman (Fernande)* of autumn 1909 was altogether different from the one made in the spring of 1906. Although to a lesser degree than the well known wax figure, the *Madman* (1905), the earlier head still had something of the soft, wax-like superficial modelling of Medardo Rosso, which this artist, as the "impressionist sculptor," had made known through his exhibition at the 1904 Salon d'Automne. As in Rosso's *Ecce Puer* (1906), the face of Picasso's 1906 *Head of a Woman (Fernande)* is covered with a light veil of painterliness, a visual impression not yet fully materialized in plastic terms. Also in common with Rosso's style is the uneven realization of the different angles of vision. Rosso, besides, only wanted to see his heads of women and children from the front, whereas Picasso's *Fernande* is shown above all in two semi-frontal oblique views, emphasizing his dissimilar treatment of the two eyes. This was still before Picasso's Iberian phase in the same year and, of course, before his study of tribal art. These features in the 1909 *Head of a Woman (Fernande)*, although they appear there in sculpture in the round, are characteristic of relief. (In 1928 Giacometti, in his sculptured plaque *Head of a Man Looking*, carried this to the name slightly to Nadelman. For him the last word in modernity were the theories of his compatriot Mecislas Golberg, who died in Paris in 1907 and whose treatise on "The Ethics of Lines" (published in 1908) reduced all art to the geometry of curves. From then on, Nadelman drew the expression of his faces using segments of circles, and this succeeded so well that in 1908 he applied the same principle in a portrait bust, no longer in existence. Picasso called on Nadelman in his Paris studio in 1908, and his 1909 *Head of a Woman* (so the story goes) must have been at least inspired by Nadelman if it was not a direct plagiary.

Even if Picasso did notice Nadelman's broken surfaces, this theory takes no account of the quite different and novel treatment of volumes in the 1909 *Fernande*. It is true that the volume of the head is modelled as a mass, but in the concept Picasso set forth in his drawings and statements, volume is interpreted as space devoid of mass and produced by intersecting planes and the hollow angles between them. In 1912, Picasso drew the corresponding conclusions (see the *Guitar*) and in Moscow in 1916 the Constructivists, notably Naum Gabo, followed his lead in theory and practice, as can be seen from a comparison of Gabo's *Constructed Head* of 1916 (page 145) with Picasso's charcoal study for *Head of a Woman* of 1909.

The *Head of a Woman* seen as a whole is at once recognizable as such, with upswept hair. On closer inspection, however, the soft parts of the face at least lose their anatomical identity and become purely plastic elements. To conceive the ridge of the nose, the curve of the cheeks and

Pablo Picasso (1881-1973):
Head of a Woman (Fernande), 1909.
Bronze, 16″ high.

Pablo Picasso (1881-1973):
Study for Head of a Woman (Fernande), 1909.
Charcoal, 12½″ × 9⅞″.

chin in terms of the underlying bone structure, the arcs round the eyes and the cheeks as the orbicular and masticatory muscles, the ridges in the neck as tendons, Picasso would have had to be a surgeon, as indeed his contemporaries Apollinaire and Proust called him, but only metaphorically. In reality, it was once more from African masks that Picasso had learnt that a head could be built up of small plastic elements, the convex and the concave being equivalent and interchangeable and independent of any natural model. The vault of the brow, for example, is certainly a convex curved unity, but Picasso constructed it from hollow and bossed surfaces, which was precisely what he had done in the summer of 1909 in many painted portraits he made of Fernande and modelled in three dimensions afterwards, in the autumn.

Although never exhibited during those years, the *Head of a Woman (Fernande)* from 1909 quickly had a European impact. One of the very few bronze versions the dealer Vollard allowed to be made of it found its way already in 1910 or 1911 into the avant-garde collection of the Prague art historian Vincenc Kramář, and made its influence felt from there. Before that the new departure had already given rise to fruitful discussion among ambitious modernist artists in Paris.

CUBO-EXPRESSIONISM

In Paris, in the spring of 1911, the Salon des Indépendants featured a particular type of cubist painting: it caught on at once as the long-sought and now fully worked out style of the modern age. Further exhibitions and many review articles soon made this Salon Cubism well known all over Europe. From 1912-1913 on, it influenced the work of other avant-garde movements: Italian Futurism, English Vorticism, the Blauer Reiter group in Munich, and the Berlin Expressionists centring on the gallery and periodical *Der Sturm*. Artists all over Europe found in the break-up or fragmentation of the object and in the bewildering fusion of a figure with its background the means of expression best suited to formulating the vital spirit of Europe in the years just before the First World War – a spirit which for some lay in the dynamism of the new means of communication by land and in the air, for others in a theosophical intellectualization or indeed a religious apocalypse, for still others in the quest for a non-objective and yet not merely ornamental art. The painters having shown the way, the sculptors followed up at once, and their style may best be described as cubo-expressionistic, for cubist sculpture it certainly was not.

Otto Gutfreund (1889-1927):
The Father II, 1911.
Plaster, 17¾″ high.

Something has already been said about the key work of this new departure: Picasso's 1909 *Head of a Woman (Fernande)*. Taking it in conjunction with Picasso's paintings of 1908-1911, we find here further sources from which these sculptors drew inspiration, and which account for the fact that their sculptures are so often reliefs or, even when done in the round, have the character of relief carving.

Among the Parisian artists may be mentioned Roger de La Fresnaye (*Italian Woman*, 1911) and Raymond Duchamp-Villon (*Lovers*, 1913). Diffusion through the rest of Europe, however, was brought about by younger artists from abroad, who had come to Paris, learnt their art under Rodin or Bourdelle, and then discovered the new advances either from Salon Cubism or directly from Picasso's works.

Particularly noteworthy among them are those sculptors from Bohemia (present-day Czechoslovakia) and Hungary who had been prepared for the new art forms by visits to the Kramar Collection in Prague and to exhibitions in Budapest. A good example of the resulting change of style, made within a brief space of time, is the sequence of portraits of his father modelled by Otto Gutfreund. After two traditional busts, he proceeded to treat the head first as a high relief with discontinuous volumes, frag-

Otto Gutfreund (1889-1927):
Cubist Bust, 1912.
Bronze, 23½″ high.

Otto Gutfreund (1889-1927):
The Father III, 1911.
Bronze relief, 15¾″ high.

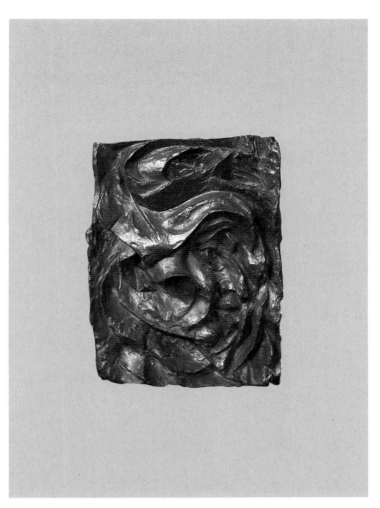

Otto Gutfreund (1889-1927):
The Father IV, 1911.
Bronze relief, 10¼″ high.

mented silhouettes and deeply shadowed transitions to the ground plane; then as a low relief full of dynamic, almost non-objective humps and hollowings. Form and content are pointedly expressionistic, not only in his *Father* (1911) but also in *Anguish*, in *Don Quixote*, in *Hamlet* (all of 1911). From 1912 on, he detached the relief form from the ground as cubified shapes in the round, which are only comprehensible in front view (*The Cellist*, 1912, where musician and instrument are fused together), and which derive from the facetting of Picasso's 1909 cubist paintings.

Gutfreund's most significant work is the *Cubist Bust* (1912), for here he carries the breakdown and recombination of the head parts to its furthest point. The result is an interplay of convex and concave forms devoid of figural meaning. Built up of surface fragments, the mass of volumes merges with the planes and openwork parts which constitute the background and surroundings. How bold this conception of sculpture is can be seen from a comparison with the bronze *Head* (1913-1914) of his fellow Czech Emil Filla. The contour of the latter is like a cut-out from one of Picasso's 1909 paintings, whose sharp-edged surface patterning is reproduced here as small relief cubes. What in this *Head* is literally "set up," is so in a figurative sense as well, for the famous "little cubes" of an early cubist picture of 1908 and 1909 are in fact only simulated shapes, appearing to project relief-wise from the canvas and yet by their tonality and non-contouring, remaining strictly on the picture surface, while Filla's step-shaped forms really do jut out.

Similar cubo-expressionist works were produced about the same time by the Hungarian sculptor Josef Csaky. His

Emil Filla (1882-1953):
Head, 1913-1914.
Bronze, 15⅜″ high.

stereometic compositions, however, like *Abstract Sculpture* (1919), derive rather from Léger's paintings and the early constructions of Henri Laurens related to them. A few years later the young Giacometti was to develop these compositions further and, using similar elements with the significance of "head," "arm" or "leg," bring them to the point of sculpture in the round.

To the Lithuanian sculptor Jacques Lipchitz, working in Paris, goes the credit, from 1915 on, of taking Salon sculpture and clothing it in the fashionable novelty of those cubist formulations which he took over year by year from Picasso's latest paintings. To his repertory belong sequences of planes set out one behind the other or built up at an angle, together with aerial forms enclosed by their silhouettes. Their plastic weaknesses become apparent when they are seen in non-frontal views. The Berlin sculptor William Wauer became acquainted with the new style at the exhibition of recent French art held in Herwarth Walden's Der Sturm Gallery. In his *Monumental Bust of Herwarth Walden* (1915), Wauer tersely rendered not only the sitter's facial features and brow, but also conveyed in cuboexpressionist terms the avant-garde side of Walden's personality. The new concept of sculpture spread to the United States, where an outstanding example is to be found in Max Weber's *Spiral Rhythm* (1915), best seen in relation to Maillol's *Torso* of 1906, for Weber had worked in Paris from 1905 to 1909. The massed volumes of a female body are dynamized in a screw-shaped manner, stereometrized in rounded-off vaultings and presented with an effective concavity as a continuum of "inner" and "outer."

Josef Csaky (1888-1971):
Abstract Sculpture, 1919.
Stone, 45″ high.

William Wauer (1866-1962):
Monumental Bust of Herwarth Walden, 1915.
Bronze, 21¼″ high.

Jacques Lipchitz (1891–1973):
Man with a Guitar, 1915.
Limestone, 38¼″ high.

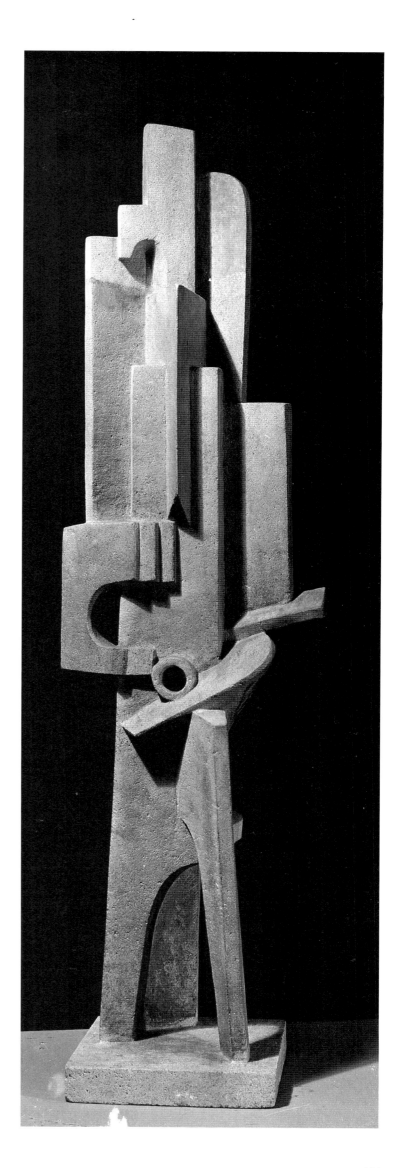

Max Weber (1881–1961):
Spiral Rhythm, 1915. Enlarged and cast, 1958–1959.
Bronze, 24⅛″ high.

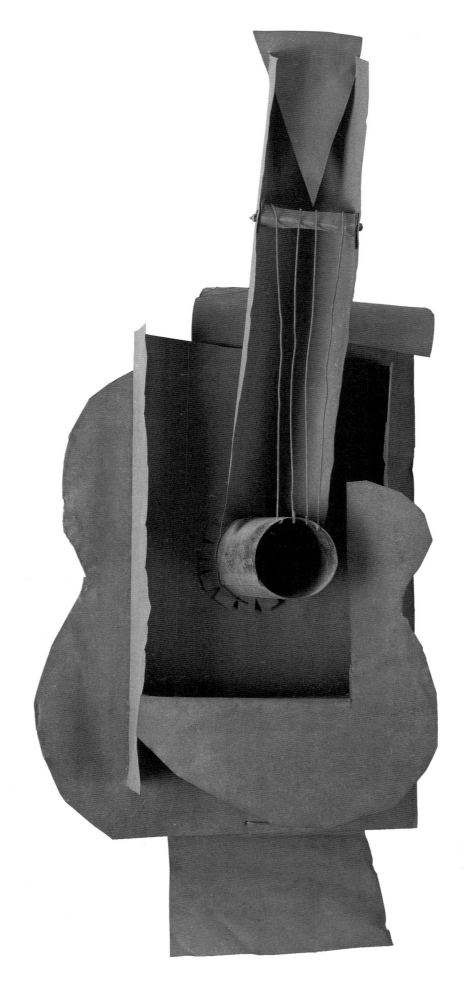

Pablo Picasso (1881–1973):
Guitar, 1912.
Sheet metal and wire, 30½″ high.

A NEW TECHNIQUE: THE ASSEMBLAGE
CUBIST CONSTRUCTIONS

If any work can be singled out as altogether transforming the notion of sculpture, it is Picasso's *Guitar* of 1912. One glance is enough to see that it is neither carved nor modelled. For such works of sculpture another term must be used from now on, and "construction" is the aptest. For the themes, too, a new category has to be defined, for nothing here is represented that corresponds to tradition, such as a human figure or an animal or an allegory bound up with them, or even a still life. What we have instead is an object: a guitar, lifesize. And there is a third peculiarity: this sculpture (using the word again as a generic notion, in contradistinction to painting) has no base and can neither stand nor lie, but hangs on the wall and in this respect is more like a picture than a relief. An even closer comparison, however, is with a mask of tribal art or with a real guitar.

Pablo Picasso (1881-1973):

◁ Bottle of Bass, Glass and Newspaper, 1914.
 Painted tin and paper, 8⅛″ high.

▽ Still Life with Glass and Knife
 on Table (Le Casse-Croûte), 1914.
 Painted wood and cloth, 10″ high.

Henri Laurens (1885-1954):
Fruit Dish with Grapes, 1918.
Polychrome construction
in wood and
sheet metal, 26¾″ high.

It does not much matter if Picasso's *Guitar* derives from the collages and papiers collés which, together with Braque, he began making in 1912. A moment simply came when Picasso decided to go on from the version in cut-out papers and construct another out of lead and wires (probably helped in this by his compatriot Julio Gonzalez who had also settled in Paris). In doing so, he deliberately moved on to sculpture, that is to a three-dimensional work in space. The resulting *Guitar* is therefore the incunabulum of Constructivism and of the later sculpture deriving from Constructivism. By virtue of its theme, it is also the incunabulum of object art and its later derivatives. But it is distinguished from Constructivism and object art in two essential points: Picasso's *Guitar* extends indeed into our real space, but it also shows us an inaccessible imaginary space (as in a painted guitar), for it lets the eye penetrate into what is in reality the invisible space of the body of the instrument. For the round sound-hole, whereby the internal and external space of a guitar communicate, Picasso contrived a pictorial effect: seen in front view, the metallic cylinder forms in the middle a circular plane which ap-

pears black. It is known that the artist got this idea from African Grebo masks on which a cylindrical form is placed perpendicularly to the surface of the piece. Picasso also took over from them the assemblage of concave and convex shapes. But his understanding of tribal art is expressed here in a deeper, broader way: just as the protuberances of the Grebo masks indicate not so much "eyes" as "glances," so the metal cylinder of Picasso's construction signifies not simply the sound-hole of the guitar, but the very source of its sound.

This work is distinguished from object art by the fact that it is not an actual playable guitar, but the plastic representation of a guitar. The same is true of the other cubist constructions on still life themes which Picasso made in considerable numbers between 1913 and 1916, sporadically in 1921 and 1924, and again in large numbers in his later years. What we have with these is always a transformation of reality, of the actual space and often actual found objects, into objects endowed now with a purely imaginary existence. His wit and fancy are given play, for example, in *Bottle of Bass, Glass and Newspaper* (1914):

taking the cover of a can of milk (still visibly labelled "Compagnie française de lait sec, Paris. Exigez la marque sur chaque couvercle"), he turns it into a beer bottle. Or again in the *Casse-Croûte* still life (1914) where a whole interior is conjured up in trompe-l'œil perspective.

Coming in 1910 from Russia to Paris, where he seems to have been stimulated more by the Futurists than by Picasso, Vladimir Baranoff-Rossiné constructed the musician of his *Symphony No. 1* (1913) with coloured fragments of wood. After returning to revolutionary Russia for several years (1920-1925), he moved on to a constructivist style, putting together non-objective material compositions made of metal, wire and plexiglass, which he called Polytechnic Sculptures. Though he was active chiefly as a painter, Baranoff-Rossiné's small group of fragile constructions have an originality entitling him to a significant position in the rise of modern sculpture.

Apart from Picasso, the only cubist sculptor worth mentioning is Henri Laurens. His earliest extant works, like the *Clown* or the *Juggler* (both 1915), may have drawn inspiration from Baranoff-Rossiné, Picasso's still lifes and Léger's paintings *Contrasts of Forms*; in their details they also owe something to tribal art. From 1915 to 1918 his sculptures came under the influence of his friend Braque. While polychromy plays an important part in them, the guiding principle behind them is the sculptural interpretation of themes like *Head* or *Fruit Dish with Grapes* by way of cut-out planes either arching or standing end to end slantingly: the result is to turn these real sculptures in real space into imaginary objects. One is reminded of the maquettes of a stage designer, using perspective foreshortenings and colour to produce three-dimensional pictorial objects and the illusion of space.

Henri Laurens (1885-1954):
Head, 1915-1918.
Painted wood and iron, 6″ high.

Vladimir Baranoff-Rossiné (1888-1942):
Symphony No. 1, 1913.
Polychrome wood, cardboard, crushed eggshells, 63½″ high.

135

THE MANIFESTO OF FUTURIST SCULPTURE

The artists hitherto dealt with came to modern sculpture by way of academicism and Rodin; they found their way forward through successive innovations based on a knowledge of archaic and non-European sculpture, together with the added stimulus of modern painting, spearheaded by the School of Paris.

Futurist sculpture (and futurist painting) had a different origin. It has to be understood as the manifesto of a total break with the past. Here the creation of forms was preceded by theories and principles. The philosophical ideas of Nietzsche and Bergson, the glorification of engines and speed, the dynamic experience of big city life and the pulsing impact of its lights and noises, all these manifestations of driving, collective forces on a heroic scale were seen as requiring entirely new forms of expression. And this new art was seen as an art of matter whose emanations of energy and flashes of movement would be swept up into the surrounding atmosphere. An ambitious if wordy programme. The trouble was that the artists' intelligence and powers of invention were insufficient to cope with it.

These shortcomings are already evident in Umberto Boccioni's programmatic sculpture *The Development of a Bottle in Space* (1912). And the big striding figure of his *Unique Forms of Continuity in Space* (1913) belies the assertion of the *Futurist Manifesto* of 1910 that a racing car is more beautiful than the Greek statue of the *Victory of Samothrace* in the Louvre. For in fact Boccioni's striding figure does little more than repeat Rodin's *Striding Man* in a form modernized by Jugendstil (one thinks of Gaudi's decorative architectural forms) and early Cubism, as exemplified by Picasso's *Head of a Woman (Fernande)* of 1909. Its representation of movement in space, furthermore,

marks no advance on the breakdown of movement in the chrono-photographs of Etienne Marey and his Italian followers, which Boccioni had obviously seen. Here and in some other sculptures of this period, now lost (portraits of his mother in the round and in relief), he keeps to the traditional concept in which the volume of a body is a modelled mass, more or less closed.

For all that, it is only fair to recognize the European significance of this group of young Italians (Boccioni, Balla, Russolo, Severini and others) who called themselves Futurists and created a furore in Paris with their exhibition of February 1912. Also shown in London, Berlin, Budapest, Zurich and Vienna, then in St Petersburg and Moscow, this exhibition made it clear to artists and public that Cubism and Salon Cubism had now been charged with a new, electrifying ideology.

In the early summer of 1913 Boccioni exhibited in Paris some hastily produced sculptures intended to exemplify the theories he had set forth in the *Technical Manifesto of Futurist Sculpture* of August 1912 (falsely predated to 11 April 1912). The most significant of these, *Fusion of a Head + Window* and *Head + House + Light* (modelled plaster busts with fragments of a window and wooden slats acting as Venetian shutters), are only known from old photographs. Inventive though they are, they still represent a somewhat awkward preliminary stage on the way to constructions and object art.

Much more influential than these works (which Picasso regarded as plagiarizing his own) were the ideas for a sculpture of the future which Boccioni set forth in the *Technical Manifesto* of 1912, and which at once found a wide response (notably in Russia). A few quotations from it may help to an understanding of the coming chapters:

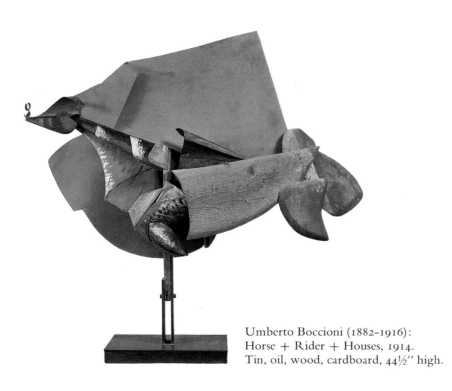

Umberto Boccioni (1882-1916):
Horse + Rider + Houses, 1914.
Tin, oil, wood, cardboard, 44½″ high.

Umberto Boccioni (1882-1916): Unique Forms of Continuity in Space, 1913. Bronze (cast 1931), 43⅞″ high.

Giacomo Balla (1871-1958):
Boccioni's Fist – Lines of Force II, 1916-1917.
Reconstructed in 1956-1958, cast in 1968.
Painted brass, 31½″ high.

"When will sculptors understand that trying to build and create with elements taken from Egyptian, Greek and primitive art or inherited from Michelangelo is as absurd as trying to draw water from an empty well with a stove-in bucket?... Sculpture could make absolutely no progress in the narrow field allotted to it by the academic conception of the nude. Sculpture will find a new source of emotion and consequently of style, by extending its plastics into the immense field that the human mind has foolishly considered hitherto as the realm of the divided, the impalpable, the inexpressible. Sculpture should impart life to objects by making their extension into space tangible, systematic and plastic, for no one today can any longer deny that one object continues where the other begins, and that all the things surrounding our body (bottle, motor car, house, tree, street) cut into it and slice it up by forming an arabesque of curves and straight lines.

"Neither in sculpture nor in painting can there be any renewal except by seeking out the style of movement.

Raymond Duchamp-Villon
(1876-1918):
The Large Horse, 1914, cast in 1966.
Bronze, 42″ high.

Futurist sculpture will be produced by the systematized vibrations of light and the interpenetration of planes... Transparent planes of glass or celluloid, sheets of metal, wire, electric lights inside and out, will go to indicate the planes, trends, tones and halftones of a new reality. Likewise, a new colouring can step up the emotional force of planes, while a coloured plane can violently emphasize the abstract import of a plastic value... It is time to destroy the alleged nobility, merely literary and traditional, of marble and bronze and bluntly deny that one should keep exclusively to a single material for a sculptural whole. The sculptor is free to use twenty different materials in a single work—glass, wood, cardboard, cement, concrete, horsehair, leather, fabrics, mirrors—provided that the plastic emotion calls for them. If a sculptural composition should need some special rhythm of movement in order to increase or contrast the rhythm set for the sculptural whole, a small motor may be added to it, which will provide a rapid movement suited to this or that plane or line.

"It must be loudly proclaimed that in the intersection of planes there is far more truth than in all the intertwined muscles, all the breasts and all the thighs of the heroes and Venuses who arouse the incurable silliness of contemporary sculptors."

This comprehensive programme was carried out by Boccioni in a single surviving piece of sculpture: *Horse +*

Rider + Houses (1914)–only the motor is missing. Brightly painted pieces of wood, cardboard and metal represent the rider as he gallops by the houses, these latter–in keeping with Boccioni's theory–moving with the same speed towards the rider and merging with him. Yet, on the eve of the First World War, this futurist vision of a traditional equestrian monument was as anachronistic as cavalry itself, soon to be annihilated by armoured cars on the battlefields of a war foreseen and glorified by the Futurists. (Boccioni himself joined the Italian army in 1915 and, as it happened, died behind the lines in August 1916 of injuries sustained in a fall from his horse.)

In France Raymond Duchamp-Villon was doing war service in the medical corps. He too treated the Baroque theme of the equestrian monument, turning it into a hybrid form, half horse, half one h.p. engine. The element between the fore-hoof and head (as only became clear much later in the enlarged version called the *Large Horse*) is not a horse's leg but a connecting-rod.

In a painted construction of wood and cardboard Giacomo Balla represented the *Lines of Force of Boccioni's Fist*. This is a free-standing upright relief with no background plane. It brings out the dynamic lines which were so marked a feature of Boccioni's paintings and drawings, usually expressed in horizontal terms. Balla's relief would perhaps have been more effective if it had been mounted against a

Alexander Archipenko (1887-1964):

△ The Bather, 1915.
Painted wood, paper, metal, 20″ × 11½″.

▷ Woman Walking, 1912.
Coloured bronze, 26½″ high.

wall, with the lines of force developing in space at right angles to the wall.

Setting aside the historical analysis of the stages of modern sculpture, we may pause for a moment and consider a more fashionable form of creation: that of those sculptors who, in their day, catered successfully to a certain clientele and figured prominently in the columns of art critics with some pretension to wit and culture. Even today they are dear to a generation, now dying out, of older art-lovers and journalists. It may safely be predicted that, in a few years' time, their names will mean little to the historian of modern sculpture. To omit them today, however, might still be open to criticism. As they hardly call for any historical or artistic evaluation, we shall simply put them in a category of their own which we shall call "*la haute sculpture*" (the "higher sculpture") on the analogy, typically French, of *haute coiffure*, *haute cuisine* or *haute couture*.

It so happens that one of them, Brancusi, made his first well-paid sale to a master of French *haute couture*, Paul Poiret. In 1912 Poiret purchased a polished bronze from Brancusi to decorate the showrooms where his mannequins presented his exclusive dressmaker's creations. This work was the fabulous bird *Maiastra*, which in the next decades in ever slenderer shape became the *Bird in Space*, now of gleaming metal, now in black or white or grey

Constantin Brancusi (1876–1957):
Bird in Space, 1925.
Marble, 45¾″ high.

Alexander Archipenko (1887–1964):
Flat Torso Walking, 1914.
Gilt plaster, 15¾″ high.

marble, always set on multipartite stands, tastefully fitting into the interior–even and especially when this interior was an esoteric "temple of wisdom" next to a Maharaja's palace. Not surprisingly, it was an interior decorator, Henri-Pierre Roché, who sent Brancusi's works out to India (together with his own designs for interior furnishings).

Brancusi cannot be held responsible for the Art Déco style, but he is for the pseudo-mythical and quasi-mystical trimmings in which his works have been wrapped till now. He is to modern sculpture what Marie Laurencin is to modern painting. In twentieth-century Paris he liked to disguise himself as a Rumanian peasant and delighted in having himself and his works photographed.

The first of this century's higher sculptors had been Elie Nadelman, whose social and artistic successes were amusingly described by André Gide in his *Journal* (24 December 1908 and "Monday 24 or 25 April" 1909). Among others, he describes "a plaster head, or anyhow the project for a head, with no eyes, no mouth, no nose, in a word as formless as a chick three days after hatching." After some haggling it was purchased by the art dealer Druet. It was this ovoid form that inspired Brancusi's burnished egg-shaped heads, such as the *Newborn* (1920). Nadelman's success in fashionable circles must have been one of the topics of the day among younger sculptors, for Matisse posted up a notice in his private art school: "No talk of Nadelman is allowed here!" His success continued unabated, and it was from Nadelman that Helena Rubenstein ordered a dozen polished heads of Aphrodite to set up in her beauty salons.

Constantin Brancusi (1876-1957):
The Newborn II, 1920 (?).
Stainless steel, 9¾″ long, on
polished metal disk, 17¾″ diameter.

Rudolf Belling (1886-1972):
Sculpture 23 (Head), 1923.
Polished bronze, 16⅜″ high.

There have always been drawing-room sculptors of this kind who meet a fashionable need; they are still with us today. Before the turn of the century, it was the erotic polychrome marbles of Jean-Léon Gérome that were relished; today it is the constructivizing metal multiples of Max Bill with their mirror finish. In the 1920s it was Rudolf Belling's smoothed expressionist and cubist forms, with which he had conveyed his (also politically progressive) modernity. His robot-like human figures were as well tooled as industrial products; for example, his *Sculpture 23 (Head)*, of 1923, with its meaningful allusions and witty foreshortenings and refinement of design. This talent for fashionable design made Belling an ideal collaborator for architects in the post-war period of utopian illusions. It was then that Alexander Archipenko, coming from Paris, met with an eager response in Berlin (1921-1923), before he found a wider public in America.

Archipenko stands out as the highest of the higher sculptors. Born in Kiev in 1887 and schooled at the distinctly philistine Moscow Academy, he went to Paris at the age of twenty, where he contrived to keep himself in the forefront of novelty and catered to the ever fresh demand for the female nude. In 1912 he popularized Salon Cubism with his *Woman Walking*. This work, with its perforated head and hole in the belly, looked like a revolution in sculpture to those art-lovers who knew nothing of Picasso's Cubism. From Picasso too he got the idea for the polychrome relief constructions, to which he gave the generic title of "sculpto-painting." In the *Flat Torso Walking* (1914) and its later versions, Archipenko took up the torso theme of Rodin and Maillol, refining their robustness away to a timeless elegance which would not be out of place in a show-window.

OBJECT ART AND APPROPRIATION

Marcel Duchamp (1887-1968):

Bottle Rack, 1914 (replica 1964).
Real object, 23¼" high.

Cycle Wheel, 1913 (replica 1964).
Real object (assemblage), 59¼" high.

Marcel Duchamp was a middling painter with an ingenious turn of mind that has made him one of the most influential artists of the twentieth century. He may be likened to a middling football player who would never have reached the big leagues, but for the fact that at the right moment he changed the rules of the game and thereby made himself the captain of his private national team. He was the grand master of punning in art. And with that word we have already adapted the term "art" to his rules of the game and acknowledged that this punster with his irrepressible wordplay affords some searching insights into the nature of art, or rather Art in the traditional sense, with a capital A.

Two years after the popular success of the Salon Cubists, one year after the *succès de scandale* of the Futurists in Paris, and one year too after Picasso's *Guitar*, that incunabulum of modern sculpture, Marcel Duchamp with a wave of his hand shifted the points of modern art and set it moving in a new direction, one with a long future before it. In 1913 he simply took the front fork of a bicycle with its wheel, set it upside down on a studio stool and signed this object construction with his name as a work of art. And from then on such an assemblage *did* pass for a work of art, not because it was art in the traditional sense (or was it? the question remains unanswered), but because we as public,

museum-goers or collectors behave before this object as if it were a work of art. With the studio stool he solved the problem of the pedestal at one blow—a problem which Brancusi with all his hybrid and mongrel forms of decorative art could never solve. But the stool here is more than a pedestal: it represents the bicycle seat.

And then we notice that Duchamp has turned the world topsy-turvy, the seat below, the wheel uppermost. The wheel moves, without making any headway, and thereby sets the surrounding air in motion like a whisk-broom—much more convincingly than Boccioni's *Unique Forms of Continuity in Space*! (Why exactly Duchamp chose a bicycle wheel is a point that belongs to the still unwritten history of the bicycle in art from 1890 to 1914.)

Duchamp pulled off his second stroke in 1914, when he purchased a bottle rack at the Bazar de l'Hôtel de Ville department store in Paris, signed it and so turned it into a work of art; an art of the "ready to wear" in contradistinction to the unique model of *haute couture*. A work of art? Yes, because *this* bottle rack of Duchamp's has no other purpose but that of aesthetic contemplation; and when the original object got lost, and such old-fashioned bottle racks were no longer obtainable, replicas of it were made and sold on the art market.

That we enter here an entirely new realm of sculpture is shown by comparison with Picasso's *Glass of Absinth* (1914), which combines a real object (the strainer with a lump of sugar used by the absinth drinker) with an imaginary "glass," in this case a small bronze sculpture. There exist six versions of Picasso's bronze "glass," which was originally modelled in wax. Each is painted differently. One of them is even coated with sand, in flagrant contradiction with the use and transparency of a glass, yet in keeping with the object represented, since glass is made from sand. The strainer is identical in all six versions (being sold no doubt by the half-dozen). Reality may thus be multiplied; it is a wholesale article, while the work of art is ever unique. Such was Picasso's reply to Duchamp.

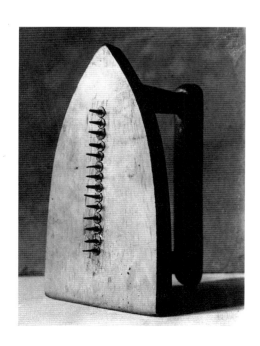

Man Ray
(1890-1976):
Cadeau (Gift),
1921 (replica 1963).
Iron with fourteen
nails glued to the
base, 16¼" high.

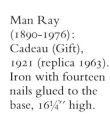

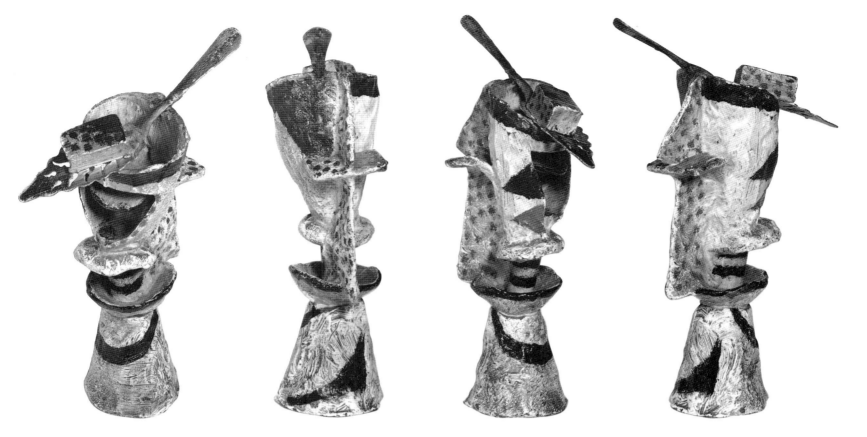

Pablo Picasso (1881–1973): Glass of Absinth, 1913–1914. Painted bronze with silver sugar strainer, 8½″ high.

Marcel Duchamp's new concept of art was promptly taken over by individual artists in Italy (Alberto Magnelli, *Still Life with Bottle and Cup*, 1914: a real bottle and cup on a futuristically modelled table), in Russia (Ivan Puni, *Plate Relief*, 1915) and the United States (Man Ray, *Cadeau*, 1921), before Duchamp enriched and extended his ideas, first in Switzerland and Germany with the Dada movement, later in France with the Surrealists.

Puni, who worked in Paris in 1910–1912 and again in 1914, subjected the object assemblage of his *Plate Relief* to the stricter pictorial order of his Suprematist friend Malevich in St Petersburg. The result is the most radical still-life representation that one can conceive of (it may be compared with Daniel Spoerri's "trap-pictures"). What is represented is the thing itself, but as a relief hanging on the wall and thus removed at one stroke into the realm of the unusable.

The idea of the readymade originated with Marcel Duchamp, who coined the term. He brought the idea with him to New York in 1915, where he worked until 1918 and attracted attention with his famous *Fountain*, a urinal exhibited upside down.

Morton Schamberg and Man Ray extended the range of the readymade, taking it straight from reality but adding titles and further objects to it and giving it an underhand, insidious effect. These were called assisted readymades. In 1918, combining a siphon with a sawblade, Schamberg entitled it *God*. Man Ray, after his arrival in Paris in 1921, studded the underside of a flatiron with nails, thus making it unusable, and entitled it *Cadeau* ("Gift").

Ivan Puni (1894–1959):
Plate Relief, 1915–1919.
Limewood tableboard with
walnut veneer
and pasted ceramic plate,
13″ × 24″ × 2″.

SCULPTURE CONQUERS SPACE
THE BEGINNINGS OF CONSTRUCTIVISM

combining collage, painting and plastic elements which were produced at the same time, as well as reliefs constructed of bits of wood and sheet metal. Because he was short of money and Picasso could not employ him as an assistant, Tatlin soon returned to Moscow and exhibited a material relief there before the end of 1913. This *Still Life with Bottle* still uses trompe-l'œil wallpaper and shaped metal in the figurative painterly style of Picasso. Behind the cut-out silhouette of a bottle criss-crossed with wire filigree we think we can see a gleam of light around a circular shape which seems to represent the internal shape of the bottle as seen from above.

From 1914 onwards Tatlin went his own way with material reliefs. He took the radical step from representational to non-representational sculpture. The bits of wood, metal and glass that he assembled represent nothing; they

Vladimir Tatlin (1885-1953):

◁ Still Life with Bottle, 1913.
Metal relief with collage (presumably destroyed).

Corner Relief, 1915 (reconstructed 1980 by Martyn Chalk).
▽ Iron, wood, wire, 31″ × 31½″ × 27½″.

Vladimir Tatlin was the man who created the historical link between Picasso's cubist constructions in Paris and the beginning of Constructivism in Moscow. From 1914 he was one of the Russian avant-garde painters who paved the way for an original art style through their group exhibitions and stage designs. They were familiar with the painting of Cézanne, Picasso, the Salon Cubists and the Futurists, as well as their manifestos. They gave the western artistic revolution a new direction influenced equally by icons and Russian folk art, and the combination of cosmic speculations and radical living revolution. (At first the Constructivists had nothing to do with the political revolution in Russia nor, after a disillusioning period of cooperation from 1918 to 1922, were they connected with it again.)

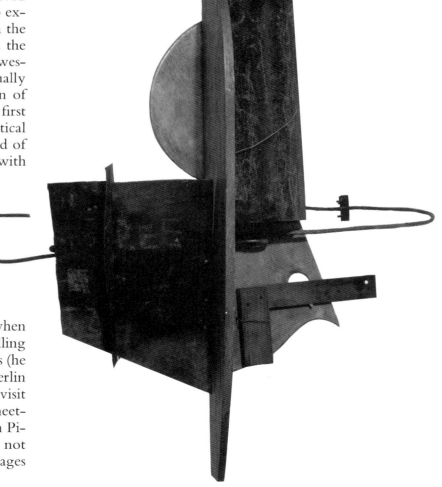

It was a significant event for this group of artists when Tatlin, who was a member of the Society of Travelling Art Exhibitions known as the Itinerants or Wanderers (he played the bandura and balalaika for them), went to Berlin in 1913 and in May left for Paris (his real objective) to visit Picasso in his studio at 242 Boulevard Raspail. (This meeting is incorrectly dated to the autumn of 1913, when Picasso lived at 5 Rue Schoelcher). There Tatlin saw not only Picasso's *Guitar* of 1912, but also the assemblages

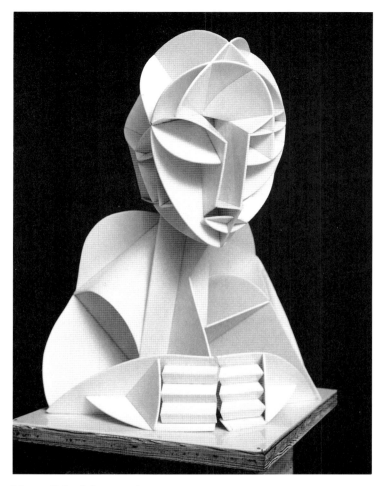

Naum Gabo (1890-1977):
Constructed Head No. 2, 1916 (reconstruction c. 1923-1924).
Celluloid, 17″ high.

the real walls of the corner of a room. Now Tatlin's material assemblages, clusters of three-dimensional forms, were suspended in space by curved metal rods or wires spanning the corner of the room. He called them "counter-reliefs" and "counter-corner-reliefs" on the analogy of the word "counter-attack" which was in constant use in contemporary newspapers (1915).

Other Russian artists followed different paths until they jointly represented Constructivism as the revolutionary art of a new age for mankind in Moscow in 1920. The brothers Anton and Neemia Gabo Pevsner (the younger brother adopted Naum Gabo as artist's name) had stayed in Paris several times between 1910 and 1914, before spending the war years 1915-1917 in Oslo and joining the revolutionary non-representational Constructivists in Moscow in 1917. So it is not surprising that once again a work of Picasso's was the forerunner of an early Constructivist sculpture, Gabo's *Constructed Head* of 1916. What was intended as a sculpture of surfaces and intermediate spaces in Picasso's *Head of a Woman (Fernande)* of 1909, but which was still modelled in the mass, Gabo now logically composed out of sheet iron surfaces which signify the volume of head, bust and hands as massless spatial compartments. The modern transparent material, celluloid, used in a later version, emphasized the renunciation of traditional sculpture, particularly in this conventional sculptural theme of a bust. In the twenties Anton Pevsner was to interpret Picasso's cubist paintings of female nudes as transparent relief constructions, using curved celluloid surfaces. From 1917 Gabo and Pevsner, together with Tatlin, Baranoff-Rossiné, Malevich, Rodchenko, Kandinsky and others, were active in the Moscow State Free Art Studios, where art teaching directed against the bourgeois academies was based on entirely new principles.

The artistic credo of the brothers Vladimir and Georgii Stenberg, born in 1899 and 1900 respectively, was as much the product of these experimental studios as of the October Revolution. They belonged to a new generation for which sculpture was from the first a non-representational, non-symbolic work of engineering. Like industrial products, their metal constructions have serial numbers

are material forms in space. Real materials in real space— that was now his programme, as opposed to Picasso's metamorphosis of materials with partially imaginary space. From 1915 consciousness of space was central to Tatlin's constructions and the foundation of Russian Constructivism. Rodchenko's *Space Construction*, hanging from a wire, is the prototype. Significantly enough, it can also be understood as a model of cosmic convolutions, but this radical solution of the base problem in sculpture did not appear until the winter of 1919-1920. (Tatlin's gigantic counterpart to it will be discussed later.) From 1915 to 1918 Tatlin's material constructions in space needed a more solid support; no longer a relief ground (an attribute which sculpture still has in common with painting), but

Alexander Rodchenko (1891-1956):
Space Construction, 1919-1920.
Wood, 18½″ high.

Georgii Stenberg (1900-1933):
KPS 58 N XIII, 1919 (reconstruction 1973).
Chrome iron, wood, glass, 88¼″ high.

represent the Utopia of artists who see themselves as the engineers of the society to come. The Realistic Manifesto of Pevsner and Gabo issued in Moscow in 1920 proclaimed the same goals, although it was based on different premises. This gives us a theory of Constructivism which understands it as a purely artistic modern style without social revolutionary references. The word "realistic" means the realities out of which a work of art is constructed: materials and space in their reality without "abstraction." The demands for dynamism, movement and an extra-temporal dimension are related to Boccioni's manifesto for a Futurist sculpture, but they do not pursue a modernistic, expressionist goal. They were, however, rapidly included in this "realistic" Constructivism, almost like scientific concepts. The main principle of this sculpture is the building up of a volume out of lines and planes which produce three-dimensionality free in space, instead of out of three-dimensional masses. Gabo and Pevsner were to remain true to it even after they emigrated to the West in 1922.

Kasimir Meduniezky (1899):
Construction No. 557, 1919.
Tin, brass, iron, 7″ high, 17¾″ with base.

instead of titles. Their bases are not massive blocks, but more like the pylons of civil engineers, balancing pressure and tensile power with structural iron and cables. Their artistic message is the materialization of dynamic forces in space. This is admittedly "Lef," but certainly not proletarian sculpture (*Lef* was the organ of leftist practitioners of the arts).

Here we only want to mention two of the countless rival manifestations of avant-garde–and at times Communist–revolutionary art in Russia. They were as diametrically opposed as their theories, one party giving preeminence in art to the object produced, the other putting the intellectual element first. One manifestation was the Exhibition by the Society of Younger Artists (Obmokhu) in May 1920 in the Moscow Higher State Artistic and Technical Studios (Vkhutemas). Here Rodchenko's *Space Construction* and Meduniezky's *Construction No. 557,* together with the rod constructions of the two Stenbergs founded genuine Constructivism. Common to them are weightlessness and dynamic movement in space. Although completely renouncing the use of symbols, they

DADA ASSEMBLAGES

Max Ernst (1891–1976):
Fruit of a Long Experience, 1919.
Dada relief with wood and painted wire, 18″ × 15″.

French Surrealism produced relief pictures in this spirit. The use of unartistic materials and unpainterly strong colours forms part of their art of dispute. And we should remember that Greek temple sculpture was once painted in bright colours, something we should certainly consider rather vulgar today. However, because of the artist's innate need to achieve the ultimate goal of a work of art as a harmonious whole, assemblages and reliefs of outstanding beauty were constantly produced in spite of their intention to shock. In the framework of the centuries-old dispute over the precedence of painting or sculpture and the ill-defined demarcations between those two arts an art form was found which proved definitively that such a categorical aesthetic is meaningless.

Jean Arp's painted and screwed on wood reliefs are especially beautiful examples of this. The ironic poetry peculiar to this artist gives his non-representational material silhouettes the mystery of a representational allusion or a chance creation, but its artistic value consists mainly in the happy configuration of curves and counter-curves. As one of the most important surrealist sculptors, Arp was to develop these curves into fully rounded sculptural masses. To a greater degree than Max Ernst or Kurt Schwitters, for example, Arp was already working with purely artistic sculptural values in his Dada reliefs.

The relief in modern sculpture follows two entirely different art forms. On the one hand, it is related to the architecture-linked semi-plastic fields of the Greek metope and the Roman decorative frieze and so retains a classical or neoclassical character. Examples of this are Hildebrand and

Jean Arp (1887–1966):
Portrait of Tzara, 1916.
Dada relief in painted wood,
9½″ × 7¼″ × 4″.

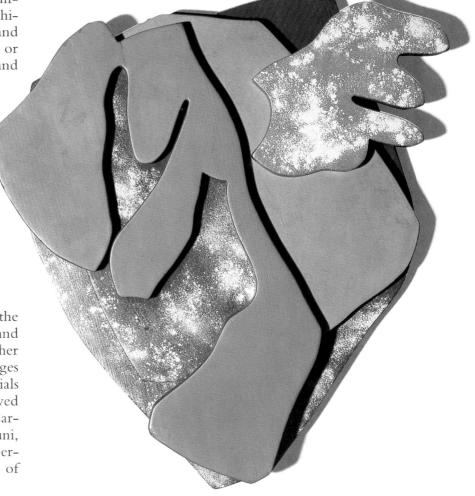

Maillol, Duchamp-Villon, Laurens and Lipchitz in the post-cubist period of the "return to order" of 1919, and Schlemmer at the Bauhaus in Germany. On the other hand, the relief continues the tendency of cubist collages and painting to act as a support for assembled materials (Picasso, 1912–1913; Tatlin, 1914–1915) and is endowed with a content opposed to traditional art in Futurism (Carrà, Balla and Severini, 1914–1916) and Suprematism (Puni, 1915–1917). The artists of the Dada movement in Germany (Arp, Ernst, Schwitters, Hausmann) and later of

At all events, Ernst and Schwitters did not pursue plastic values. Their relief works, and in Max Ernst's case also the sculptures of his later years, are works at second-hand. Primarily they made "anti-art." Ernst found a happy frame for this message in his *Fruit of a Long Experience* (1919), quite literally a traditional picture frame which simultaneously allows the apparently chaotic coloured forms and materials assembled inside it to appear as the absolute opposite of an art theme suitable to such a frame and yet connects it with the frame by its chamfered profile. Relief and "picture" are made of the same relief substance and attain from form and content a superimposed unity.

Schwitters' *Wide Schmurchel* of 1923 hangs on the wall as an unframed relief picture. If the word "Schmurchel" in the title recalls the German word "Schnorchel" (for the airpipe of a submarine or a diver's equipment), only on reflection does there arise an association of content with those waste bits of wood which are assembled into an aesthetic object from their contemptible existence as something worthless and rejected. But Raoul Hausmann's *Spirit of Our Time* (1919) expresses the whole spirit of Dada. A wigmaker's hand-turned wooden head ludicrously ridicules the professions of the telegraphist or pilot of the future, by the various contraptions screwed on to it.

Raoul Hausmann (1886-1971):
The Spirit of Our Time, 1919.
Wood, metal, leather, cardboard, 12¾″ high.

Kurt Schwitters (1887-1948):
The Wide Schmurchel, 1923.
Wood relief, 14¼″ × 22″.

148

SPREAD OF CONSTRUCTIVISM

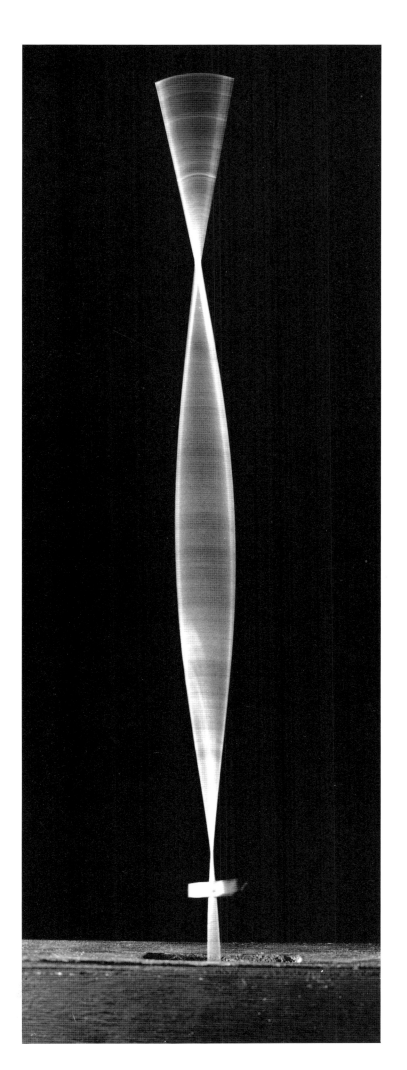

Although some groups of artists after World War I expressed their world view with nihilistic irony or expressive pathos and others wanted to preserve traditional artistic values, still others were captured by the belief of the revolutionary Russian Constructivists that artists ought to take part in building up a better, juster and more industry-orientated world through their work. Their visions may quickly have turned out to be Utopias rather than political reality (the powers of stupidity and brutal violence are always stronger). Nevertheless, they created centres for a modern visual culture which led to the most important artistic achievements in the twentieth century, at first in Europe and later in the United States of America. They saw themselves as laboratories for a basically original and consequently contemporary aesthetic. Their sculptural creations were basic researches with materials, space, movement, writing and light, and their results were reflected in art teaching, experimental photography and film, and in such urban manifestations as posters, emblems, slogans and stage settings, as well as in the design of industrial products. The stage for this movement was primarily

◁ Naum Gabo (1890-1977):
Kinetic Sculpture (Standing Wave), 1920 (replica 1983).
Metal rod with electric motor, 24¼″ high.

Wladyslaw Strzeminski (1893-1952):
Suprematist Architecton, 1923 (reconstruction 1979).
Painted wood, 15⅜″ × 14⅛″ × 14⅛″.

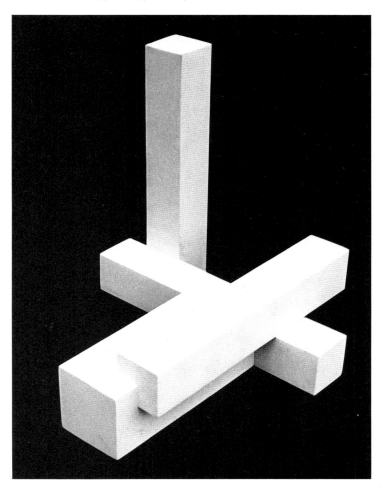

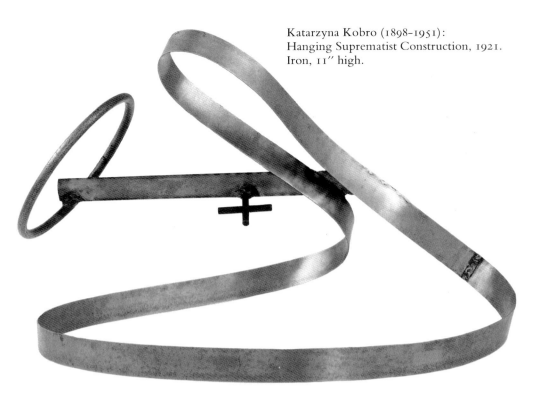

Katarzyna Kobro (1898-1951):
Hanging Suprematist Construction, 1921.
Iron, 11″ high.

Georges Vantongerloo (1886-1965):
Construction of Volume Relations, 1921.
Mahogany, 16⅛″ high.

Germany and Holland (particularly the Bauhaus in Weimar, Dessau and Berlin), whereas France, England and America only accepted this fundamentally new attitude after the pseudo-modernity of Art Déco and the arrival of emigrants from Russia, East Europe and Germany.

The most valuable sculptural achievements in this brief promising decade between the end of the war and the advent of totalitarianism are not sculptures in the usual sense of the word (memorials, for example), but the models made of basic elements. It would be wrong to call them "abstract," because they do not represent anything objective, but they do confront us in pure form with the plastic realities of volumes, surfaces and the dynamics of space and time. With his *Kinetic Sculpture* (1920), Gabo produced an unsurpassed example of the kinetic art that was not taken up again until the thirties and sixties. What the photograph shows as "volumes in space" is, like the chronophotographs, the massless body of a thin perpendicular metal rod vibrating by means of a motor. In contrast, Wladyslaw Strzeminski's *Suprematist Architecton* (1923) is a structure of massive blocks which rise up vertically from a flat three-dimensional coordinating cross, but slightly offset from its centre. The name "Suprematist" comes from the works of the Leningrad artist Kasimir Malevich who, after the period of Suprematist painting (*Black Square*, 1914), advocated such stereometric block constructions as the basic forms for a new architecture. Strzeminski's wife Katarzyna Kobro had taken part in Russian Suprematism and Constructivism in the art studios at Moscow and Smolensk until 1922 and after moving to Lodz in Poland spread their message with white surface compositions with corners, curves and primary colours expressing the presence of space.

In Holland Georges Vantongerloo was the artist who created Constructivist sculptures almost as teaching aids,

making mathematical equations visible in the process. They are executed in that small model-like format which corresponds to the scale of the hand and meets the eye as a unity that looks different from different sides and is nevertheless acceptable as a whole.

Examples from the Bauhaus studios are the *Cube Composition* (1919) by the Swiss Johannes Itten and the *Light Requisite* by the Hungarian Laszlo Moholy-Nagy. This Light-Space Modulator, as the artist called the theme he treated in paintings and constructions, is a motor-driven apparatus which breaks up rays of light into agitated rhythms, reflecting and projecting them into space, and makes it the total work of art for the industrial age, especially when combined with music in stage settings.

◁ Johannes Itten (1888–1967):
Cube Composition, 1919 (destroyed).
Plaster, 55⅛″ high.

▽ Laszlo Moholy-Nagy (1895–1946):
Light-Space Modulator, 1930 (replica 1970).
Glass, metal, wood, electric motor, 59½″ × 27½″ × 27½″.

151

MONUMENTS FOR A NEW ERA

Auguste Rodin (1840-1917):
Balzac, 1898 (cast in 1937).
Bronze, 9′ 2″ high.

Significantly enough, modern sculpture has only produced a single important public monument: Rodin's *Balzac*, on the plot of ground in Paris at the crossing of the Boulevard Montparnasse and the Boulevard Raspail. Completed in 1898 and intended by Rodin to be executed in dark-grey granite, the statue was not cast in bronze until 1937 and erected in 1939 as a monument to Balzac *and* Rodin (the inscription on the base reads: *A BALZAC/A RODIN*). Otherwise the twentieth century only erected conventional artistically feeble statues to its heroes. (The theme of modern war memorials is another equally dismal story.)

But there was no shortage of attempts to create monuments in keeping with the spirit of the age. When academic portrait statues and allegorical figures had become impossible (with the exception of totalitarian state art), artists sought to express the aspiration to a new culture and a new spirituality in public monuments. The ascending screw/spiral which aspires to endless space is the constantly recurring symbolic form of this utopian aim. Even Rodin had envisaged a spiral ramp structure as a monument to labour in 1898. In the Jugendstil period Hermann Obrist (a Swiss working in Munich) designed a public monument with the same spiral structure. We do not know what ideal it was supposed to express, but we may reasonably assume that it had a symbolist cosmic content. A similar concern lies behind the *Tower of Fire*, which Johannes Itten had

already conceived during the formative years he spent in Vienna (1916-1919) and then had executed in 1920 at the Weimar Bauhaus as a 12-foot high model made of metal and coloured glass. He created it as a symbol of the mental and spiritual reunion with his dead sweetheart and simultaneously—and this transition from the spiritual to the material is typical of the years 1916 to 1920—as a signal tower for air traffic. Here the symbolic content of a Gothic cathedral tower was combined with modern functionalism based on technology and mathematics.

Hermann Obrist (1863-1927):
Movement, c. 1895.
Plaster, 72½″ high.

Johannes Itten (1888–1967):
Tower of Fire, 1919–1920 (destroyed).
Metal, glass, wood, 12′ high.

Vladimir Tatlin (1885–1953):
Model of the Monument to the Third International, 1919–1920.
Photograph of the original model (now destroyed).
Metal, wood, glass, etc., height of model 20 ft.,
intended height of monument 1300 ft.

Walter Gropius used this ascending development of form from terrestrial to celestial space for the monument in the main Weimar cemetery to the memory of the workers shot during the National Conservative Kapp putsch of 13–17 March 1920. Made of reinforced concrete, it followed the Constructivist programme for a sculpture which uses surfaces to create a spatial volume.

The historical source of these tower-like monuments is the Eiffel Tower of 1889. Tatlin wanted to make his Monument to the Third International twice as high as the tower and the Woolworth building in New York, at the time the world's highest skyscraper (the word itself is a programme!). It never got beyond the stage of the 20-foot high wood model which is known from photographs of the Exhibition Hall of the 8th Soviet Congress of December 1920 in Moscow and later reconstructions. The steel skeleton of a spiral ramp more than 1,300-feet high was intended to hold three mobile glass rooms suspended by cables on a common asymmetrical axis. The cubic congress hall on the lower storey was supposed to rotate on its axis once a year. The central pyramid-shaped room for the International Executive, etc., was to rotate once a month and the uppermost cylindrical information centre, revolving once a day, was intended to broadcast the latest news and proclamations to the universe by radio and writing projected on to the clouds. Until 1926 the wooden model was a feature of the May Day parades in Moscow,

Walter Gropius (1883–1969):
Monument to the Victims of the Kapp Putsch
(Weimar, March 1920), 1922.
Concrete.

carried on a horse-drawn cart. A young lad concealed in the lower part of the tower turned a handle to produce the planetary and cosmic processes.

Gabo's Constructivist interpretation of a Greek temple column is the opposite of this utopian future project. As if in a teaching aid showing the difference between traditional and modern sculpture he replaced the massive fluted superimposed drums forming the column by transparent surfaces assembled at an angle to each other and a large flattened ring. Yet the idea of the towering monument in modern sculpture was also realized in non-Constructivist techniques. Otto Freundlich created a socialist memorial with the mutually supporting superimposed blocks of his *Ascension* (1929), whereas Brancusi's *Endless Column* was erected as a war memorial by a fascist regime, in spite of the popular motifs from Rumanian cemetery monuments and farmhouse structural elements or (in hindsight?) Tibetan mystifications. It would be a mistake to think that these vertically arranged rhomboids were piled up one by one, each one supporting the other. In fact, they were threaded on a steel core like pearls on a string.

▷ Constantin Brancusi (1876-1957):
The Endless Column, at Targu Jiu, Rumania, 1938.
Gilded steel, 98½ ft. high.

Otto Freundlich (1878-1943):
Ascension, 1929.
Bronze, 78¾″ × 55⅛″ × 55⅛″.

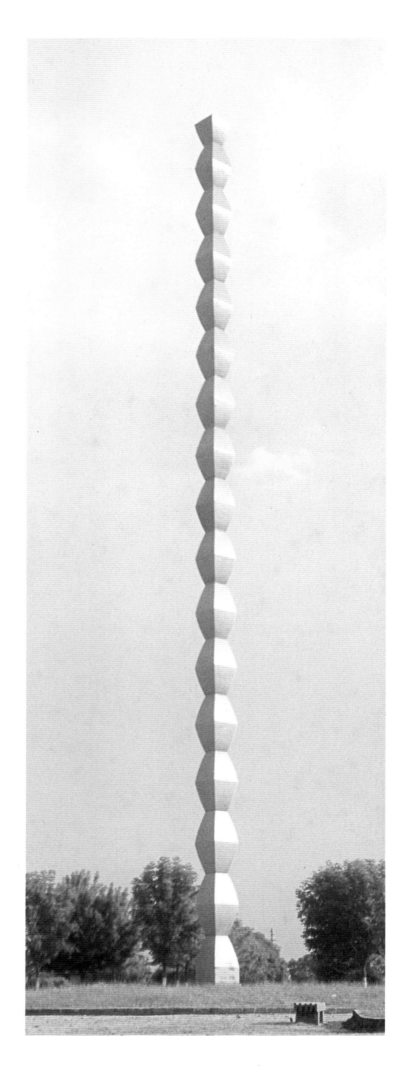

Naum Gabo (1890-1977):
Column, 1923. Enlargement of 1975.
Glass, plastic material, wood, metal, 41½'' high.

TOWARDS THE TOTAL WORK OF ART

Raymond Duchamp-Villon (1876-1918):
Cubist House, 1912.
Plaster maquette.

It was the success of the Munich modern style at the Salon d'Automne of 1910 which led the Paris Salon Cubists to design a Cubist House for the 1912 Salon d'Automne. The sculptor Raymond Duchamp-Villon and other artists created a cubist façade and decorative wall friezes. The Suprematists (and later Constructivists) Tatlin, Yakulov and Rodchenko transformed the Café Pittoresque in Moscow into a total work of art with reliefs of brightly coloured wood built on to the existing four walls and objects hanging from the ceiling. In both cases the artists strove not only to create works of art to be looked at or even handled, but also to inject their whole personalities into the pictorial and sculptural spaces, much as they were asked to do when commissioned to design pictorial-cum-spatial stage settings and a little later Cubo-

It is part of the definition of every stylistic period, Gothic, Renaissance or Rococo, for example, that the decorative forms peculiar to them are reflected both in the works of the fine arts and in the everyday objects of interior decoration. This was an all the more urgent need for modern art styles from Cubism to Constructivism and Surrealism because they wanted to introduce a new era for mankind (at least in their manifestos). Thus the representatives of a new tendency in sculpture and painting continually strove to impress their own special style on exhibition rooms or interiors. The Russian revolutionary proletarian culture even led to Tatlin designing new clothes for the workers and the members of the Bauhaus gave themselves a group identity by the individual style of their haircuts.

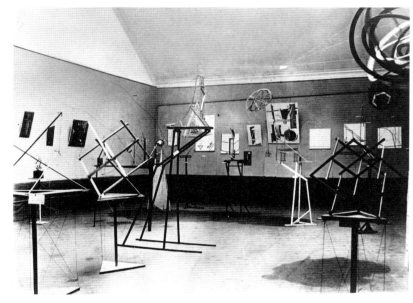

Space Constructions by the Stenberg brothers at the Obmokhu Exhibition, Moscow, 1921.
Photograph by Rodchenko.

El Lissitzky (1890-1941):
Proun Room, 1923 (replica 1965).
Painted wood, 118″ × 118″ × 110″.

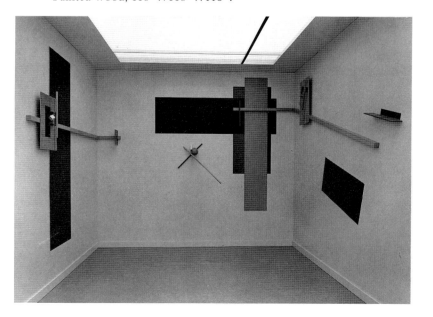

Expressionist film sets (like the *Golem*, 1915, or the *Cabinet of Dr Caligari*, 1919). Kurt Schwitters' Dada building (it extended through several floors and rooms of his own home in Hanover) is to be understood on much the same lines. From 1918 until he emigrated in 1935, he transformed his house into a series of caves or grottoes full of ludicrous found objects and natural objects, applied reliefs, tortuous narrow corridors and weird irrational vistas. At first he called it Merzbau after one of his collages containing the fragment of a word (Com)merz(bank), from which he took the title of his Merz style. Later he called the house the "Cathedral of Erotic Misery" for personal reasons.

From this point we see a parallel development in the bewildering exhibition installations of the Paris Surrealists in Charles Ratton's gallery rooms, 1936, and the International Surrealist Exhibition of 1938. More than the sum of

Jean Arp (1887-1966), Sophie Taeuber-Arp (1889-1943)
and Theo van Doesburg (1883-1931):
Dance Hall at the Café Aubette in Strasbourg, 1926.

International Surrealist Exhibition,
Galerie Beaux-Arts, Paris, 1938.

all the objects exhibited, these installations were "environments" before the word had come into common use.

The first Obmokhu Exhibition in the Vkhutemas in Moscow in May 1920 had turned the exhibition room into a vigorous manifesto for Suprematism and Constructivism through the combined effect of individual works of art with the same stylistic tendency. Even though the Constructivists understood the installation of a room as a special artistic commission, a much purer "meditation" room emerged with a few colours and shapes. Under the influence of the works exhibited by Malevich and Lissitzky in Berlin in 1921, the Berlin painter Erich Buchholz had transformed his living room at Herkulesufer 15 in the Suprematist style as early as 1922, but Lissitzky's PROUN room in the Berlin Art Exhibition of 1923 was the more original and significant achievement. Like Schwitters' Merz, PROUN was the artificially coined name for an original personal artistic style. The name comprises the initial letters of the Manifesto slogan PRO U (twerschdenije) NOW (yenform) IS (kusstwa), which means "Foundations of New Forms in Art" in English. In the small mathematically proportioned empty room, the colourful and mostly rectangular wood reliefs attached to the walls and placed across corners could radiate in space with marvellous insistency and put the observer, who was completely surrounded by them, into a mood in which sense perception acquired a spiritual quality. It was the same story in Mondrian's Paris studio in the Rue de Départ where the imaginary white meditation space of his painted compositions was given concrete form in real inhabited space. Yet the same purely artistic elements used in small-scale brightly coloured arrangements could also lead to cheerful large-scale installations of the kind carried out by Mondrian's friend, the De Stijl painter Theo van Doesburg, together with Jean Arp and Sophie Taeuber-Arp in the Grande Salle of the Café Aubette at Strasbourg.

157

REALISM AND SURREALISM
FIGURAL SURVIVALS

Antoine Bourdelle (1861-1929):
Equestrian Statue of General Alvear (Buenos Aires), 1923.
Bronze, 9'7½" high.

So far in this history of modern sculpture we have only discussed the artists of the avant-garde. We were mainly interested in the creative forces which periodically introduced new concepts. This way of looking at things is surely right if we seek to find the prototypes for the controversial sculpture of the present in the history of modern sculpture as a whole. The public is very quick to say that present-day sculpture is not art any more. Today no one would dream of saying that Rodin's sculpture was not art, but in his day, during the first public exhibition of the *Bronze Age* (1876) or *Balzac* (1898), that was the universal allegation, because people adopted the rules of the Académie des Beaux-Arts as the criterion for what was art (and sculpture in particular). The public always knows what the art of yesterday was, but we are interested in the art of the specific "today" which has transcended yesterday's rules. Yet all the avant-garde tendencies mentioned in previous chapters were links in the chain which connects the present with Rodin.

To be sure, a "revisionist" and "pluralistic" art history, of the kind in fashion today, criticizes our predilection for the avant-garde and calls it "modernistic," "formalistic" and "elitist." We accept the objection and admit that so far we have limited our discussion to certain sculptors and works constituting only a fraction of the production of statues, monuments, busts and decorative applied sculpture. Nevertheless, we believe that our position is justified. The army of traditionalists behind the avant-garde received their just rewards in their day when critical praise, public commissions and high fees were lavished on them by their contemporaries. At the time such sculptors as Bourdelle, Despiau and Kolbe were feted as heroes, and some of them were still celebrated in the decades of totalitarianism.

We have nothing against them. A neo-Baroque equestrian statue by Bourdelle still retains its power. The agitated plastic masses of his interpretation of Beethoven still have the power to move us. His *Head of Eloquence* from the period of World War I (part of one of the figures accompanying the gigantic *Monument to General Alvear* in Buenos Aires, 1923) is, in its neo-Grecian stylization and yet very sensitive modelling, as much a guarantee of the power of culture against the power of destruction as Picasso's *Head of a Woman (Dora Maar)* (1941) executed during the occupation of Paris. Was Bourdelle a great sculptor? We do not hesitate to answer yes. Nevertheless any art-lover with only a few days to spend in Paris would be well advised to visit the Musée Rodin rather than the Musée Bourdelle. Such value judgments are part of the history of modern sculpture, for they are based on the development of the history of sculpture as a whole. And it mentions Bourdelle's name today as much as anything for the critical comments he made once a week in the twenties in the Académie de la Grande Chaumière on the studies after the

Antoine Bourdelle (1861-1929):
Eloquence, full-size head study, 1914-1917.
Bronze, 17¾" high.

Charles Despiau (1874-1946):
Assia, 1937.
Bronze, 74¾″ high.

model and the early works of Alberto Giacometti and Germaine Richier.

When contrasting avant-garde and traditional sculpture, we also question the attitude of these two tendencies to contemporary political and social events. We do not ask whether art expresses this, but whether it conceals the suffering of the present (it is permanent) by adopting beautiful themes and forms from the past, or whether—as the autonomous force that it is—it opposes something creative to this suffering. We shall see this opposing force of sculpture operating in Surrealism and especially in Picasso's works which make serious demands on the spectator, by bringing in the economic crises, unemployment and political events of the day. As opposed to it, the period between the wars saw the continuation of the neoclassicism that glossed over reality (with a hedonistic character in France and a symbolist note in Germany) and led directly to totalitarian state art.

Undoubtedly Despiau's house and garden sculpture is "eternally" beautiful and an exaggerated female nude by Gaston Lachaise is eternally sensual (at least to a heterosexual male observer), and a chaste woman guardian of the Holy Grail by Kolbe always mysterious. But are they also important?

Georg Kolbe (1877-1947):
Assunta, 1921.
Bronze, 6′4″ high.

159

Gaston Lachaise (1882–1935):
Standing Woman, 1932.
Bronze, 7′4″ high.

Charles Despiau's *Assia (Naked Woman Standing)* of 1937 looks back with Maillolist stylization to Joseph Bernard's Salon sculpture *Young Girl with Pitcher* and is halfway to the heroic sculpture of his friend Arno Breker. Kolbe's *Assunta* (1921) takes over the figure of Archipenko's *Woman Walking* (1912) and hands it on to Giacometti's *Invisible Object* (1934). With this the importance of both works within the history of sculpture seems to be documented. But are they important as *modern* sculptures? The answer must be no.

In contrast, Käthe Kollwitz's *Self-Portrait* (1926–1936) and Ernst Barlach's *Memorial to the Dead* are important in the context of contemporary suffering. They possess a straightforward unpretentious seriousness which simultaneously consoles and expresses suffering. The face of the committed woman and artist was so stamped by both her personal force and the general suffering of the age that Barlach transferred it in 1927 to his angel in Güstrow Cathedral which hovered above the tablet recording the names of the dead until 1938. It is significant that a state which was served by the art of Despiau, Kolbe and Breker removed the bronze and melted it down. And it is not only a part of sculpture, but also of broader contemporary history that the plaster version was taken to a safe place and that during the war, in 1942, a new bronze cast was made in secret and that it now hangs in divided Germany, in the Antoniterkirche in Cologne (Federal Republic of Germany) since 1952 and later in a duplicated version (1953)

Ernst Barlach (1870–1938):
Angel for the Güstrow
Memorial to the War Dead, 1927.
New cast of 1942 in the
Antoniterkirche, Cologne.
Bronze, 85½″ long.

in Güstrow Cathedral (German Democratic Republic). The angel for the Güstrow *Memorial to the Dead* clearly shows that Barlach was primarily a sculptor in wood. His modernity led him from Jugendstil by way of Expressionism (mainly as draughtsman and writer) to small-scale sculptures verging on the soulful which, unlike Matisse's small sculptures, lack a special awareness of plastic space. To him and to many other successful sculptors of his day, modern sculpture was the stereometric stylization and angular treatment of natural forms whose volumes were conceived as variably compact masses (in Barlach's case more so than with others). In terms of the history of sculpture, this is a deliberately conservative attitude in comparison with the now well-known composite works of tribal art carved out of wood. It also appears conservative in the wake of cubist constructions and in comparison with contemporary international Constructivism. It would have had its merits if geniuses had been at work, but they were only talents.

Even a work by the eighty-year-old Maillol exceeds them all in power and adventurousness: the *River*, from the days of World War II. The voluminous agitated nude had a complicated history (it was composed of rearranged parts of the *Mountain* which were not intended for a reclining figure, not even by Maillol), but as it now both yields to and braces itself against space, so that head and left arm are forced to hang down below the plinth, it is a genuine plastic event far transcending its ostensible content.

Käthe Kollwitz (1867-1945):
Self-Portrait, 1926-1936.
Bronze, 14½'' high.

Aristide Maillol (1861-1944):
The River, 1938.
Bronze.

PICASSO'S SURREALIST CONSTRUCTIONS

Pablo Picasso (1881-1973):
Construction with Glove, 1930.
Cardboard, plaster and wood on canvas,
covered with sand, 10⅝″ × 14″.

Between Picasso's cubist and surrealist constructions come his designs for ballet settings, such as *Parade* (1917) and *Mercure* (1924). These were the works which, together with events in his love-life, led his Cubism into two new periods, the Classical and the Surrealist. Here we do not use the word Surrealism in the usual sense connected with the movement, but in the sense it acquired from Picasso's drawn, painted, constructed and modelled works in the decade 1920-1930, namely as the metamorphic reconstruction of the real world. His friend, the poet Guillaume Apollinaire, emphasized this in his programme notes for *Parade* in May 1917 and repeated it in June with the subtitle "Surrealist drama" for *Les Mamelles de Tirésias*. Ten years later, in the context of a memorial to Apollinaire, who died in 1918, Picasso created the most important sculptures of this decade. They were free-standing constructions of iron rods such as *Woman in Garden* (1929-1930).

As an intermediate stage between the cubist *Guitar* (1912) and the sheet metal still life of 1914, we mention here only the *Guitar* of 1924, painted black and white, which has a monumental effect. It has a much stronger, more spectacular "sonority" than the 1912 version and was inspired by the example of theatre properties, of which Picasso later said that they were most effective when black and white were contrasted. Like the 1912 *Guitar* (or like a real guitar so long as it is not played) it hangs on the wall, yet it is not a relief. The lower part reproduces a lambrequin to left and right and in the centre, as a continuation of the upper body cover, what may be a cloth to effect the connection with a table standing in front of the wall. In other words it is intended as a theatre-like interior with a still life. With the exception of the cocoa tin painted white and mounted on the area representing the sound-hole across which wires are stretched as vibrating strings, the instrument is cut out of one or two large flat sheets of metal. Picasso had obviously made a pattern for them beforehand, because they are bent and folded in the most

complicated way, so that we see parts of the front and rear sides. But what looks like rounded borders and edges is trompe-l'œil painting.

Nothing about the all white *Woman in Garden* is trompe-l'œil, even if everything is aimed at spatial and objective illusion. What can we recognize and name? Welded, screwed and soldered iron surfaces and structural rods make up the composite image of a naked woman with flowing hair. A small horizontal area below head and long neck denotes the shoulders. The oval shape below with two protruding bolt heads is the bosom. Two of the rods must represent the arms and two the legs. Where is the body? Is the woman standing or is she sitting in a deck-chair? Long stems carry Philodendron leaves. Yet all these allusions to forms may be misleading, like the title *Woman in Garden* (not Picasso's choice). Woman-garden would be

Pablo Picasso (1881-1973):
Guitar, 1924.
Painted sheet metal and wire, 43¾″ × 25″ × 10½″.

more correct for this metamorphic union of woman and plant. That is how Picasso saw his young secret lover Marie-Thérèse and painted as plant/woman in a room in the early thirties, whereas previously he turned this sport-loving girl swimming or playing ball into a balloon/woman (in paintings) or sea anemone/woman in a small modelled statuette entitled *Metamorphosis* (1928).

Marie-Thérèse lying on the beach (Picasso managed to take her to Juan-les-Pins behind the back of his wife Olga) was also the inspiration for his picture relief *Construction with Glove*. Here, too, the title was an unhappy choice, for the (stuffed) cloth glove is of course the right hand next to the cheek of the woman sleeping like a child. Her tiny head can be seen above thumb and index finger. The body is cut out of cardboard and depicts her bosom and womb half realistically, half frivolously. Beach plants complete the

Pablo Picasso (1881-1973):
Woman in Garden, 1929-1930.
Painted iron, 81⅛″ high.

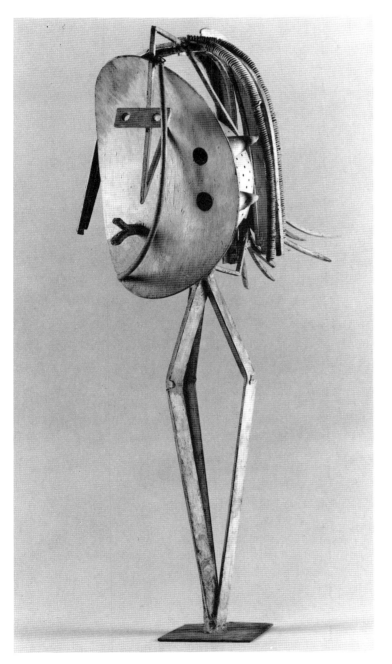

Pablo Picasso (1881-1973):
Head of a Woman, 1931.
Painted iron, sheet metal, springs and strainers, 39⅜″ high.

picture which is set into the obverse of a stretched canvas. The sand sprinkled over the whole and glued on unites the various materials and of course represents the beach.

The nails, bedsprings and salad strainers, which together with sheet metal fragments and iron rods–all unified by painting–represent the *Woman's Head* of 1931, underwent a similar metamorphosis. We see the volume of the head (the two opposed salad strainers), the hair (nails and feathers), the profile lines (bent metal rods) and the bosom. The result is an extremely witty transformation of a bust– a classical theme in sculpture–and presumably also the representation of a cook or housewife. The bust does not stand on stone plinth of the kind used for portrait busts, but on a sort of tripod which fills the base volume not as mass but as empty space and is reminiscent of a rococo stele in outline.

With such surrealist iron sculptures, which he amplified into genuine caricatures of his marital relations with the addition of found objects, Picasso introduced the period of iron sculptures in which Julio Gonzalez was to dominate. Gonzalez was also the artist who taught Picasso how to work iron, starting in March 1928, and helped him to execute these constructions.

WELDING AND FORGING

Pablo Gargallo (1881-1936):
Harlequin Mask II, 1927.
Copper, 7½'' high.

Julio Gonzalez (1876-1942):
Head known as the
Swiss Woman, 1932.
Iron and stone, 20⅞'' high.

It will be remembered that the decisive step towards *modern* sculpture consisted in the addition of combination and construction to previous methods of sculpting (of wood or stone) and modelling (of clay or plaster, mostly with a view to making bronze casts). From the beginning the use of sheet iron and wires was connected with it, in particular after Picasso's *Guitar* (1912). Indeed, as early as the *Head of a Woman (Fernande)* Picasso chose to use wires for the hair in order to take the mass to the volume and to effect the cubist penetration of form and ground (in sculpture of bodies and space), but at the time he found that solution too intellectual and stuck to modelling. But he took the decisive step towards iron sculpture with his surrealist constructions.

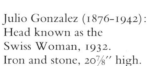

Julio Gonzalez (1876-1942):
Harlequin, 1929.
Iron, 17'' high.

Of course, Picasso did not invent iron sculptures, although it may be true that there is a Spanish tradition behind them. At all events, the Spaniard Pablo Gargallo, who shared a studio with Picasso in Barcelona in 1901 and followed him to Paris in 1906, was already cutting figures and masks out of sheet copper. Given the contemporary general interest in tribal art, he may have linked the Spanish tradition with observations of hammered and chased African metalwork. Later Gargallo made it his own speciality, although his virtuoso craftsmanship did not go far beyond remarkable transformations of traditional forms. Nevertheless, his *Harlequin Mask* (1925-1927) interests us because of the representation of body volumes by concave and bent surfaces with ribs and bars soldered on to them vertically, as well as precise outlines for Harlequin's three-cornered hat.

Julio Gonzalez, who lived in Paris from 1900, would probably not have gone far beyond Gargallo's craftsmanship if Picasso had not renewed an old friendship with him in 1928 because he needed his expert knowledge of smithing and welding to execute his countless projects. At first their collaboration took place in Gonzalez's studio. Their main works were created from 1929 to 1937 and established the new art form of iron sculpture, which was taken up even before the war by the American David Smith (he mainly knew Gonzalez's work from reproduction) and found new adepts after 1950.

Owing to the material and the technique, the volume of a figure was reproduced by rods reaching into and surrounding space, by surfaces and rounded walls. This involved that inner penetration of figure and space that Gonzalez made the principle of his sculpture. Consequently the representations became, if not exactly abstract (as in the international Constructivism of those years) at least figurative spatial diagrams. We recognize the *Harlequin* of 1929 by his comical mask in front of the funnel-head and the lozenges on his costume, which even suggest colour through the areas of light and shade created by the perforations. However excellent this allusive representation, Gonzalez's great talent (and his advantage over Gargallo) lies in the strongly non-representational power of the constructive elements creating interior and exterior space. We see this particularly clearly in the "head" entitled *Swiss Woman* (1932). Here rectangular and rounded iron surfaces are welded together and completed with a curved bar in such a way that we are almost confronted by an abstract material and spatial construction, like those of the Vkhutemas and Bauhaus schools. Of course the charm of the strong hand-made (instead of industrial) material plays a much greater part in the overall effect, not least through the block of stone that serves as a base for the Swiss woman.

The more delicate wire sculpture whose works are like drawings in space has different origins and results. Alexander Calder was a mechanical engineer when he learnt to paint in New York. Settled in Paris from 1926, he invented the toylike partly mobile wire figures more suited to him and used them to populate a miniature circus. He put into practice (probably unconsciously) the futuristic programme of a sculpture made mobile with the help of hand- or motor-driven apparatuses, before he discovered in 1933 the Mobiles that were set in motion by the air around them and then moved on to ever larger Stabiles: poetic colourful engineer's work. The Swiss Walter Bodmer, on the other hand, who kept in touch with the latest artistic developments in Paris from Basel, constructed non-representational filigree compositions of soldered wires from 1936 as reliefs and small sculptures which give substance to the linear doodling of Klee's pencil on the surface of the paper. This makes Bodmer a precursor of the wire sculptures of, say, Günther Haese, which appeared from 1950 onwards.

Alexander Calder (1898-1976):
Spring, 1928.
Wire and wood, 94½" high.

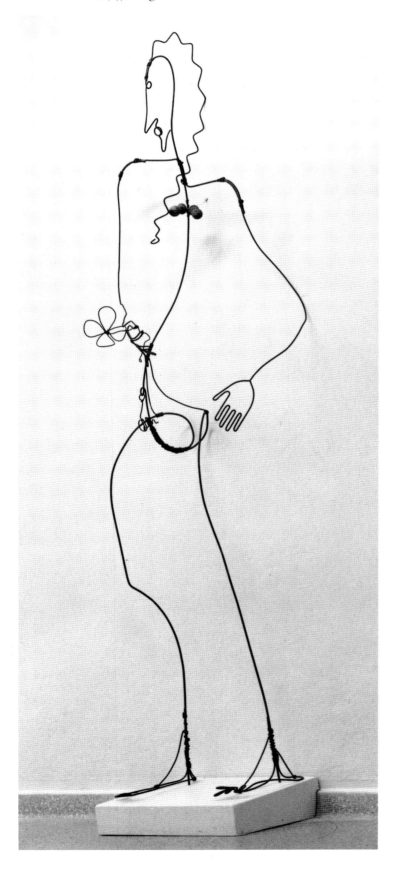

Walter Bodmer (1902-1973):
Wire Picture, 1936.
Wire and sheet metal on wooden board painted white,
17⅜" × 13⅞".

GIACOMETTI OVERTAKES THE AVANT-GARDE

If there is one special feature which makes our history of modern sculpture different from previous treatments of the theme, it is the importance attached to Picasso and henceforth to Alberto Giacometti, too. His plastic work will be constantly analysed in the chapters that follow. Of course this arrangement of the material is dependent on periods and dates. No doubt this emphasis leads us to one-sided judgments, because anyone who once gets involved with the art of Picasso and Giacometti measures all other works of sculpture by the standard of their creations.

Picasso also transformed the art of his century as a sculptor and was a unique stimulus to its artists. Numerous exhibitions, the publication of an exhaustive catalogue of his sculpture and the possibility of studying the works and the notebooks left after his death (now in the Musée Picasso, Paris) all bring this out quite clearly. Giacometti, on the other hand, appears increasingly as a unique figure in the history of modern sculpture, indeed in the history of sculpture as a whole, who did not open up the way for other artists, too, like Picasso, by tackling new artistic problems and constantly providing new solutions, but emerged with a new vision of sculpture which could have imitators at best, but no successors. You will read in our last chapter that "vision" is to be understood literally. But first we must show in this chapter and later how Giacometti asserted himself among the Post-Cubists and Surrealists.

When the twenty-one-year-old Giacometti came to Paris from the remote Swiss valley of Bergell in 1922, it was for the sake of Bourdelle's teaching at the Académie de la Grande Chaumière, which indirectly means for the sake of Rodin. As a high-school pupil he had become familiar with Rodin's portrait busts from illustrations and copied them in plasticine. His two younger brothers and his mother sat as models for him. Once in Paris he soon realized that modern sculpture had moved a long way from Rodin, although for preference he sought out the tendencies that were new to him, too, among the great men of the day, Laurens, Lipchitz and Brancusi, rather than among the genuine avant-garde of Constructivism and Object Art. (He came across the sculptures of Matisse and Picasso at their 1930 and 1932 exhibitions at the earliest.) Thus Giacometti began his own career with a post-cubist *Torso* (1925), which stereometrically stylized the body and legs and is not far behind Maillol's *Action in Chains* in plastic force, although it is much harsher. In those years he caught up with the lessons of archaic and Egyptian sculpture, as well as African and Oceanic tribal art that were so important for the previous developments of modern sculpture.

Interest in prehistoric sculpture and painting was also awakened in the twenties, so Giacometti was able to share in their novelty. The *Man and Woman* group (1928-1929) is evidence of this new plastic vocabulary and his large *Spoon Woman* (1927) formulates the theme of the torso using these new premises.

Alberto Giacometti (1901-1966):

◁ The Artist's Mother, 1927.
Bronze, 12¾″ high.

▽ Head of a Man Looking, 1927-1928.
Bronze, 15½″ high.

△ ▷ Man and Woman, 1928-192
Bronze, 17⅞″ high.

▷ The Couple, 1926.
Bronze, 23⅝″ high.

But his chief theme remained the likeness. It remained so until the end and spurred him to those extraordinary researches which turned Giacometti into the unique artist we know. A decisive step in that direction was *The Artist's Mother* (flat head) of 1927, because this sculpture does not reproduce the volume of a head like previous sculpture (i.e. what we know about a head in advance), but the seeing face of the mother as the artist *saw* it in front of him. The perspective three-quarter view is contained in the frontal disc outline, as if it was a painted likeness. Perhaps Bourdelle had his share in this solution, because his model for a war memorial in the Chambre des Députés envisaged the head of the allegorical female figure "La France" in a similar flattened perspective; but the whole was conceived as a relief in a flat wall niche (between Delacroix's painted figures). Giacometti placed this painting-like conception of sculpture (which Picasso had anticipated with his still life compositions of 1912-1916) as sculpture in the round in free space; the flat reverse shows the flattened hair knot.

The whole range of this painting-like treatment of sculpture, as well as the concept of an "observed face which observes" is obvious a little later in one of Giacometti's series of *Plaques*, the thin almost abstract sculpture *Head of a Man Looking* (1928). It is not saying too much if we interpret the vertical depression in the gently

curved surface as a "nose" and the horizontal depression as the seeing eye of a head turned to the left. In the same year the work inspired Picasso to create the well-known lithograph *Face* (Bloch catalogue No. 95: Marie-Thérèse in 7/8th profile facing left) and this transformation is by no means astonishing. For with the principle of the flat plaques–Giacometti made a few others with the attributes and title of *Woman* up to 1931–he made sculpture the bearer of the pictorial sign as if it were paper. The enhanced sculptural power immanent in these disc sculptures came from their prototypes in the Louvre, the Cycladic marble idols from pre-Grecian times. For of course they lie behind the great originality of the *Man Looking*. But it is irrelevant and superfluous to trace it to those models alone, or to see an imitation of Etruscan bronze figures in Giacometti's later matchstick figures. Giacometti's own work goal led him to these solutions. The prototypes encouraged him to make a style out of the result of his researches.

The formal context of Giacometti's figure discoveries before 1930 is more easily justified by tribal art because different models for different compositions can be accurately named. Thus *Man and Woman* (1929) is linked with the antelope dance masks of the Bambara and the Bwami figures of the Balega. But Giacometti's thin pointed silhouette forms have acquired an unembarrassed sexual significance. In addition, copulation is represented as aggression. With this Giacometti joins the surrealist avant-garde, in particular the writer Georges Bataille, who wrote about the connection between sexuality and violence, and his periodical *Documents*. From 1930 Giacometti's sculptures showed what Surrealism really is.

PICASSO AT BOISGELOUP

With the onset of the thirties, the period of exile and of new political and economic crises begins for modern sculpture in Europe and Russia. The Wall Street crash of 1929 brought an end to the "Golden Twenties." Art Déco, rampant since 1925, and an elegant classicism or populist realism superseded the topicality of abstract Constructivism; Object Art mutated into Surrealism. All this, as well as state art of the thirties, will be discussed in the following sections.

A sculptor has to be very rich if he is not to suffer privation or betray the autonomy of his creative drive in commissions for decorative sculpture. Matisse and Picasso were in this fortunate position. An exhibition of Matisse's bronzes in the Galerie Pierre in Paris, 1930, together with the plastic sensual corporeality of his beloved Marie-Thérèse Walter, now in full bloom, spurred Picasso on to

new realizations. He also wanted to execute at least some of the projects he had conceived since 1927 and recorded in countless drawings and notebooks, among them a series of large monuments with tumefied fragments of bodies along the La Croisette promenade in Cannes. Thus a new model and a new sculptural stimulus met.

A third element was added and gave the name to this period of Picasso's plastic work. In June 1930 he bought the property of Boisgeloup 60 kilometres north-west of Paris. In its buildings he installed his first sculpture studio, in addition to a printing press for graphics and a painting room, in order to create iron sculptures in the grand manner (still with the help of Julio Gonzalez) and above all to model in plaster. Even if he had classical sculpture just as much in mind as Matisse's *Large Heads* and *Reclining Women*, he also surrounded himself with casts of the prehistoric Venus of Lespugues found in the Grottes des Rideaux (Haute-Garonne) in 1922 and a monumental African Nimba sculpture. All these had their connections with the plastic metamorphoses which Marie-Thérèse experienced at Boisgeloup.

Nevertheless the adherence to Surrealism of this period suggested by the word "metamorphosis" is not enough and a look at the large bust or the relief *Head of a Woman (Marie-Thérèse)*, both from 1932, shows that in those years Picasso the sculptor was equally preoccupied with the

Pablo Picasso (1881–1973):

◁ Head of a Woman, 1932.
Bronze, 33½" high.

▽ Sculptor, Crouching Model and Sculptured Head, 23 March 1933.
Etching, 10½" × 7⅝".

classical Greco-Roman tradition. So just as Picasso had begun to modify his cubist style when interpreting Olga Khoklova's Ingresque beauty and designing ballet decors, he now saw the Surrealism of previous designs for monuments and constructions as a restrictive "period" style compared with the classical profile of Marie-Thérèse Walter and his graphic sequences for Ovid (1931) and Aristophanes (1934). He showed how he himself understood his work with his model at Boisgeloup, in the 43 etchings with the theme Sculptor and Model (in the *Vollard Suite*,

Pablo Picasso (1881-1973):

△ Head of a Woman (Marie-Thérèse), 1932.
Bronze relief, 27″ high.

◁ Bather, 1932.
Bronze, 27½″ high.

1933), which form a critical and lively commentary on the sculptures he made at that time. In them he handled the polarity between age and youth (Picasso aged fifty, Marie-Thérèse aged twenty-one), between reality and art (the model confronting the work of art), as well as between classical tradition and Surrealism, in so doing quoting his own sculptures and constructions pictorially.

In the etching of 23 March 1933 the bearded sculptor is completing the last of four busts of Marie-Thérèse, while the model sitting for it admires her radiant portrait emerging. In a sheet etched on 4 May the standing naked model facing a surrealist composite figure asks herself, "Is that meant to be me?"

The large *Head of a Woman* (the penultimate version after a classical portrait head and a bust with resplendent volumes) stands between likeness and interpretation. The fact that the base was originally a lath tripod on a found wood disc, i.e. that it is a construction, is barely concealed. The head, especially the face, is composed of spherical, tumid, curving elements which provoke formal associations with the male and female sexual organs (nose and lips between the full cheeks), but it is only the harmless realization of studies which sought to compose such a head out of five swollen male genitals. The grotesque impression made by the sculpture and its antecedents lasts only for a moment. In reality, this is a striking likeness of Marie-Thérèse, combined with the sensuality which lay at the base of their love. For many details of form one must consult Matisse's bronze *Jeannette V* (1916) to see that it grew out of the dialogue with Matisse which spanned the decade. That applies equally to the standing *Bather* who is turning round or a reclining distorted *Bather*. Both potentiate the rhythmical bronzes of Matisse and come alive because the swollen forms can be interpreted in so many ways.

169

PSYCHODRAMAS
OF GIACOMETTI

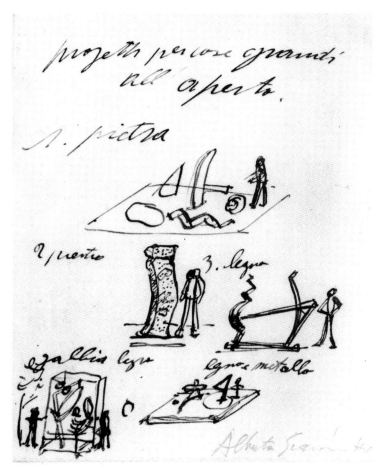

Alberto Giacometti (1901-1966):

△ Surrealist Drawing, 1932-1933: "Projects for large things in the open."
Ink, 7⅜″ × 6¼″.

▽ The Palace at 4 a.m., 1932-1933.
Wood, glass, wire, string, 25″ × 28¼″ × 15¾″.

The most penetrating of the many commentaries on Giacometti's sculptures by Parisian authors is undoubtedly Michel Leiris's article in George Bataille's periodical *Documents* (September 1929): "Everything he does is like the petrification of one of these crises, living from the intensity of an adventure swiftly captured and fixed." He compares them with "the true fetishes, i.e. those which resemble us and are the objectified form of our desire." This insight also applies to Giacometti's later compositions, but above all it is a prescient interpretation of the surrealist constructions he made from 1930 to 1934.

The best example of these is *Suspended Ball* (1930). A ball, from the lower part of which a segment has been removed, hangs on a cord in a cage of metal rods. It hovers above a similar, but much larger segment (quarter of a melon, crescent) which could only serve to make the ball whole again–both bodies are made of plaster–in the mind of the observer. The potential perpetual motion of the ball, which can be made to slide along the segment lying on a platform, means that there can be no healing reunion. No matter how we interpret the two bodies, they remain metaphors of an irreconcilable polarity (e.g. man and woman, although the relationship of the forms is ambiguous, or sensuality and pain). That is also the theme of Giacometti's other constructions with cages and chessboard–like bases. We do not know how he arrived at these original creations, because although primitive art, international Constructivism or works by Picasso may be precursors, their potent sign content creates a total transformation. They make the drama of human existence visible to us and resemble "petrified crises," embodied psychodramas, or small-scale settings and maquettes for Antonin Artaud's Theatre of Cruelty. And in fact one drawing

with five sketches for such sculptures has the title (in Italian): "Projects for large things in the open." Four of them have a human figure. (The second work, 8 feet high, was executed in stone for the property of Marie-Laure and Charles de Noailles on Hyères.)

The *Palace at 4 a.m.* is exactly like a model for a stage setting. A poetic text by Giacometti makes a reference to the drama being enacted, the seriousness and intensity of which the observer senses, although he can still only interpret it as a fragment of a dream; a bad dream of the ego caught between childhood, present and future, between sexuality and death. We register the active role allotted to the spectator in the process. It is even more strongly expressed when we encounter the *Woman with her Throat Cut* from the same year. The metamorphic crustacean woman with her throat slit lies on the ground at our feet in a convulsion combining the act of love and the death throes. Is the guilt ours? Even though there are historical precedents for a recumbent sculpture like this (Rodin's *Martyr*, 1884; Degas's *Woman in a Tub*, c. 1886), the situation and the paroxysm are unique. Like all important works of art, Giacometti's surrealist constructions and sculptures live because of their significant plastic formulation and the endless possible ways of interpreting them. Yet for all the past sculptural references which link the *Invisible Object* (1934) with Kolbe's *Assunta* of 1921 or with an Oceanic death figure from the Basel Ethnological Museum (Giacometti knew about it; in addition he had a copy of the No. 2, 1930 issue of *Documents* containing an article on the carvings of the Solomon Islands), it remains enigmatic. Thus, through Giacometti's work in the early thirties, sculpture acquired that disturbing dimension which characterizes the best of Surrealism.

Alberto Giacometti (1901–1966):

△ Invisible Object, 1934–1935.
Bronze, 60¼″ high.

◁ Woman with her Throat Cut, 1932–1933.
Bronze, 8″ × 29½″ × 23″.

SURREALIST OBJECTS
AND SCULPTURES

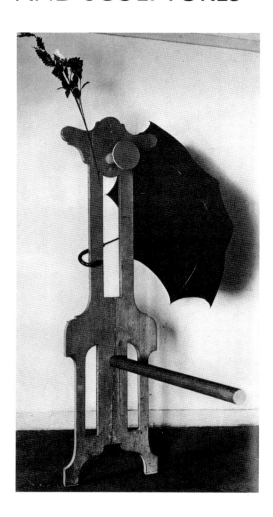

As heirs to the Dada assemblages of Marcel Duchamp, Man Ray and Raoul Hausmann, surrealist assemblages of objects differ from the surrealist constructions of a Picasso or a Giacometti and from surrealist sculpture by their apparently unartistic random improvisation and the new latent content they aimed to convey. Disparate found objects are presented by combining or slightly altering them in such a way that they suggest a hitherto unexpressed ("deeper," "unconscious") meaning through the association of ideas and thoughts aroused in the observer. As a result the real things of the real world change into poetic messages from a "surreal" sphere in which sensual and often sexual impulses have a stronger effect than rational and aesthetic criteria.

In 1925 the architect and painter Le Corbusier (a rational man *par excellence*) demonstrated how important the irrational and improvised content of these objects was to art after Cubism and parallel to Constructivism and Neoclassicism. He completed the painted and sculptural decoration of his pilot apartment in the exhibition pavilion *L'Esprit Nouveau* with pebbles, fragments of bone and pine cones, and called these natural objects "objects with a poetic reaction." At the same period Paul Klee, in his Bauhaus studio, surrounded himself with similar objects found in nature.

In December 1926 the poet Jean Cocteau held his own one-man show with assemblages made of cardboard, drawing pins, string, pipe-cleaners, matches, hairpins, etc., under the title *Plastic Poetry*. Ten years later a genuine

"cabinet of curiosities" was installed in the Charles Ratton Gallery in Paris as a Surrealist Exhibition of Objects in which modern works of art, ethnological collectors' pieces and grotesque natural objects filled walls and showcases on equal terms. An entirely different affair was the decoration of the 1938 Paris International Surrealist Exhibition in the Galerie Beaux-Arts which deliberately created an irrational total work of art of bewilderment and confusion, like Schwitters' Merzbau at Hanover.

Poetic, not "unconscious" actions by the artist lie behind poetic reactions to such objects. Joan Miró's *Figure with Umbrella* (1931) is based on a ballet figurine that was never executed. Hidden behind a moveable shield, its purpose was to keep an umbrella permanently in view. An old sideboard frame found at a cabinet-maker's, which Miró duplicated symmetrically, forms the support for the umbrella. The upper part, resembling a three-cornered hat, owing to the symmetry, produced the association "man," which was now mischievously embodied with a disc (for

◁ Joan Miró (1893-1983):
Figure with Umbrella, 1931 (replica of 1973).
Wood furniture, frames, dowel, umbrella and
artificial flowers, c. 6′ high.

▽ Object, 1936.
Assemblage with different objects, 31⅞″ high.

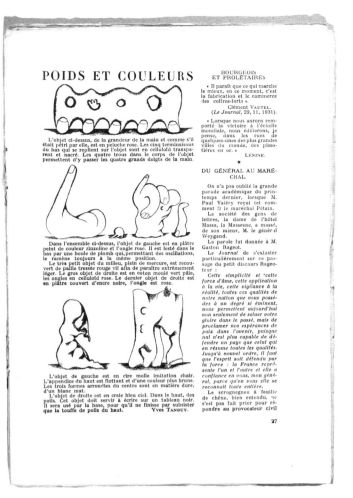

Joseph Cornell (1903-1972):
Soap Bubble Set, 1936.
Glazed box with different objects, 15¾″ high.

Yves Tanguy (1900-1955):
Weights and Colours, 1931.
Projects for sculptures, drawings and text.

"face"), wooden rod (for "phallus") and paper flowers (for "panache" in every sense of the word). A business man's hat is also the point of departure for the interpretation of Miró's *Object* (1936). It represents the head and supports a number of objects incarnating man's most secret desires, namely for sexual adventures and a voyage to the South Seas.

Such poetic journeys and places are also evoked by the collection of objects which the American Joseph Cornell (a Surrealist although he had never been to Paris) arranged

in small glass cases. In 1936 Meret Oppenheim needed much less–a fur-covered cup, saucer and spoon–to realize the most powerful side of surrealist assemblages that play with the perverse. Similar projects published by Yves Tanguy as early as 1931 and challenging stimuli by Man Ray and Picasso may well have had their influence, but here the maximum effect was achieved with the minimum of means and the last word said on this chapter of modern sculpture–not least by the ambiguity of the title: *Furry Breakfast*.

Meret Oppenheim (1913-1985):
Object ("Furry Breakfast"), 1936.
Fur-covered cup, saucer and spoon,
cup 4⅜″ diameter; saucer 9⅜″ diameter;
spoon 8″ long; overall 2⅞″ high.

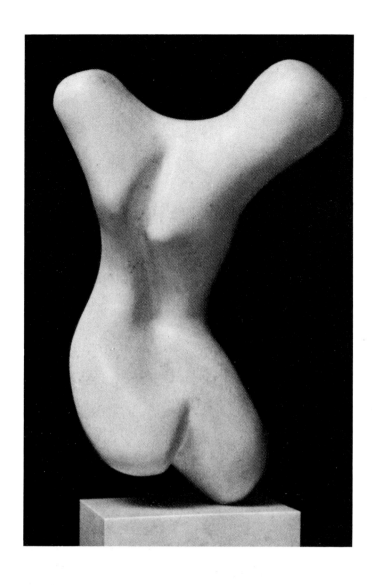

The previous chapter about plastic constructions and objects from the surrealist period allowed us, after the sculptures of Picasso and Giacometti, to consider works which already exceed the traditional bounds of sculpture by their workmanship and materials. In the process we have found a broad base to give a specific meaning to the concept of Surrealism. In particular we named the principle of metamorphosis, the modelled incarnation of psychosexual dramas and compositions and transformations of objects with poetic or irrational associations.

These principles and effects are also applicable to works that are sculptures in the narrower sense and make Surrealism a sculptural style. Perhaps this would be the place to mention the early work of Henry Moore, but it follows too closely in the footsteps of Picasso and Giacometti to be of special interest to us. Miró's surrealist sculpture (as opposed to his objects) grew from small clay models and assemblages which were later cast in bronze (after 1950). In contrast Jean Arp is certainly the sculptor who gave the surrealist style in the thirties its loveliest plastic form.

Arp's sculptural creations start from the "pure," i.e. from primarily contentless non-representational plastic form, as Brancusi had consciously made his works by his stereometric stylizations and smoothings and then gone on to make them into abstract creations using cubes, cylinders and ovoids. Arp now went the opposite way and created animate, often humanoid beings out of abstract figures

Jean Arp (1887–1966):

△ Torso, 1932.
White marble, 24⅜″ high.

▷ Human Concretion, 1935.
Plaster, 28¾″ × 19½″ × 17¾″.

made of white plaster or stone. The outlines and curves follow a biomorphic creative feeling which is only a step away from the representation of a female torso but does not take this step itself, leaving it rather to the spectator.

So we encounter plastic works which we can recognize (like composite figures in our dreams) and almost name, without being able to give them a concrete identity. In the suggestive forms of Arp's *Torso* (1932), our interpretation of it as a female body is prompted by our innate sensual desire, as surrealist "ensnaring art" expects from us. The colour white is so much a part of these surrealist sculptures that it is needed to endow the bronze casts (including those by Picasso, Giacometti and Max Ernst) with their full effect, namely the unreal and often fragile presence of an apparently known yet unidentifiable being from another world who has landed in our real environment.

The poetic alienation achieved by painting works white is supported by their titles which refer to their extraterrestrial origin, for example Max Ernst's *Moon Asparagus* (1935) or Miró's *Lunar Bird* and *Solar Bird* (both 1966). Arp often gave his surrealist sculptures the felicitous title *Concretion* or even *Human Concretion*. These titles precisely designate the transition from the non-representational and general to the representational and specific. We see a plastic form "becoming man" so to speak and not the opposite process, an abstracting stylization of the human form. Therein lies one of the most beautiful and original achievements of surrealist sculpture.

If such a product also looks so completely different when seen from different aspects that the identity of the object is not immediately recognizable in four different photographs, then we find the process of coming into being exemplarily expressed before our eyes and encounter the plastic object as an animated personality. Lying on the grass with no base, a sculpture such as *Human Concretion* (1935) may strike us as a defenceless helpless creature and intimate in a unique way that we humans, too, are fruits of the earth.

Max Ernst (1891–1976):
Sculpture, 1934.
Stone eroded by the torrent Maïra, 7⅛″ × 11¾″ × 13¾″.

Max Ernst (1891–1976):
Moon Asparagus, 1935.
Bronze, painted white, 64⅜″ high.

Hans Bellmer (1902–1975): The Doll, 1934. Six photographs of various positions.

Other sculptures by Arp draw their power to enchant by being grouped with the analogy of a human family or being exposed to a special fate recorded in their title, e.g. *To Be Lost in the Woods*.

In the summer of 1934 Max Ernst entered this intermediate world between original product of nature and representational art form when he and Alberto Giacometti were staying at Bergell, in the Swiss Alps. They salvaged stones made round by the moulins and the mountain torrent Maira and used them as a base for delicate reliefs. Max Ernst combined the existing egg shape with the bird myth he also cultivated in his paintings, so that the creative process summons up the analogy of the chicken hatching from the egg. The common denominator of such surrealist sculptures is the flowing birth of art from nature which leads us to the source of the creative and defines the work of art as a surrealist product of nature.

An analogous but contrasting creative process led by quite different ways to a similar result. *Moon Asparagus* and other surrealist sculptures by Max Ernst result from assemblages of industrial products (piled up milk bottles,

for instance). On the "detour" around the art form, the plastic finishing touches, the bronze cast and the white paint have turned them into newly discovered species of vegetable, so to speak. Max Ernst populated a personal mythology with such creatures, yet often we cannot ignore how much they owe to some of Alberto Giacometti's sculptures from the thirties and are thus sculpture at second-hand.

Of course that applies even more to the works of those sculptors who transform the repertory of forms from Yves Tanguy's paintings, for example–those petrified hominids in barren landscapes with distant horizons–into plastic bodies. Even though surrealistically stylized, they bypass the miracle and enchantment of genuine surrealist sculpture (that of Arp and Giacometti) and basically belong to the field of modern marketing and advertising. The same thing happened to some of the enigmatic figures in René Magritte's paintings, but he himself knew how to handle things better. His *Future of Statues* (1932) is a valid sculptural equivalent of his astonishing painting themes. The plaster head painted with a blue sky and summer clouds resembles a death mask because of the closed eyes; the death mask of a man who has entered an entirely different timeless (or, as the title says, future) world. This is the embodiment of the state of trance or second state of the Paris Surrealists who precisely at that time were photographing themselves with closed eyes in photo-machines, both to document their "unconscious" method of working and pay homage to Giorgio de Chirico's famous painting *Child's Brain* (1914). In a later object sculpture (1959) Magritte turned a bottle of red wine into a doll-like female nude by trompe-l'œil painting.

The role of woman in surrealist painting and sculpture expresses antagonism to traditional art especially clearly. Instead of Aphrodite or ideal she is mannequin and object, indeed the helpless passive object for satisfying man's wildest sexual desires. As the oldest and permanent theme of sculpture since prehistoric times and classical idealization, the modern Pygmalion treats woman with the utmost viciousness and cruelty, possibly revealing a deeper psychic layer in man in the process, in accordance with surrealist aims.

The Berliner Hans Bellmer was such a Pygmalion in reverse. In the figure of a doll he created as fetish of his desires a child-woman which he subjected to sexual tortures without being able to wipe the effortless air of superiority off her innocent face. He used the camera as his instrument of torture to document the dislocations, dismemberments and brutalization of his Lolita. Out of this grew a small book, very few copies of which still exist, although in 1934 Albert Skira reproduced a sequence from it in his Paris review *Minotaure*, which was devoted to Surrealism.

The images in *Die Puppe* would be almost unbearable if we were not constantly reminded that she is only a doll. She would not be half as full of content and effective if the doll were not endowed, like Pygmalion's statue, with the credibility of a living being who constantly triumphs as a human individual in spite of all the tortures undergone.

She would have to lose her head in order to become wholly an object. And that happened to the doll when Bellmer joined the Surrealists in Paris. His flesh-coloured *Doll* (1936) is a monster, an abortion, born for no other purpose than to be mistreated. Here we must return to Maillol's *Action in Chains* of 1906 to see where we now stand. One could almost say that classical sculptural form is, though exaggerated and mechanized, still dominant, but how much crueller and more disillusioned the message is now. Instead of shoulder and neck, the torso symmetrically repeats the lower body and womb. The artistic formulation is as strong as that of Meret Oppenheim's *Furry Breakfast* from the same year as Bellmer's work, but we can no longer speak of a witty play on words or a poetically surrealist assemblage, or even of lascivious double meanings as in Picasso's *Woman's Head* and *Bathers* of 1932, nor of a mere sensual accentuation as in Gaston Lachaise. Here, as if by a gene mutation, there has been an intervention in natural creation and even a surpassing of the phantasm of those men who rave about a woman with neither arms nor legs whose trunk is mercilessly submitted to their criminal passion. Moreover the *Doll* is made for copulation *à trois*. Because we are seduced by this work to give it a multifaceted interpretation and we cannot look at the illustration with indifference, it can be called the quintessence of surrealist sculpture: the work of art as artificial product of nature.

The difference between the statements made by Arp's *Torso* (1932) and Bellmer's *Doll* (1936) depends primarily on the difference between the two artists. Nevertheless, it also reflects political developments in Europe between 1932 and 1936. Even before the terror of Guernica, the Spanish Civil War had already seen carnage and torture of which twentieth-century man was considered incapable, but which stem from his innate desire for cruelty and still happen today. The expressive power of surrealist sculpture is exhibited precisely in the range between budlike growth into form (with Arp) and instinctive dismemberment.

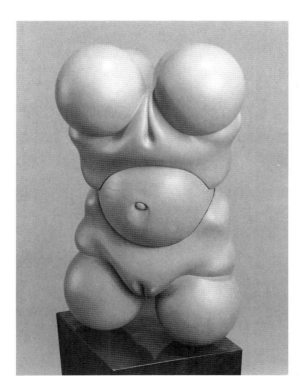

Hans Bellmer (1902-1975):
The Doll, 1936 (replica of 1965).
Painted aluminium, 18¼" high.

René Magritte (1898-1967):
The Future of Statues, 1932.
Painted plaster mask, 12¼" high.

ABSTRACTION AND FIGURATION
ABSTRACT SCULPTURES AND MOBILE CONSTRUCTIONS

Sophie Taeuber-Arp (1889-1943):
Relief, 1936.
Painted wood, 21⅝″ × 25½″.

physical form to an algebraic equation as a polished nickel silver object standing in space. Max Bill's *Endless Ribbon* embodies (originally in plaster, later in the modern material concrete) the Möbius concept of a surface which becomes a spatial structure by being twisted 180° around its lengthwise axis. The result is the mathematical paradox of a strip which has only a single surface and edge, but takes the form of a continuous loop.

In her *Relief* (1936) Sophie Taeuber-Arp permutes differently coloured cut out discs which lie on, in front of and behind the wood ground. As a result the relationship between form and ground is constantly susceptible of different interpretations. The disc cut out of the board is a hole, an absence (the "original version" is obviously the sound-hole in Picasso's *Guitar*, 1912). As the front side of a cone projecting from the board, it is a plastic body. By allowing the observer to look through to the wall on which the relief hangs, the disc admits that the work is an artefact.

Ben Nicholson's *White Relief* (1935) makes a similar statement, but much more quietly and statically. It represents almost the minimum of a concrete statement by

Georges Vantongerloo (1886-1965):
Space Construction, 1935.
Polished nickel silver, 15¼″ high.

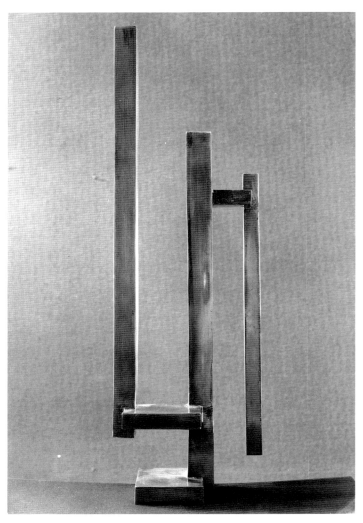

During the years 1931 to 1936 non-representational painters and sculptors working in Paris formed a vaguely defined group which was named after the periodical *Abstraction-Création* which also appeared in those five years. It represented the shared exile of the different currents in international Constructivism. In this chapter we use the term *Abstraction-Creation* in a wider sense for sculptors who did not belong to the Paris group but followed the same goal, namely to create modern sculpture (and painting) as rational, almost naturally pared down constructions with elementary forms and colours. They certainly do not renounce poetry or emotion, but to them they are moments of feeling from a more abstract reality. They are plans for a brave new world, promises of a happier future, models for memorials to a better mankind. Today, of course, we know that these were Utopias.

In spite of the usual word "abstraction," the state of the sculptures shown here is completely concrete. If we recall Arp's title *Human Concretion* for his biomorphic creations, we are now dealing in an analogous way with "mathematical concretions." Georges Vantongerloo's *Space Construction: $Y = ax^3 - bx^2 + cx$* (1935; the work is also entitled *Construction: $Y = 2 \times^3 - 13,5 \times^2 + 21x$*, which an expert mathematician would know was identical) gives

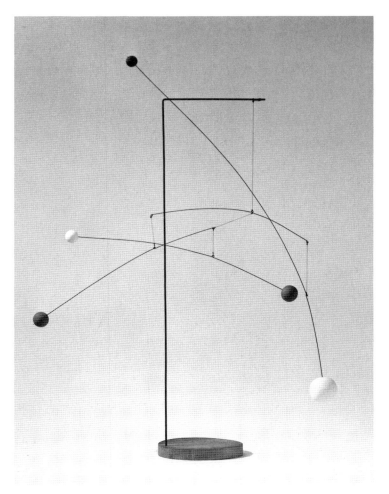

Alexander Calder (1898-1976):
Mobile, 1935 (?).
Wood, metal, string, 31″ high.

Max Bill (1908):
Endless Ribbon, 1935-1953.
Bronze, 49¼″ high.

way of such elementary items as square and circle, single and double, large and small, before and behind, light and shade, etc.

The first successful products of mobile sculpture also belong to this period and its groups. After Alexander Calder (and others) had built in small electric motors to activate them (something Tinguely was to employ far more impressively in the 1960s), he relied exclusively on gravity and currents of air to move his mobiles. For all the popularity which the principle of the mobile later enjoyed (nowadays they are produced in kindergartens), we should never forget the wonderful demand Calder made on his constructions of wire and painted balls: "I want to make Mondrians that move..."

Ben Nicholson
(1894-1982):
White Relief, 1935.
Painted wood,
40″ × 65⅜″.

179

OFFICIAL SCULPTURE UNDER THE DICTATORS

Vera Muchina (1889):
Factory Worker and
Kolkhoz Woman, 1937.
Stainless steel, 80′ high.

Paris World's Fair, 1937, with facing pavilions of the USSR
and the Third Reich.
Upper left, Muchina's Factory Worker and Kolkhoz Woman.
Lower right centre, Josef Thorak's sculpture group Comradeship.

The historical basis for Fascist sculpture is a doctrinaire exaggerated neoclassicism which strives to express a timeless heroic age. This is often supported by a close connection with architecture (often linked with town-planning) and underlined by gigantic dimensions. Both architecture and street perspectives as well as sculpture are at the service of an ideology, so the ultimate critical judgment about whether we are dealing with stage architecture and decorative sculpture, or even historicism and kitsch, matters little. The model was not the Grecian polis or acropolis, where temple buildings and sculpture programmes were conceived on a diagonal view so that they could be seen in free space and as repeatedly told epics, but imperial Rome. The dominating principles of axes, frontality and symmetry, of the colossal and the nudity of the figures are means of expressing the total state power which seeks to suppress man's individuality, indeed must suppress it. Given such premises, highly talented sculptors may have been at work, but not great artists, who are individuals by definition.

State art is propagandist art, whether in Mussolini's Italy, National Socialist Germany, the USSR or its satellites (and only too often in the democracies). It is always anti-modern art, reaction to the avant-garde, ostracism of the creative.

And so it was no coincidence that at the Paris World's Fair of 1937 the houses of the USSR (by Boris Iofan) and the German Empire (by Albert Speer), which opposed each other as massive wings to the overall layout on the Trocadéro site, were very similar, not only architectonically, but also because of the crowning and accompanying figures (by Vera Muchina and Josef Thorak); and that the Pavilion of the Spanish Republic (by José Sert) with Picasso's Marie-Thérèse sculptures and his Guernica painting was so entirely different.

Comradeship, Thorak's sculpture of two naked heroes hand in hand, with crossed legs, has been lost or hidden. It was more or less a replica of the Roman marble copy of the *Murderers of the Tyrants* (after the lost Greek bronzes of Harmodius and Aristogeiton), but we must assume that the sculptor did not know (or that *he* assumed that the

Constantin Brancusi (1876-1957):
Gate of the Kiss at Targu Jiu, Rumania, 1936-1938.
Stone, 16′10″ high.

party did not know) that in antique art the crossed or intertwined legs of two figures meant the act of copulation.

Today Vera Muchina's 80-foot high group *Factory Worker and Kolkhoz Woman* stands outside the building housing the permanent Agricultural Exhibition in Moscow. It was produced in the "Hammer and Sickle" factory in sixty-five separate laminated stainless steel pieces and erected in Paris in thirteen days by a team of stakhanovites, according to the Paris press of 1937. The works of Arno Breker, about whom Charles Despiau published a very appreciative book under the Flammarion imprint in 1942, were the quintessence of Nazi sculpture.

Now let us take a look at Rumania where Brancusi (living in Paris from 1904, without any contact with his homeland from 1914) created the monumental axial layout of Targu Jiu from 1936 to 1938. It consists of the 97-foot high *Endless Column of the Gift of Memory* (that was its original title), the *Stone Portal* (called *Gate of the Kiss*) and a massive round stone table with twelve massive round stools (originally without a title, now known as the *Table of Silence*). Brancusi's *Endless Column* was commissioned and paid for by Aretie Tatarescu, President of the National League of Women of Gorj and wife of the then National Liberal Prime Minister of Rumania and later Ambassador in Paris under the fascist dictatorship of King Carol II. It was erected as a memorial to the fallen in the First World War. Later Brancusi executed the gate as a portal to the Gorj town park at his own expense. In so doing he changed the originally planned site in such a way that it stood in the axis between column and table. The model for all this was the Parisian Arcs de Triomphe (after the triumphal arches on the imperial axes of ancient Rome) with their arrange-

Enrico del Debbio (1891):
Foro Italico, Rome.
Detail of the stadium with marble athlete statues.

ment on the triumphal axes of the Champs Elysées and the Tuileries (with the obelisk in between). The motif of the kiss, endlessly repeated in large- and small-scale reliefs, stems from much earlier symbolist projects of Brancusi's for a *Column of the Kiss* and a *Temple of Love*. Brancusi had used it before in many sculptures and projects stylistically suited to the times before he now executed it in the monumental Mussolini style. He embellished both the vibrant war memorial, the motif of which comes from Rumanian folklore, as well as the kiss design, with his brand of nature mysticism, which after World War II was swallowed and advocated all too gullibly by the very historians of sculpture (such as Herbert Read and Carola Giedion-Welcker) who had previously espoused the cause of the avant-garde.

Albert Speer (1905-1981):
The New Chancellery in Berlin, 1938
(destroyed).

Arno Breker (1900):
The Party, 1938.
Bronze.

POST-WAR PROSPECTS

Pablo Picasso (1881–1973):

△ Head of a Woman (Dora Maar), 1941.
Bronze, 31½" high.

▽ Head of a Bull, 1943.
Assemblage (bicycle seat and handlebars), 13¼" × 17¼".

▷▽ Death's Head, 1943.
Bronze and copper, 10" high.

Picasso's wartime and post-war sculptures are so important that they deserve a chapter to themselves. They are manifestos, not only because of their subjects, but also of the period when they were made–manifestos of defiance at first and later of recaptured *joie de vivre*. We shall pass over the numerous light-hearted small-scale works of those years and concentrate on the handful of magnificent works which are far more important in the history of modern sculpture than all the sculptures from totalitarian states put together–as Picasso meant them to be.

Shortly after war was declared, Picasso went to Royan on the Atlantic coast in early September 1939. Until the occupation of Paris on 14 June 1940, he frequently spent a few days or weeks in the capital. At the end of August 1940, after the Germans entered Royan and Pétain's armistice, he returned to Paris permanently, living and working in that old building at 7 Rue des Grands-Augustins in which he had painted *Guernica* in 1937. It seemed as if his committed anti-fascist stand was destined to continue there, because he could easily have emigrated to the USA or Mexico. His sculpture studio at Boisgeloup was inaccessible, but there was enough room for his sculptures at No. 7. He had some of them cast in bronze (friends undertook secret missions to arrange this) during the occupation, when even church bells were commandeered to be turned into cannon, which was yet another demonstration of art taking a stand against the power of the state.

The large plaster *Head of a Woman (Dora Maar)* (1941), however, was not cast in bronze until 1958. The classically burnished likeness with the serene expression links up with the Marie-Thérèse heads of 1931. The head and its base form a single *piece*, i.e. they are a sculpture and so hark back to the art of Rodin or in broader terms to the art of sculpture which was expressed in earlier periods by the allegori-

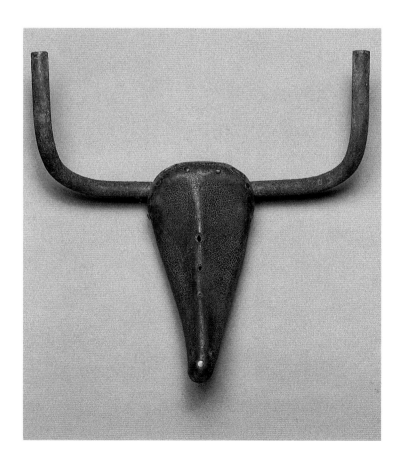

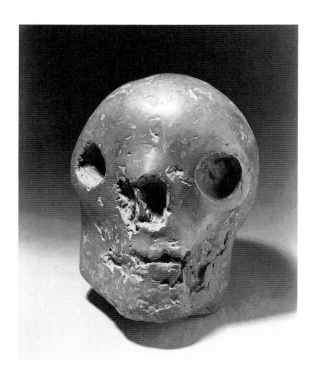

cal figure of a muse. This testimony to exuberant life is contrasted with the image of death. Picasso's *Death's Head* (1943) is an object without a base or pedestal which makes it look like a skull from a charnel-house. The reproduction clearly shows the expressive power of this bronze, but not the equally important quality of its dense heavy mass. As a gesture of defiance, it, too, was cast during the occupation using essential war materials.

Both works–like the *Man with Sheep* (1944), a bronze cast of which was erected in the market place of Vallauris in 1950–are traditional sculptures executed as a whole (in other words, they are not constructions) and are akin to public monumental sculpture. Later, in 1959, a bronze cast of *Head of a Woman (Dora Maar)* was erected outside the Paris church of Saint-Germain-des-Prés as a monument to the poet Guillaume Apollinaire. The assemblage *Head of a Bull* (1943) is the exact opposite: a brain-wave by which recognizable material objects, the handlebars and saddle of a bicycle, are transformed by the artist's imagination into something quite different. As a result the iconography of the bicycle (we are reminded of Marcel Duchamp's *Cycle Wheel*, 1913) has found its most remarkable expression. Nevertheless Picasso imagined an even more miraculous transformation: a cyclist arriving and finding the spare parts needed for his bicycle in a work of art. The figure of the *Man with Sheep* extends the iconography of the Good Shepherd, because the farmer with the serious and resolute expression holds the animal in front of him like a sacrifice.

However, the post-war *Goat* (1950) is a purely sculptural joke, to appreciate which the observer needs to know that its exuberant vitality is the product of wicker basket, ceramic flower-pots, palm leaves, metal, wood, cardboard and plaster.

Pablo Picasso (1881-1973):

◁ Man with Sheep, 1944.
Bronze, 88″ high.

▽ Goat, 1950.
Original plaster, 47½″ high,
56½″ long.

Fritz Wotruba (1907-1975):
Seated Figure, 1951.
Bronze, 20½″ high.

the USA), Jean Arp and Sophie Taeuber-Arp (at first in the South of France, then in Switzerland), while the artists who stayed in France (Maillol, Brancusi, Laurens) continued their work in silence. Barbara Hepworth had her studio in Cornwall and Henry Moore succeeded Sir Jacob Epstein as England's foremost sculptor. Other sculptors who have not been mentioned so far prepared for their decisive impact on the post-war artistic scene in Switzerland (Marino Marini in the Ticino, Germaine Richier in Zurich, Fritz Wotruba in Zug). However, one artist who confined himself to his studio from 1935 to 1945, Alberto Giacometti (living in Geneva from 1943 to 1945), will be discussed in detail in the next chapter. His experimental work was the biggest step taken in the history of sculpture in those years.

Altogether the new ideas of the thirties produced some wonderful works during and after the war. Picasso's biomorphic *Bathers* from Boisgeloup inspired Henri Laurens to a fully modelled style with opulent sensual curves with

Jean Arp (1887-1966):
Shepherd of Clouds, 1953.
Bronze, 65¾″ high.

War and post-war years are usually reactionary periods, especially so in the history of sculpture dealing with public and memorial works. Nothing stifles art more than closed frontiers and long years of exile, and in this respect World War II was far more repressive than World War I. The latter was preceded by one of the most eventful decades in recent art history when Expressionism, Cubism, Futurism and Object Art effected a break with century-old traditions. During the war the Dadaist movement appeared, transcending European frontiers and even crossing the Atlantic, and Constructivism was introduced. The Surrealist movement, however, had come to a standstill during World War II. It was still in existence on several continents, but the International Surrealist Exhibition held in Paris in 1947 showed that it was a rather vitiated existence. And the competition in 1951 for a monument to the Unknown Political Prisoner had the same effect on international Constructivism. For in Europe World War II was preceded by a decade of economic privation as well as reactionary and totalitarian repression of the avant-garde. In the United States of America, much Surrealist and Constructivist thinking had to be absorbed in the isolation of the artist's studio (by David Smith, Arshile Gorky and Richard Lippold, for example), so that brand-new concepts of sculpture and hence the sculpture of the present could emerge in the mid-fifties.

On the other hand, the years of war and exile gave the avant-garde artists mentioned in previous chapters the opportunity to develop and propagate their concepts, and so ensure the establishment of modern sculpture after 1950. This applies to the Americans Alexander Calder and Joseph Cornell, and to the artists who were active as emigrants, Naum Gabo and Anton Pevsner (in England and which he interpreted the female body as an arrangement of plastic masses. His *Crouching Woman* (1940-1941) associates them all in a compact cube shape and merits comparison with the crouching figures of Maillol and Derain from the early period of modern sculpture (1905 and 1907). In a sense it marks the conclusion of the trends and tendencies introduced in those years. What is different is the formal innate personal value of the plastic basic form even without representational significance. The impact on the senses does not result from the motif nor do the structural features spring from the enforced stereometry; if anything both belong to the plastic independent life of this figure, as if the work were primarily a sculpture and only secondly a figure.

The works by Maillol and Derain already mentioned also form the basis for Wotruba's *Seated Figure* (1951), but here we see the beginning of something new that was most strongly expressed in Wotruba's work in the sixties, namely the architectonic articulation of a lying, sitting or standing figure built up of angular stereometric blocks. It is impossible to imagine a greater contrast to Arp's *Human Concretions*.

A development of the Surrealist "natural products" of the thirties, Arp's *Shepherd of Clouds* (1953) confronts us as a 6-foot high monument—a monument to the faculty shared by the dream and the poet to look on the constantly changing and evanescent cloud formations in the sky as more real and lasting than earthly realities. Unfortunately the snow-white plaster version which alone did full justice to the theme has been destroyed.

To express European vital consciousness in the years immediately after World War II, Marino Marini found a most fertile theme under the generic title of *Miracle*. Most versions represent a rider falling from his rearing horse. Both of them escape with their lives, miraculously and spiritually purified. In other sculptures with the same title, the miracle consists in the virility exhibited by the rider. These are all paraphrases of the traditional equestrian statue (and extensions of Boccioni's transformation of that theme), which Marini first calls in question using Expressionist means (polychrome wood sculpture: *Miracle*, 1955) and then pulls from its pedestal.

Marini modelled the southern French sculptress Germaine Richier in 1945 as a personal monument to the years spent together in exile in Switzerland. This ended their artistic friendship, because from then on Marini's art came to a halt, whereas Germaine Richier's sculpture progressed and made her one of the more forceful figures in the postwar years. (Other tendencies and new goals appearing in the early post-war years, in the works of Chillida and Robert Müller, for example, will be treated in the third part of this volume.) Her total oeuvre is like a summation of the age of modern sculpture. Schooled in the modelling tradition of Rodin (by Guigues in Montpellier and Bourdelle in Paris), briefly affected by the conventions of Maillol and Despiau, deeply moved by the expressive mythic power of Surrealism and aware of the concepts of Constructivism and Giacometti's post-war works, Germaine Richier achieved a style which expressed nature's fierce hostility to man. With her *Praying Mantis* figure (1946) she

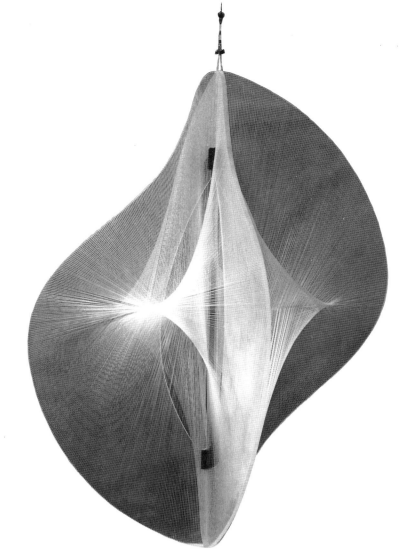

Naum Gabo (1890-1977):
Linear Construction in Space No. 2, 1949.
Plastic material and nylon threads, 36″ high.

Anton Pevsner (1884-1962):
Developable Victory Column, 1946.
Bronze, 41″ high.

Germaine Richier (1904-1959):
The Praying Mantis, 1946.
Bronze, 50½″ high.

Henri Laurens (1885-1954):
Crouching Woman (The Farewell),
1940-1941. Bronze, 27½″ high.

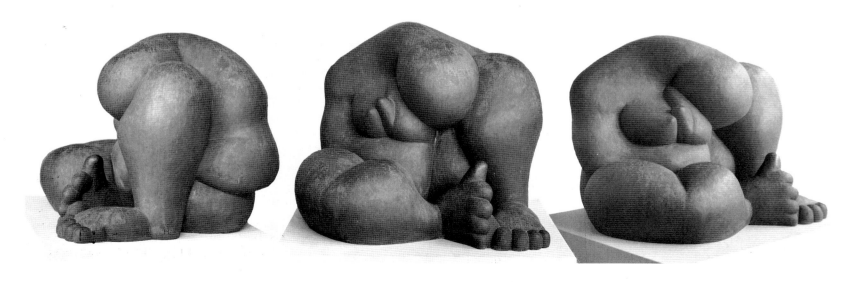

186

acknowledged the fascination of the Surrealist circle around 1930. It represented an insect, the female species of which kills the male gruesomely in the act of copulation. The hybrid combining woman and insect (cf. Giacometti's *Woman with her Throat Cut*, 1932) incarnates an existential nightmare that is not an image of the terrors of external nature, but of the growing cruelty and destruction in man's inner self. This "crusted" style of modelling is capable of expressing the transience of corporeality by calcification and decay and consequently of representing temporality. Germaine Richier's bronzes are also "human concretions," but how different their message is from Jean Arp's!

Constructivism enabled the post-war period to produce large-scale, indeed monumental works. The maturity of the style is shown by the fact that it discovers the means to create plastic bodies and volumes with lines of force. To this end Gabo, in his *Linear Construction in Space No. 2* (1949), stretched nylon threads over a curved frame, in such a way that curved surfaces containing spatial volumes arise from the parallel lines. (In the fifties architects used similar surfaces for concave and convex roof vaulting.) In Pevsner's *Developable Victory Column* (1946), the metal rods of which the model (later cast in bronze) was constructed possess their own stability and supporting force. The dynamic shaping process which produced the lower and upper curved forms is easy to reconstruct. A bundle of upright rods arranged to form a surface was fixed in the middle and then twisted above and below so that the rods fanned out into a spatial shell or cover. The title "Column" betrays the work's aspiration to achieve the timelessness of the Greek temple, but the qualifying "developable" reflects the modern experience that triumphal monuments are a transitory affair and only fulfil their promise of lasting moral usefulness if they can be dismantled and re-erected elsewhere.

Marino Marini (1901-1980):
Great Friends were the True Ones (Portrait of Germaine Richier), 1945.
Original plaster, 13″ high.

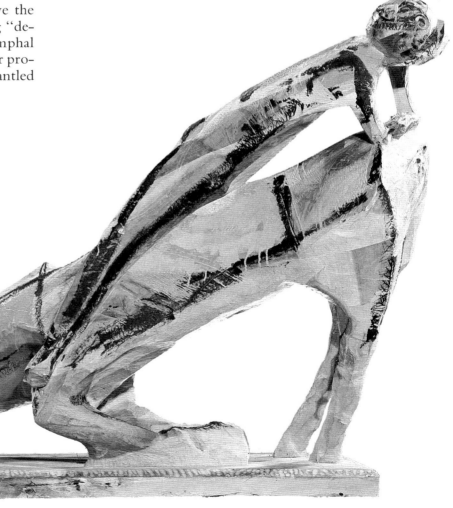

Marino Marini (1901-1980):
Miracle, 1955.
Polychrome wood, 65″ high.

GIACOMETTI'S RENEWAL OF REPRESENTATIONAL ART

"It's not life any longer," wrote Antonin Artaud in February 1947 to André Breton to explain why–in addition to many other reasons–he was unwilling to take part in the International Surrealist Exhibition held in Paris in the summer of 1947. It could equally well have been said by Alberto Giacometti, whose name appeared in the catalogue against his will, although his *Invisible Object* (1934) was not actually exhibited. What Giacometti did exhibit that year in Avignon and Paris was an entirely different kind of sculpture, which attracted no notice until the exhibitions in New York (Pierre Matisse Gallery) and Berne (Kunsthalle) in the spring of 1948, but became world famous from 1950 onwards. Both in style and content, it was closer to life than sculpture had ever been before.

The key work is the *Square* (1948), which unites four matchstick-like little men walking and a small spindly woman standing, all on a communal platform raised to eye height by a stand. It is to be understood as a model for a lifesize monument in a public square. We have to compare the concept with the *Burghers of Calais* and to change a phrase of Cézanne's, "remaking Rodin after nature," call it "remaking Rodin after life" or more precisely after the phenomena of perception. In 1960 Giacometti again took up this project for the Chase Manhattan Plaza in New York creating lifesize and larger than lifesize figures, but they were never erected. In the courtyard of the Fondation Maeght in Saint-Paul-de-Vence, especially when visitors animate the scene, we realize what Giacometti was aiming at: "the totality of life," the simultaneous presence of art (*Large Head on Base*, after the colossal head of Constantine in Rome), everyday life (*Walking Man*) and myth (giant

Alberto Giacometti (1901-1966):

△ Head Study (Rita), 1938.
  Bronze, 8¾" high.

▽ Public Square, 1948-1949.
  Bronze, 8¼" high.

▽▷ Project for Chase Manhattan Plaza, New York, 1960.

Alberto Giacometti (1901–1966):
Composition with Seven Figures and a Head (The Forest), 1950.
Bronze, 22½″ × 18″ × 23″.

Alberto Giacometti (1901–1966):
Chariot, 1950.
Bronze, 65¾″ × 24½″ × 27½″.

Alberto Giacometti (1901–1966):
Bust of Annette IV, 1962.
Bronze, 19″ high.

Standing Woman). And so a project from Giacometti's Sur-realist period (*Project for a Square*, 1930) was realized in the style which is connected with his name even in colloquial French when people talk of a Giacometti woman to des-cribe someone who is the opposite of Rubenesque.

From 1935 to 1945 Giacometti sought to reproduce the outward appearance of figures and head as we see them in reality: always in the distance, always in space, always as part of a much larger field of vision–and as living vis-à-vis, not as dead object. He strove to introduce perspective into sculpture, at first making use of the methods employed by painters: a decrease in size and vaguer definition as the distance increases, large bases to set the figures off. In 1943 in Geneva he had reached the stage when his tiny plaster masses "fell into dust at the very last touch of the spatula." When he returned to Paris in the autumn of 1945, legend has it that he brought his sculptures with him in match-boxes.

In 1946 Giacometti made many studies of passers-by in the street (with reference to the *Square*) and after models in his studio (as a continuation of his researches into the phenomenology of perception) and transferred the short-hand style of his drawings to sculpture. He discovered that

Alberto Giacometti (1901-1966):
Large Head of Diego, 1954.
Bronze, 25½".

making distant figures smaller was an unsatisfactory way
of recreating reality. If anything, it made approaching figures seem to shoot forward and he found their existence in
space was more accurately expressed by their extreme el-
ongation and slimness. He now made sculptures like drawings in space with armatures of iron rods and plaster. From
1947 onwards he formulated the results of his observations
and his reflections on life as style in the original sense of the
word, namely as an art form, for the way in which he saw
visual reality and for the personal expression of what he
had recognized as life and being alive. 1950 was the year
when he produced a great many works for exhibitions in
New York and Paris. His *Chariot* and *Composition with
Seven Figures and a Head (The Forest)* incarnate the image
of woman as the visionary artist sees her. From then until
1965 he indefatigably pursued a single goal–giving life to
a modelled figure by reproducing his active vision. From
the hatchet-like Diego heads of 1954 and the lively Annette busts of 1962 to his very last work, *Bust of Elie Lotar*,
all the plastic forms and masses of the upper part of the
body serve solely to transform the bronze as seen from the
front into the outward image of a real encounter. They
express the nuclei of personalities.

Alberto Giacometti (1901-1966):
Bust of Elie Lotar III, 1965.
Bronze, 26½".

PICASSO'S FINAL TRANSFORMATIONS

Picasso's sculpture studio in 1950.

The frequently quoted, but abbreviated remark made by Picasso in 1923, "In my opinion research in painting is useless, what matters is finding," applies perfectly to the plastic works which he created between his seventieth and ninetieth years. Most of them are actually found objects, whose material or form gave him ideas for sculptures with a quite different figurative significance. Often flashes of inspiration enabled him to discover brand new technical realizations. Let us record that what began at the beginning of the century as small-scale bronze "painter's sculpture" became public monumental sculpture in steel and concrete in the second half of the century. (*Head*, 1967, in Chicago; *Sylvette* in New York, 1967, and in Rotterdam in 1970). Picasso the painter also dominated the history of sculpture in his century by the number of works (more than 600, not counting his pottery) and the abundance of entirely new concepts.

The years 1947-1950 brought Picasso not only a life-enhancing new start after the war years with another young companion, Françoise Gilot, who bore him two children (she was the *Pregnant Woman* of 1950), but also the photographic book by Brassaï, *The Sculptures of Picasso*. More than before Picasso showed henceforth that for him the essence of art was metamorphosis. As a painter he turned a fish into a hen in the last twenty minutes of Henri Clouzot's film *Le Mystère Picasso* (1955). As a sculptor in 1952, he transformed two toy cars, a Renault and a Panhard, which the art dealer Kahnweiler had given to Claude, aged four and Paloma, aged two, into the head of a baboon, and then by adding the handles of two cups which became ears into a mischievous portrait of Kahnweiler. The round body of the baboon was originally a ceramic jug (the head and breasts of the *Pregnant Woman* were also ceramic vessels), its tail with a curled up end, a spring from a car. All the forms, including the baboon's

Pablo Picasso (1881-1973):

▽ Goat Skull, Bottle and Candle, 1951-1952.
Painted bronze, 31″ × 37⅝″ × 21½″.

▷ Baboon and Young, 1952.
Original plaster (ceramic, metal, plaster), 22″ high.

young, were covered with plaster and completed, for it was ultimately meant to be a genuine sculpture, and not just a witty joke, which is why Picasso had these assemblages cast in bronze.

One often senses the vulgar materials magically transformed into moving sculptures behind the painted bronze and experiences their substantial significance all the more expressively. *Goat Skull, Bottle and Candle* (1951-1952) means life and death, those opposites so frequently represented by Picasso. Death is obviously represented by the goat's skull, the surface of which clearly shows the imprint of corrugated cardboard (for the pelt) and whose horns are once again the handle-bars of a bicycle. The rays of the "candle" stuck into the bottle are large carpenter's nails. The bottle is made of wood and only looks round because it is painted. But since the late Middle Ages a burning candle has denoted man's generative power, here

a symbol of life. (That is why it is extinguished in the room of the Virgin at the moment of the Annunciation.) The picture frames and odd bits of wood out of which Picasso produced a cheerful group of six bathers in 1956 so that each figure has its own character underwent a much less drastic change. Finally, five years later, a new period began in Picasso's sculpture: his folding sculptures. Of course, nothing is absolutely new; Picasso was actually carrying out ideas from earlier years, when he cut out chains of little men from folded paper for his and Marie-Thérèse's daughter Maia for example, or they may hark back to his Cubist constructions. He did this with the aid of such experts as Lionel Prejger for the works in metal and Carl Nesjar for the concrete sculptures. Essentially the principle remains valid that the sculptural works, like the objects in a painting, are imaginary objects which stem from the perspective plane and bring their imaginary spatial per-

Pablo Picasso (1881-1973):
Bathers, 1956.
Bronze, from 53½″ to 104″ high.

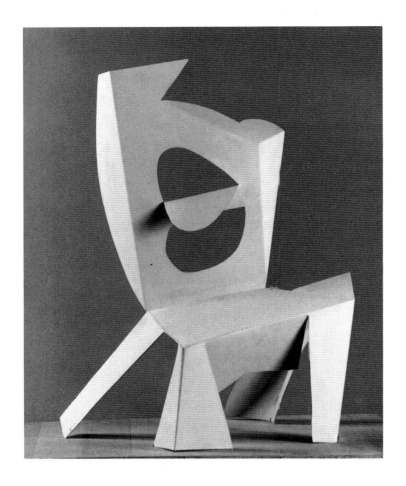

Looking back on modern sculpture in the fifties, we see a change in both the theory and technique of sculpture–mainly through the principles of construction and the assemblage of objects–which was much more radical than the development from Michelangelo to Rodin. The sculpture of the present was to introduce even more radical changes, compared with which "modern sculpture" is like that of yesterday. The criterion was mostly that of the human figure or the creating human hand and the themes, too, mostly dealt with mankind. Last but not least in this context there was a completely new beginning in the post-1950 period, in which we have included the later works of Giacometti and Picasso.

Pablo Picasso (1881-1973):

◁ The Chair, 1961.
Painted sheet metal, 43⅞″ high.

▷ Sculpture (Sylvette), 1970.
White cement and black crushed granite, 26′ high.

▽ Woman with Hat, 1961-1963.
Painted sheet metal, 49⅝″ high.

spective into real space and at least mentally can be changed back into the surface from which they come. The constructive problem of free standing is solved by the folding and unfolding of the surfaces.

The *Chair* (1961) shows all that very clearly. It is not a real chair, any more than the *Guitar* (1912), with which he initiated modern sculpture, is a real guitar. It would be impossible to sit on the sloping and foreshortened seat. At the time Picasso said to Lionel Prejger, who executed his cut paper patterns in sheet metal: "That is a chair and it is also an explanation of Cubism. Imagine a chair that has fallen under a steamroller. Wouldn't it look something like that?" But he cannot have meant it seriously. A squashed chair would not look like that, but like César's and Chamberlain's scrap-iron compressions. Yet the form and spatial principles of Cubist constructions from 1913 to 1916 are actually resumed and this time executed completely in the round and not merely in relief. Other cut out and folded sheets of metal become lifesize women, alone or with a kicking baby. A touch of black paint on the otherwise totally white figures either filled out anatomical details or created "shadows" and hence three dimensionality on the surface, or interrupted the figure as "space." In the brightly coloured *Woman with a Hat* the real shadow below the sheet metal surface cut into a round "models" the bosom. The painting of the rear sheet which is rolled forwards at the bottom left and right resembles the golden-brown velvet upholstery of an armchair. The woman represented is Jacqueline (married to Picasso in 1961) who is wearing her hat, ready to go out, but waits for a moment until her nail varnish has dried. The immaterial gleam of the finger nails and eyes is evoked when we look through the spaces cut out at those points.

Alexander Calder (1898–1976):
La Grande Vitesse, 1969.
Red painted steel, 43′ high.
Vandenberg Center Plaza, Grand Rapids, Michigan.

MONUMENTALITY AND NEW TECHNIQUES
SCULPTURE RETURNS TO THE PUBLIC SPACE

Reg Butler (1913-1981):
Working Model for the Unknown Political Prisoner, 1951-1952.
Bronze wire and metal maquette, welded on to stone base, 88″ high.
First prize.

From the social and political failure of the great monuments of Rodin up until the years just after the end of World War II, in other words from 1900 to 1950, almost everything innovative achieved in three-dimensional expression was at the level of the object, the "private work." This basic reflection by the pioneers of contemporary art on the reality and expressive power of the components of their image remained, because of its dimensions, hidden from the public eye. Despite the will of the Russian Constructivists and the dream of the idealists of De Stijl and the Bauhaus, sculptural investigation, though it had discovered a fourth dimension–empty space–, had but slight impact on the renewal of town planning, architecture and objects of everyday use. Worse still, with the economic depression of the thirties and the advent of totalitarian powers, a deep gulf opened between artistic creation and political demands.

To be sure, monuments were still put up between 1905 and 1939, but these social commissions kept away the genuine creators, especially so in that the rise of Fascism slanted aesthetic standards toward psychological propaganda. The "promotional" distortion discredited the monument with a pedagogic purpose devised by republics to honour its heroes; under the Vichy regime in France it was to receive ultimate condemnation. By sending to the scrap-heap for the sake of military savings the bronze that had been used in casting such monuments, Pétain and his friends also found the opportunity of ridding public areas of "dangerous" examples.

The attitude emerges clearly in the words of Abel Bonnard, Minister of Education under the Vichy government: "The painful circumstances in which we find ourselves can lead to a fair and wholesome reappraisal of our glorious achievements so that, a few years from now, there will be no more intruders, nor any that are unworthy among that small community of statues which everywhere must set noble examples." Replacement in stone had been promised, but even the victorious Resistance forgot the Republic's former glories. The pedestals remained empty; the function had been drained of meaning, and sculptural creation was no longer suited to commemorative representation.

The paradox of the monument became apparent on the occasion of the international competition for the Monument to the Unknown Political Prisoner organized by the London Institute of Contemporary Art. The judging took place in 1953; 3,500 artists had entered, but only 200 maquettes were submitted to the international jury; and they were signed by the most prestigious artists. The winners were Butler, Gabo, Basaldella, Pevsner, Hepworth. It became obvious that the obligation of-illustrating a theme was a hindrance to the freedom of expression of modern sculpture. This antinomy stood out clearly in the opinion of Jorge Romero Brest: "It must be admitted that in all cases the necessity of sticking to a given subject only weakened the expression of each project... We come up against a burning question of our time, one that calls into question the relations between the quality that each artist may be presumed capable of giving his creations and the possibility of inventing a style that would formally result from the spiritual demands of an epoch."

The best entries were abstract, since for the time being the gesture or the symbol no longer held any reality for the modern sculptor. Henceforth the only projects feasible on a monumental scale would be those in which the intuition and desire of the creator came before those of the patrons commissioning the work. Now it was just when social demand, however noble, was being recognized as inadequate to the claims of creation, that there was a move afoot almost everywhere to institutionalize–in the form of a budget allocation reserved to art in public constructions–the aim of integrating artistic creation into building structure. Such measures, furthermore, were taken less in order to bring art into the city than to express social solidarity with the artists.

It is nonetheless paradoxical to observe that an attempt was being made to concretize the ideas of the Constructivists, with a thirty-year time-lag, just when they had already become out of date. For as a matter of fact, in the post-war context, town planners and architects, obsessed by industrial programming and economic exigencies, no longer took an interest in artistic creation, and the best workers in the plastic arts refused to meddle in a hostile milieu where their creation would perform none but a decorative function. Condemned to be only a "soul-supplement," the art work could not be satisfied with the narrow setting permitted to it. Restricted to ornamentation, this sculpture had even less of a future insofar as sculptors had once more taken possession of real space. But if contemporary sculpture had won back public space it owed that fact to the daring of a few patrons or communities with cultural aspirations. Moore and Calder were the first to blaze that new trail; their universal renown made them the first to receive commissions for monumental works. And it was by rediscovering urban space that contemporary sculpture would soon encounter its new function: from token-object it became gradually transformed into "living-space." At the same time the development of techniques or the invention of new technologies made it possible to give duration and monumentality to what had been ephemeral or temporary in the constructions of the pioneers.

On both these levels the example of Calder is significant. Born in 1898, he did not have his first retrospective until 1938; only in 1949 did he receive his first public commission (a work twenty feet high rejected by the Philadelphia Museum). Laureate of the Venice Biennale in 1952 and the Carnegie Award in 1958, he thereafter acquired a fame which enabled him to inscribe in space ever larger and loftier designs (65 feet high) that could be produced only by industrial methods. The citizens of Grand Rapids took up a subscription in order to acquire their Calder. Inaugurated in 1969, *La Grande Vitesse* (*High Speed*), by becoming the town sign, marked a turning point in the history of commissions. A modern city had discovered the returns in cultural prestige which an investment in art could bring.

Reproduced from Art d'Aujourd'hui, *N° 5, Paris, July 1953:*

LE MONUMENT AU PRISONNIER POLITIQUE INCONNU

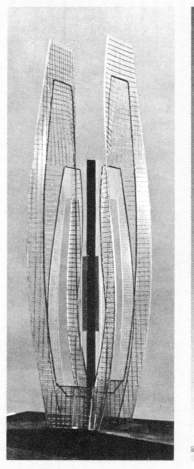
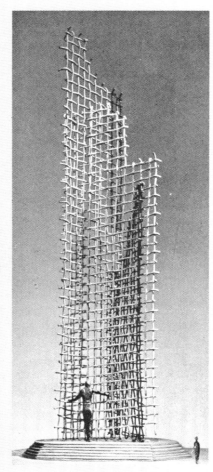

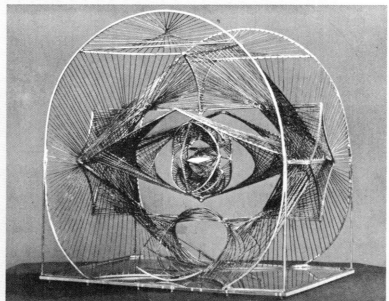

Quatre seconds prix
(£. 750)

1	2	3
	5	
4		

1. Reg Butler *(Grande-Bretagne).*
2. Naum Gabo *(Etats-Unis).*
3. Mirko Basaldella *(Italie).*
4. Barbara Hepworth *(Grande-Bretagne).*
5. Antoine Pevsner *(France).*
(Photos F. L. Kenett.)

7

MOORE, A SHINING EXAMPLE

The Englishman Henry Moore was one of the first contemporary sculptors to encounter the possibility of projecting his imagination into public space. Born in 1898, he attained international renown starting from the end of the Second World War. His first one-man show was in 1941; in 1945 he was appointed Member of the Arts Committee of the British Council and in 1946 the Museum of Modern Art of New York held an important retrospective exhibition of his work. In 1948 the Venice Biennale awarded him the prize for sculpture. These consecrations won him commissions the sizes of which were in direct proportion to the widening of his popularity. He had in fact until then produced only a very small number of works exceeding six feet in height: a relief for the St James's Park Underground Building in 1928–which he regarded as a youthful folly–and the reclining figure of the Detroit Institute of Arts in 1939. From 1947, on the contrary, his works kept on growing in height and in width: 7 feet for the *Three Standing Figures* of Battersea Park in 1948; 7½ feet for the *Reclining Figure* of the Tate Gallery in 1951; 16½ feet for the stone *Reclining Figure* for UNESCO in 1958. In 1969, with *The Arch*, he reached a height of 19½ feet; and *Vertebrae*, a sculpture in three pieces, was soon to attain 22½ in length.

Moore's previous development had directly prepared him for dealing with real space and that monumentality. The encounter with archaic art in 1929 gradually freed him from subjection to the model from nature; then the influence of Arp and Picasso steered him towards a more abstract expression that sought less to reproduce than to create organic forms justified solely by their presence and expressing by their vitality the growth he discovered in the natural elements he began to collect: bones, pebbles, tree-stumps, seashells, etc. These products of nature, which preserved in their very form the development that life demands, inspired his work as a sculptor: direct carving, which he brought back into practice, shows for instance how the specific qualities of the constituent material of the work can directly influence the artist's inspiration.

The observation of these natural elements opened Moore's eyes to another way of proceeding at the same time that it revealed asymmetry to him as a dynamic prin-

Henry Moore (1898):
Sculpture and Red Rocks, 1942.
Crayon, wash, pen and ink, 19⅛″ × 14¼″.

Four Piece Composition (Reclining Figure), 1934.
Cumberland alabaster, 20″ high.

ciple. His interest in the continuity of forms led him quite early to experiment with the mass with a hole pierced through it, from which he would renew the relation between sculpture and surrounding space. He was not unaware of the possibilities of abstraction, but most of his works preserved a biomorphic, not to say anthropomorphic character. "All art," he said, "is abstract in one sense. Not to like abstract qualities or not to like reality is to misunderstand what sculpture and art are about... But for me, I can't cut my sculpture off from living, and the forms that one sees in nature, in people, in trees are reproduced or get mixed up with one's sculpture because they are all part of living."

He achieved this osmosis between human representation and the understanding of organic forms essentially in the reclining or recumbent figure, which he preferred as a subject above all others and which gave him the pretext for his most daring constructions. "There are three fundamental poses of the human figure," he recognized. "One is standing, the other is seated and the third is lying down... But of the three poses, the reclining figure gives the most freedom, compositionally and spatially. The seated figure has to have something to sit on. You can't free it from its pedestal. A reclining figure can recline on any surface. It is free and stable at the same time."

The study of bones also showed him that external form is the direct consequence of a function, the demands of which imply a continuity of the tension of the volume extending to its interior, even when pierced with holes needed for articulation. It also revealed to him the positive-negative relation between elements of the same structure, a relation he experimented with in small constructions of several pieces that gave preponderance to internal space; for him space and form soon made the unity of sculpture.

And when Moore could finally take the step to monumentality, he developed a landscape sculpture in an especially close relationship with nature, in that he executed each of his pieces on a particular site. "I realized what an advantage a separated two-piece composition could have in relating figures to landscape," he noted. "Knees and breasts are mountains. Once these two parts become separated you don't expect it to be a naturalistic figure; therefore, you can justifiably make it like a landscape or a rock. If it is a single figure, you can guess what it's going to be like. If it is in two pieces, there's a bigger surprise; you have more unexpected views... The front view doesn't enable one to foresee the back view. As you move round it, the two parts overlap or they open up, and there's a space between. Sculpture is like a journey. You have a different view as you return. The three-dimensional world is full of surprises."

The size of commissions such as the one from UNESCO obliged Moore to work with collaborators, but he acquired such experience of materials that he was always able to restore to them their energy and reality. Large-

Henry Moore (1898):
Reclining Figure, 1945-1946.
Elmwood, 75″ long.

sized works also led him to prefer bronze, in other words, modelling. It was in maquettes he could hold in his hand that he projected his desires and experience into a manageable material; but he kept a close eye on its enlargement to make sure that it would find its full meaning in the site which awaited it.

Refusing to submit to architecture, Moore invented a counter-architecture: he was fully aware of the freedom which the artist's thought had to introduce into the constraints of the city. Their purposes opposed them: "Architecture and sculpture are both dealing with the relationship of masses," he wrote. "In practice, architecture is not pure expression, but has a functional or utilitarian purpose... And sculpture, more naturally than architecture, can use organic rhythms. Aesthetically architecture is the abstract relationship of masses... but sculpture, not being tied to a functional and utilitarian purpose, can attempt much more freely the exploration of the world of pure form."

The dream of integrating art and architecture was impossible, and Moore, with that affirmation of a landscape-sculpture, opened new horizons to expression in the third dimension while shifting its function in social space. It offered itself as a sensual experience: direct, tactile, but also spiritual in referring to another consciousness of life and its development. With Moore, representation of movement disappears in the expression of forms preserving the imprint of the demands of growth and the scars of time.

Henry Moore (1898):
Sheep Piece, 1971-1972.
Bronze, 18' high.

Henry Moore (1898):
Three Piece Reclining Figure: Draped, 1975.
Bronze, 14'8" long.

ABSTRACTION AND RESPECT FOR MATERIALS

Giò Pomodoro (1930):
Antagonistic Contacts I, 1973-1974.
Black marble, 8'2½" high.

We have already seen that, from the end of the nine-teenth century, painters had played a determining role in the liberation of sculpture; it was to be confirmed once again by Miró. He came to sculpture through reviving the primary experiences that had made him receptive to paint-ing, as he confided in that 1949 interview: "I am a colour-ist, but an illiterate as regards form. I can't tell a straight line from a curve. I manage to get a living sense of form by drawing from the sense of touch, with my eyes closed. Still today, thirty years later, the effects of that experience of drawing reappear in my interest in sculpture, when I feel the need to massage with my hands, to take a lump of wet earth and knead it. That way I get a physical satisfac-tion I can't attain by drawing or painting." At the time he said this, Miró with his friend Artigas, was beginning to devote himself to experiments in ceramics that were to become decisive; until then he had created only a few objects in the context of Surrealism. It was, moreover, just when his painting was taking on an increasingly calli-graphic aspect that Miró hit upon form as an antidote. His practice of sculpture continued to broaden between 1954, when he received the prize for painting at the Venice Bien-nale, and 1972, the year of his exhibition at the Zurich Kunsthaus, devoted exclusively to his work as a sculptor.

Miró's output is divided into two quite distinct genres: modelling and assemblage from the found objects which he collected. In the Catalan village of Gallifa, where Ar-tigas took up residence in 1951, Miró produced his pieces of pottery which soon were able to attain monumental size. The landscape here was magnificent, and the poet Teixidor, who was among the first to discover Miró's ceramic sculpture, emphasized what it owed to the site: "Nature at its highest pitch, in its most baroque exaspera-

Joan Miró (1893-1983):
Miró Labyrinth: The Triumphal Arch, 1963.
Concrete.

Raffael Benazzi (1933):
Turtle, 1971-1972.
Oakwood, 51¼″ × 88″ × 41½″.

tion; that is the supreme motive. The rocks, mountains and stones, the trees and plants of Montroig and Gallifa, form the decisive substratum of that art."

Combining the freedom to manipulate the earth with the expressive possibilities of its passage through the ordeal by fire, Miró revived the presence of biomorphic forms by binding them into a new relationship to space through his working of solids and voids. The vitality and exuberance of his creations took up again the influence of Gaudí, to which Miró was always responsive.

At the same time, Miró went back to the assemblage. Like those of Picasso, his assemblages were transmuted into bronze, but they were different from Picasso's in taking their origin from a storehouse of forms still more natural and commonplace, prompting Alain Joufroy to say: "Miró has transformed the *object* into *sculpture*. He has got the idea accepted that the objectifying of vision and its material objectification are acts of a *sculptor*. But that is not to imply that he has covered up, in the same act, the meaning of the operation... It was thought that modern art, through the antirealist principle on which it was founded, had routed all of reality from the field of its investigations... And we indeed have to admit that such was not at all the case..., that the everyday reality of men, the humblest and most common, remains the centre, and as it were the sun, round which turn the genuine inventors, all the great frontier-crossers of language."

In giving pottery and assemblages monumental size, Miró was enabled by his metaphors and metamorphoses to project his subjectivity in forms that certify our citizenship of a world without limits, in perpetual evolution, which only his freedom of imagination, starting from the encounter with the ephemeral, was able to express with such force. The return to origins and to the elementary was completed; mother earth and her ceaseless germination regained their meaning once more.

This need to make forms live in space while exalting the material that constituted them and exploiting the technology that makes it possible to give them a monumental scale (the pneumatic drill of the stone carver; the chain saw of the lumberjacks or the plasticized gelatins of the metal-

founders) also characterized the adventure of a new generation of abstract artists who rediscovered in the relation of forms and natural surroundings a silent and totemic presence of which figurative sculpture had been deprived by the representation of gesture. Thus, Giò Pomodoro worked marble to the limits of its tension, equilibrium and purity; Benazzi rediscovered the richness and vitality of wood; Aeschbacher put up millennial markers in lava or granite which found afresh the truth of their material nature. Light played a determinant role in bringing out those natural materials which stand confessed in their specific quality while the spirit they bear within them opposes the functional and economic planning that defines the image of modern cities.

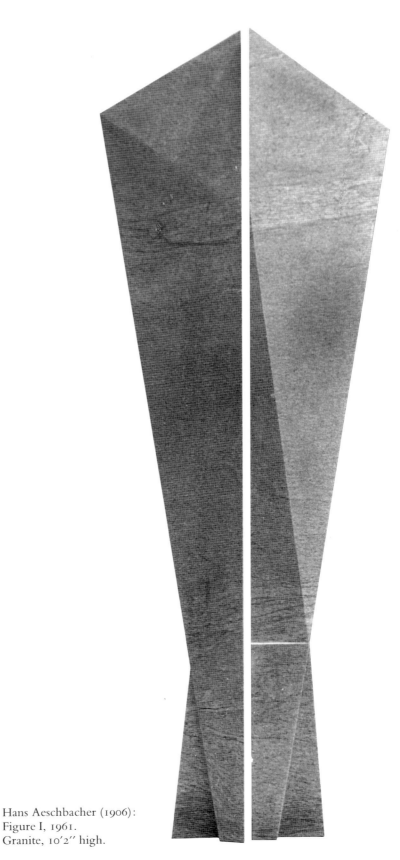

Hans Aeschbacher (1906):
Figure I, 1961.
Granite, 10′2″ high.

203

MONUMENTALITY THROUGH CONCRETE

Mathias Goeritz (1915):
Five Tower Square, satellite
town of Mexico City, 1957-1958.
Height of towers, 121′ to 187′.

In their effort to assert the freedom of creative thought in monumental constructions designed as counter-architecture, sculptors were often led to exploit the possibilities of a new technology or even to create them. Throughout history, as Pierre Francastel has emphasized, the products of technical thought have borne comparison with those of scientific and artistic thought: "The artist who composes a picture or elaborates a sculpture produces objects of civilization which, from a certain point of view, have characteristics in common with works arising from the most purely speculative activity. In every case there is production of things external to the producer of them, usable by others, and marked by interferences in judgment and action."

In this respect the relationship which sculptors were to maintain with concrete is particularly significant and sometimes even paradoxical. If concrete was one of the preferred materials of modern architecture, its utilization by artists ought to have promoted the integration of these two modes of expression. Now in adopting concrete,

sculptors lost no time in making it the object of a construction directly opposed to architecture!

Concrete might seem *a priori* to provide another possibility for casting–having the advantage over plaster of durability–or even a means of direct construction, using the resources of form-work, especially since the boldest architects, such as Breuer, Le Corbusier, Nervi, Niemeyer or Saarinen, showed that its flexibility and resistance permitted the expression of pure and unprecedented forms, and that engineers stretched its bearing capacity and opportunities for asymmetry to their limits. Artificial cement, reinforced or prestressed concrete were used in renewing the basic vocabulary and possibilities of stable structure, with concrete sheaths stimulating the imagination and renovating the occupation of space. With potentialities like these, architecture and sculpture could find common ground; and in 1963, at the University of St Gallen, Alice Penalba opened up those possibilities of integration with a splendid wall relief. It was even found that concrete could be not only formed or moulded, but carved, polished and even coloured, or have its material nature refurbished by the introduction of other constituents or by special treatment, e.g., washed-down or sand-blasted concrete. At this stage, Picasso's meeting in 1956 with the sculptor Nesjar, the first user of the Betogravure

Ervin Patkai (1937):
Group Created for the Olympic Village of Grenoble, 1967.

Pablo Picasso (1881-1973):
Woman with Outspread Arms, 1962.
Concrete and pebbles, 19′7″ high.

system perfected in Olso by Viksjö and Jystad, was significant. This system enabled Nesjar to build monumental forms in space of an original character, perfectly adapted to the execution of his latest foldings; it consisted in form-work for a concrete composed of white cement bonding crushed stones or pebbles, on which it was possible to draw with a sand jet, which, tracing a groove in the cement sheath, brought back out the colour and matter of the aggregate. For ten years Picasso built monuments by that system, which makes it possible to combine drawings with slender forms. The St Hilaire sculpture was 20 feet high, but that of Lake Vaneru in Sweden in 1965 would attain 50 feet, with a thickness not exceeding 4 inches.

Above all, the use of concrete enabled sculptors to grasp space in a durable way; to create environments in nature. Fountains today no longer have the symbolic importance they possessed up until the nineteenth century, but they

remained the starting-point for imaginary constructions. The one built by Stahly for Asnières in 1958-1960 introduced flexible forms, undulating amid the rigour of the architectural grouping. The *Signal* put up by Adam in 1961 in front of the new museum at Le Havre still relied on traditional form-work, but its dynamism and monumentality refresh the relation to space. The utilization of concrete by sculptors would change the relationship between the spectator and the building. The five towers built in Mexico City by Mathias Goeritz in 1957-1958 opened different perspectives. From 121 to 187 feet high, painted white, yellow, red and orange, put up at the entrance to the motorway leading to the United States, they had no other justification than to mark the area physically and spiritually. "I do not seek," the artist said, "to make works of art but to create a spiritual atmosphere through devoting my efforts to the service of the environment." En-

Henri-Georges Adam (1904-1967):
Signal, 1961.
Concrete, 72′ long.
In front of the
Musée des Beaux-Arts,
Le Havre.

vironment: the word had been spoken, and with it sculpture found other than decorative functions. On such a scale it was no longer a case of providing a "soul-supplement" but of stimulating a physical and mental experience by intervening in a place so as to give it a new meaning. Regular prisms of triangular section that preserve in the bands of the form-work the steps and length of time taken to complete them, Goeritz's sculptures, by boldly breaking in their colourful and kinetic relation the sinuous promenade of the highway, introduce the city into nature.

By directly stimulating the sculptor's inspiration, concrete further gave rise to other more decisive experiences in the evolution of sculpture and architecture. Concrete could be material for a physical development, as shown by Gérard Singer in exhibiting the *Ambulomire* in 1968; the inspiration for a spiritual experience of space and sound for

Dani Karavan, who the same year completed his *Monument to the Dead of the Negev Brigade*, or for Patkai the ground for creating a geological landscape in the Olympic village of Grenoble. In elaborating the form by the cavity ripped directly from the polystyrene moulds into which the cement was poured, Singer und Patkai renewed the physical presence of matter by working on a one-to-one scale. Shortly afterwards, Herbert Bayer, one of the Bauhaus pioneers, worked on a garden for a motorway, and in 1974 Dubuffet executed his *Enamel Garden* at the Kröller-Müller Museum in Otterlo, Holland: a grouping 65 by 100 feet. All these works offered themselves as so many spaces for living, calling for an active and physical participation by the spectator, and distinguished from architecture only by their poetic purpose: direct experience of place modified our awareness of space and of matter.

François Stahly (1911):
Fountain, 1958-1960.
Concrete, 90½″ long.
Asnières, Paris.

THE RESOURCES OF METAL

Since the invention of the assemblage, the distinction between painting and sculpture has become blurred and ambiguous. But until the utilization of painted metal by Alexander Calder and David Smith, sculpture remained subject to the demands of representation (anthropomorphic or geometric), with space occurring as the negative of the mass. Composed of elements which intervened directly in space, the "sculptographs" of Calder and Smith compelled the spectator to distinguish the optical space of the painting from the physical depth of the sculpture.

The possibilities dawned on Calder when he visited Mondrian's studio in Paris in 1930: "It was a very exciting room," he recalled in his autobiography. "Light came in from the left and from the right, and on the solid wall between the windows there were experimental stunts with coloured rectangles of cardboard tacked on... I suggested to Mondrian that perhaps it would be fun to make all those rectangles oscillate. And he, with a very serious countenance, said: No, it is not necessary, my painting is already very fast."

Calder found that acceleration he was looking for in his mobiles, of which the critic James Johnson Sweeney wrote in the preface to Calder's first retrospective in 1938: "Their creator defines mobiles as plastic forms in movement. Not simple translations into rotation, but various movements of different nature, speed and amplitude that combine to form a whole. One creates forms and colours; one may also create movements." Released from the mass, Calder's structures become free paintings in space. We also have that impression when facing the constructions of Smith, so much so that he was obliged to make a disclaimer: "Some critics refer to certain pieces of my sculpture as two-dimensional. Others call it line drawing. I do not admit to this, either conceptually or physically. It may be true in

Alexander Calder (1898-1976):
Mobile at Kennedy Airport, New York.

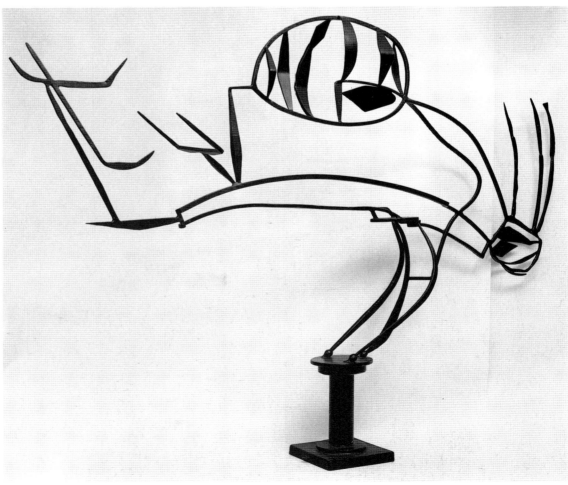

David Smith (1906-1965):
Australia, 1951.
Painted steel, 6'7½" × 9' × 16".

part, but only as one attribute of many, and that by intention and purpose. There are no rules in sculpture." This crucial assertion justifies the novelty and daring of his production.

In behaving like a sculptor drawing images in space, Smith cut sculpture off from its previous definitions. During his development he never ceased to bring into play the ambiguity of the plane which stands out in space and becomes depth as soon as it is perceived.

Smith discovered iron by seeing illustrations of the constructions of Picasso and Gonzalez in 1931 in *Cahiers d'Art*. He executed his first metal sculptures as early as 1933, but it was only after the war that they assumed their full meaning. Smith developed through working on closely linked series: "When I begin a sculpture I am not always sure how it is going to end. In a way it has a relationship to the work before, it is in continuity to the previous work–it often holds a promise or a gesture towards the one to follow..." Smith chose metal, since "Its associations are primarily of this century. It is power, structure, movement, progress, suspension, cantilever and at times destruction and brutality."

With the *Landscapes* (1946) Smith drew space, tracing violent gestures not unlike those with which Pollock spattered his canvases. Smith's works were transparent and frontal, representing the supreme abstraction of sculpture, until then defined by its mass. "I have always considered line contour as being a comment on mass space and as more acute than bulk, and that the association of steel retained steel's function of shapes moving, circumscribing upon axes, moving and gearing against each other at different speeds, as the association of this material suggests. The overlay of line shapes, being a cubist invention, permits each form its own identity and, when seen through each other, highly multiplies the complex of associations into new unities. I do not accept the monolithic limit in the tradition of sculpture. Sculpture is as free as the mind, as complex as life."

Such an attitude enabled Smith to advance with giant strides, freely associating forms discovered or created in a respect for frontality that reached its culmination in the *Letter* (1950), a kind of hieroglyphic writing in space, but set out like a sheet of notepaper. Then *Australia* revealed the potentialities of automatic writing in space: the dynamism of open, aerial forms, disengaged from the static problems of the equilibrium of masses. With Smith sculpture lost its fixed centre; it inscribed itself in the space it

defined. The *Agricola* and *Tank Totem* series brought in more subjective elements. Built from pieces of scrap often painted to emphasize their planes and identities, they led Smith increasingly to more elementary geometric structures, that still remained open. Instead of being form, sculpture secured the illusion of form. Smith's ever-growing output reached its peak in 1962; at Voltri, near Genoa, he completed twenty-six pieces in one month for the Festival of Spoleto.

Smith then tended towards more rigorously built constructions. The *Zigs* are a reinterpretation of the elements of Cubism, where planes are opposed according to rigorous orientations, but rendered ungraspable, totally abstract, by their projection in space. No longer using anything but cubes, discs and cylinders of painted metal, Smith simplified his language further with the *Cubis*, his final series: monumental forms, always frontal, defying the laws of gravity and equilibrium; "useless" pieces of architecture asserting sculpture as a real object, open and liberated from all representational or metaphorical requirements but which already introduced the formalist approaches to follow. Sculpture's only stake was in space; with Smith it no longer owed anything to painting. Reality lay henceforth in the dialogue maintained by the spectator with spatial constructions that justified themselves by their presence alone.

David Smith (1906-1965):

△ Landscape, 1949.
Painted steel and bronze, 17″ × 24″ × 7″.

▽ Zig IV, 1961.
Painted steel, 8′ high.

▷ Cubi XXVII, 1965.
Stainless steel, 9′3″ high.

209

CHILLIDA: THE SHAPING OF METAL

The long history of human affairs has rarely been disturbed by the invention of new techniques. Yet those techniques are so epoch-making that we still mark the evolution of society by such conquests: the iron age, bronze age and so on.

Now as regards sculpture, the twentieth century has brought new possibilities of construction in space, including assemblage and iron. The two, moreover, converge, with welded or wrought iron proving to be the most durable and resistant form of the assemblage. At the source of these new artistic practices is one and the same creator:

Picasso. It was around 1930 that, with the aid of Julio Gonzalez, Picasso executed his first iron constructions; but it was not until the fifties that the metal made itself the area of choice for experimentation in modern sculpture.

The introduction of iron created wholly new sculptural possibilities by favouring other forms of equilibrium, by playing freely with space and by allowing the physical reality of the finished piece to display the marks of the work that went into it: the burn of the fire which deformed the mass of matter, the scar left by the hammer that crushed it on the anvil, the welding joints that sealed together the heterogeneity of the components.

Organized in 1955 at the Kunsthalle in Berne by Arnold Rüdlinger, *Eisenplastik* was the first show to take a comprehensive look at the history of this method of construction in space which was tempting an ever-growing number of sculptors, to the point of becoming prevailing practice. There the work of the young Spaniard Eduardo Chillida was much noticed.

Of Basque origin, Chillida had studied architecture in Madrid before going on to sculpture. Several sojourns in Paris put him in touch with modern art, and he gradually turned away from figurative representation. His first iron piece dates from 1951; *Ilarik* was achieved with the help of the blacksmith of Hernani, where he had just settled. It was a revelation for him, and he set up a forge at his own residence. Iron convinced him that he had "to leave a pleasant land, in which all results seemed valid, to undertake a dangerous journey to the unknown." "Iron," said his friend Claude Esteban, "the kind of work it entailed, showed Chillida the very thing granite *falsified*: the approach to and confrontation of space by way of a dynamic

Eduardo Chillida (1924):

△ Silent Music, 1955.
   Wrought iron, 25¼″ × 59″.

▷ Comb of the Wind II, 1959.
   Iron, 11¾″ × 18 ⅞″ × 6¾″.

▷▷ Dream Anvil X, 1962.
   Iron and wood, 59″ high.

force in which the ductility of the material and the strong purpose that shapes it are combined." In 1958 he received the sculpture prize of the Venice Biennale for a body of work that was already abundant and fundamental, and no longer had anything to do with the work of the pioneers. Chillida demonstrated the meaning of the work by exploring the equilibriums that metal made possible with an undreamt-of freedom.

Working in wrought, then welded iron turned him away from the concept of mass by offering him new relations between construction and space: his assemblages embarked on the conquest of the air. His first works were still inspired by the form of the craftsman's and peasant's articles of ordinary use, but he transposed them poetically into empty space, attaching them by a single fixed point to the ground or the pedestal, from which they radiated in manifold directions. Combing space, clawing the wind, he defied the laws of statics. From the outset Chillida recognized the demands and possibilities of metal, which was rendered supple and malleable by its passage through fire, but which also retained the marks of the blows that shaped it, of the force that twisted it. This physical presence of work of which the finished piece kept the imprint and which made it possible to measure in imagination the time and effect of the process of elaboration would assume great importance in contemporary creation.

Working with tubes or bars, Chillida found that they divided up space. The core of matter was replaced by emptiness; the mass by air; but air was all the more meaningful

in that Chillida, as a good craftsman, developed his forms by following their growth: "I start the work with the heart. The heart is like the first seed. As soon as it begins to beat, it works with me. So I am no longer alone. It has its own driving force, and I feed it with my gestures; I help it to live. The work can begin to develop." Creation is a combat with and against matter, a confrontation with the elements: fire and water.

Chillida's forms abandon verticality to develop like knotted and forceful calligraphs. Refusing to let himself be guided by the technical know-how he had rapidly acquired, in 1956 Chillida turned to a thicker material which he twisted or unwound, but which kept in its folds the violence that bent it to the sculptor's will. *Dream Anvils* were both lyrical metaphors and labyrinths built from a space which he described. Strengthened by this experience as an ironsmith, Chillida was able, starting in 1958, to attempt other materials such as wood, which allowed him to work on a larger scale, while affirming once more that "sculpture is in solidarity with what revolves around it." He was to carry over this experience with metal into alabaster and granite, compact materials which react to light, that light which steel and later Cor-Ten (rusted) steel would lead him to prefer in more serene architectural compositions where the impact of gesture vanished in the continuity of spirals, drawing the spectator inward to the hollowed-out centre of the heart. These knots of metal opened onto the mystery of the infinite and the void. Chillida became the builder of the Invisible.

THE TRIUMPH OF IRON

Robert Jacobsen (1912):
Ideomotorisk Problem 2, 1954.
Iron, 12½″ high.

Robert Müller (1920):
The Heart, 1963.
Iron, 65″ high.

The traditional practice of carving, which meant extracting the mentally visualized mass from a block of stone or wood, made the sculptor dependent on static equilibriums defined by simples axes and determined by specific gravity. Forged or welded metal, on the contrary, made possible a new occupation of space. Forms did not need to be symmetrical; a single point of attachment to the ground could secure their stability. Jacobsen, who grasped the idea of metal sculpture in 1949, recognized that it overturned tradition: "As far as I am concerned, the gap is the form; the metal, the outline of that form. Therefore that makes two forms: the gap and the outline."

Although he had already made a few attempts at metal sculpture around 1936, it was in Paris, where he arrived from Denmark in 1947, that Jacobsen took iron as the exclusive material of his sculpture. He came to it that much more naturally for having previously earned his living as a mechanic. He worked "cold," cutting out and assembling: "Welding was my luck," he said. "So I've become a 'scrap-iron sculptor' and that's all... With stone you drift from one form to the next; with iron you make the form, you choose the space." Jacobsen, who constructed his pieces with cubic and scattered elements reassociated by space, lost no time in eliminating the pedestal, being able to secure equilibrium by relations of tension alone: "I think I have made one hundred per cent use of space, inside and outside simultaneously; that's how it is throughout my work... It's sculpture in the round, visible from all sides."

It was in Paris, too, then in full creative ferment, that the Swiss Robert Müller discovered the possibilities of metal. He was summoned there by his former teacher, Germaine Richier. In 1951 he made his first iron sculpture, having learned the brassware trade with a smith. Chasing and hammering metal, he discovered its expressive potential. From 1953 onwards he began to forge and weld forms with a strong sexual connotation, whose metaphorical power he enhanced, after 1957, by adding elements salvaged from rubbish tips. For the vertical equilibrium that figure-work implied, he gradually substituted a horizontal development favouring a relation that was more physical than optical. Surrealist automatism enjoyed a revival in Müller's work, through its way of exploiting the folds, cracks and joints of the metal.

It was in 1954 that Bernhard Luginbühl hit upon iron as a possibility for giving material shape to his drawings, inspired by Picasso's surrealist period. Remaining in Switzerland, Luginbühl did not seek inspiration in rubbish tips, but made direct use of the products of heavy industry,

Robert Müller (1920):
Lobster, 1955.
Iron, 23⅝″ × 49⅝″ × 11¼″.

▷ Bernhard Luginbühl (1929):
Silver Ghost, 1966.
Iron, 12′9½″ high.

Berto Lardera (1911):
Heroic Rhythm VI, 1965-1966.
Cor-Ten steel and stainless steel, 12½' high.
Maine-Montparnasse, Paris.

which he assembled, riveted, bolted or cut out in a violent way, finding, in the opposition of forms and matter and the contrasts of colour and of use, other transformational possibilities which, after 1960, attained monumental proportions.

Luginbühl humorously revived the sense of appearances by exposing the components of the work. In the seventies he even added sound and movement, under the influence of his friend Tinguely.

The Italian Berto Lardera came also to Paris in 1947. Metal enabled him to fit together flat geometric elements that, as it were, caught the sculptural tradition by the wrong foot, since he freed it simultaneously from mass, weight and sense of touch. As soon as he brought horizontal planes into his vertical equilibriums he gave a quality to space that earned him commissions for outdoor monuments. Ironwork *per se* was less important to him than the way in which it enabled him to occupy space dynamically by playing on interpenetration and the transparence of planes.

As Lardera proved, iron could take on a monumentality that would make it the preferred material of artistic monuments of our time. By its resistance, the strength of its forms and its possibilities for colouring, it entered the structured elements of architecture; it could also occupy the space of our public squares, since it typified our possibilities and capacity to feel, as Alex Liberman showed masterfully when he proposed a counter-architecture that renovated space by encouraging a different perception of our technological possibilities laid bare.

Starting with the 1960s, metal sculpture went through still other developments, emphasizing further aspects of its distinctive nature. Anthony Caro was Moore's disciple before meeting Smith and Noland in 1959. The impact was immediate: in 1960 he found in the use of steel the possibility of leading sculpture to a fundamental abstraction. Conscious that he was venturing into unknown territory, he forgot everything he knew in order to devote himself to a systematic experimentation with steel girders, testing their possibilities. That means became an end. He improvised, avoided compositional stereotypes and placed the accent on the form and process of his construction. Putting together spare parts with a logic inherent in their reality, he turned horizontality into a vital dimension.

Rejecting all external reference and metaphorical allusion, Caro modified by this minimalist abstraction the physical experience which the spectator maintained with sculpture. By admitting it to be a positioned object he stressed its relation to the environment, the ground becoming a component part of the sculpture. Lines and volumes painted in monochrome defined space: formed, divided or enclosed it. In *Hopscotch* Caro shows clearly that

Anthony Caro (1924):
Hopscotch, 1962.
Aluminium,
8'2½'' × 15'7'' × 7'.

Alexander Liberman (1912):
Covenant, 1975.
Red painted steel, 50′ high.
University of Pennsylvania, Philadelphia.

Mark Di Suvero (1933):
Storm Angel, 1973-1974.
Iron.
Square Chabas, Chalon-sur-Saône, France.

he can give space direction. Suggesting movement and equilibrium at the same time, he achieved in sculpture the Suprematism of Malevich in structures that render the spectator active, with each object offering itself as a new experience in perception.

If Caro's works remained true to the actual size of the object, those of Mark Di Suvero, on the contrary, gave that syntax of pure abstraction a monumental dimension. Arriving in New York from California in 1957, Di Suvero escaped the dominant movements of Pop and Minimal Art. He practised the assemblage, since junk construction freed the sculptor from economic dependence on the patron, and Di Suvero set up for being fiercely independent. In 1960 a terrible accident in a lift made him a cripple, but he did not give in. Seated in a wheelchair he grasped the possibilities and claims of teamwork; unable to create except by delegating authority, he projected his frustrations into space by means of machine-made components. By immense willpower he gradually regained the faculty of movement. His spatial constructions kept pace with that progress, becoming ever bolder and more monumental but remaining composed of primary structures, raw elements, fruits of technological possibilities the assemblage

of which expressed for Barbara Rose "the triumph of man's constructive and creative imagination over the destructive forces of technology which man has created."

Back again on the West Coast, Di Suvero worked outdoors on metal pieces that reached heights of up to 23 feet; soon he was including in them mobiles to promote spectator participation in his creations.

This aim of public sculpture, made with and for people, ended in spectacular fashion at Chalon-sur-Saône, where Di Suvero worked from 1972 to 1974 as the guest of CRACAP, which placed metallurgical firms and their specialists at his disposal. Each piece became the fruit of the requirements of the artist and the possibilities of technique and technicians; it represented a conceptual and physical confrontation with the real. Selected by the collaborators of that creation, the piece remaining at Chalon glorifies the creative possibilities in the local industry. Assembled by means of chains and cables, larger than life, Di Suvero's constructions have a sweep and dynamism that explicate our technical knowledge by condensing it in an *in situ* experience displacing the content of the abstraction while making it the setting for a basic perception from which symbolic resonances with human values are not excluded.

MOVEMENT REPRESENTED OR REAL

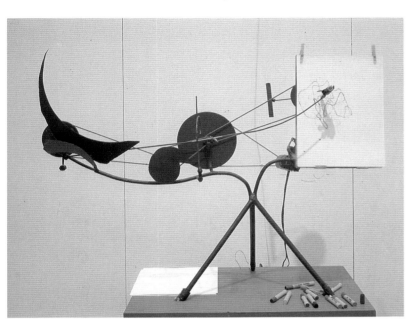

Jean Tinguely (1925):
Metamatics No. 13, 1959.
Iron, 38½″ × 71″.

Artists could not be indifferent to the fact that ours is the century of industry and machinery. Metalwork sculpture, especially when formed out of found objects, naturally brought them into close touch with the implements of life. What else distinguishes a construction made from rails, wheels, axles and pinions and called the sculpture of a machine, if not its uselessness and immobility? The Swiss, Jean Tinguely, took up the challenge of movement by adding the motor onto his creations. A Dadaist at heart, Tinguely began by reacting against the absoluteness and finiteness of painting: in 1955 he animated the surfaces of his paintings, abstract compositions whose forms moved around inside their frame through the action of an electric motor. Beginning in 1953 in Paris he formed a friendship with Yves Klein and became one of the founders of the New Realism. This context led him to a deeper reflection on art and its relations to everyday life: it gave him greater audacity. With *Metamatics* (1959) he entered the domain of sculpture. The assemblage giving rise to the mechanism became the work in itself. From then on his creations, going so far as to self-destruct, were composite but always animated constructions, and invited the public to participate in them. His friendship with César had shown Tinguely the possibilities of electric welding, enabling him to construct ironic and metaphoric mechanical contraptions. Drawing machines, for instance, directly attacked the outpourings of lyrical and gestural abstraction then at the height of fashion.

The following productions were inscribed under the generic heading of Baloubas, from the name of a tribe which carried "bizarre weaponry. They had Christmas-tree balls on their heads, machine guns on which they hung little bells–they tried, in a way, to adopt modern and dangerous weapons for their own use." The commissioning of *Eureka* for the Swiss Exhibition at Lausanne in 1964 pointed him in a different direction, confronting him with duration, monumentality and public space. It opened up a more sculptural adventure; one created out of industrial elements, of which the "infinity" of the movement had to be more minutely elaborated. For the first time he painted the group of elements black, finding in that monochromy the possibility of blotting out the heterogeneity of the components. Here, the machine becomes the sculpture. It manufactures nothing, but that uselessness brings the myth of Sisyphus back to life, invites the spectator to reflect on

Jean Tinguely (1925):
Eureka, 1964.
Height 28′10″.

a machine civilization that condemns its members to repeat the same actions forever.

By adding real movement generated by a motor, with all it implied of the inexorable and "eternal," Tinguely thus discovered that this type of sculpture had perhaps more survival value than the traditional monuments relinquished to nature. A machine endures, for it demands to be checked over, maintained and oiled; the worn out or defective parts may even be exchanged. And Tinguely concluded: "The only thing stable is movement, movement always and everywhere." By exposing the organs of the machine, Tinguely uncovered their symbolic, metaphoric, not to say sexual, reverberations. He also utilized the resulting sound, and called for growing participation by the public, transforming his shows into festivals aimed less at putting questions to art than at enabling art to join in with life; his machines involve play, but also convey feelings as powerful and different as joy or terror.

Many other artists linked with Constructivism had used the resources of the most advanced technology in a positive way. This tendency continued after the war and, out of the use or illusion of movement, and from the resources of electric light, a new aesthetic was born under the generic name of Kinetic Art. The term had already been used in 1920 by Gabo and Pevsner, and had been revived by Moholy-Nagy; but it became charged with a stronger connotation in the fifties when geometric art took a new leap forward by adding real or virtual movement and playing on the ambiguities of perception. Entitled *Move-ment*, a large exhibition at the Denise René Gallery in Paris surveyed the situation in 1955 and gave fresh impetus to investigations in these fields. Kinetic art furthered the confusion between painting and sculpture by involving the duration of perception. This could be linked either with the movement of the spectator before the motionless work or, on the contrary, with the work's own movement. Like Tinguely, Soto went from painting to sculpture. He began by introducing dynamic elements in front of painted structures: spirals drawn on plexiglass or mobile stalks suspended in front of the painting and enhancing the kinetic illusion. Gradually he came to create genuine environments made of bars, stalks or coloured threads: the *Penetrables*, coloured milieus capturing light and dematerializing the object, in which the spectator would be physically immersed.

Since the 1880s, that is to say, since the beginning of technological civilization, artists have reacted in a fundamentally contradictory way to the progress of science: some (Expressionists) by rejecting it; others (Constructivists) by seeking to exploit its achievements, either subjectively or in fact. During the formidable economic boom and scientific prosperity of the 1950s, there were many creators who shared the ideas of Vasarely on a new humanism born from modern civilization that needed to be given an aesthetic structure based on pure forms and colours. For all those artists, space was a basic element. It was no longer a void, but the *medium* of communication; the field in which forces and energies were exchanged and intersected.

Jesus Rafael Soto (1923):
Extension into Water, 1973.
Maracaibo, Venezuela.

George Rickey (1907):
The Photoplant.
Honolulu, Hawaii.

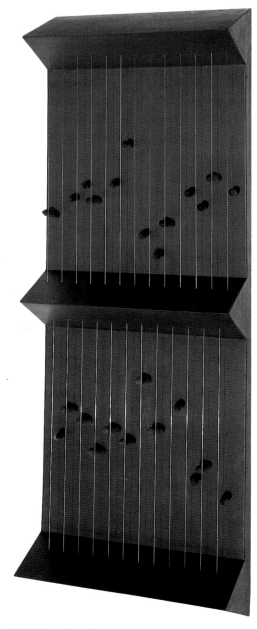

Pol Bury (1922):
12 and 13 Vertical Ropes and their Cylinders, 1973.
Wood and nylon, 55½″ high.

Takis (1925):
Signal, 1974–1980.
Bronze and steel, 16½′ high.

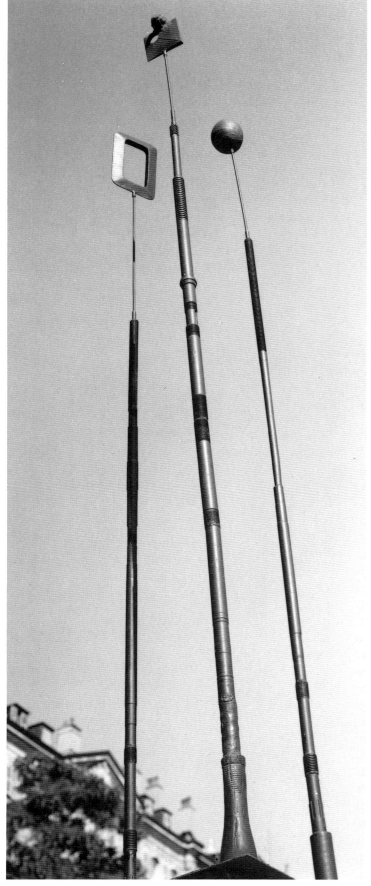

As a theorist and historian of Constructivism, George Rickey gave the Calder mobile fresh possibilities in carefully articulated mechanical constructions. His first *Mobiles* date from 1945. Starting from geometric investigations into the development of forms in space—their balance and direction—he built, with the precision of a mechanic, objects that moved and vibrated in response to the push of air, and as he himself noted, "When you build an object for movement you are always surprised by the movement itself: however premeditated the design the movement seems to come from somewhere else."

Starting also with kinetic painting but paying the closest attention to technical possibilities, Yaacov Agam highlighted the time factor in the elaboration and perception of the work. His transformable and moving images became environments in which space was active, and recreated the relationship between form and image in their perceptual dynamics.

This staging of movement is again at the heart of Pol Bury's development. He too came to sculpture from painting. "Doing abstract painting," he said, "I noticed—moreover in the same way, it seems, that Kandinsky

Carl Frederik Reuterswärd (1934):
Laser Haloes over the Centre Beaubourg, Paris.
Project, 1972.

discovered abstraction by going back to landscape–that it was quite usual for painters to turn the finished painting each way round. I asked myself why not apply that principle to the *inside* of a painting; why not cut the forms out instead of painting them and place them on axes... it's thus for quite pictorial reasons that I went on to do relief."

The necessity for movement prompted him to use motors placing the forms in constant variation, and before long those forms became pure volumes, the materials and colours of which soon rendered the dynamism still more complex. For the works of Bury moved with an extreme slowness the better to refer to the consciousness of time. In an essay entitled "Dilated Time" he describes how slowness causes trajectory to be forgotten whereas speed emphasizes it. In all his sculptural work he tried for the minimum threshold of time perception in order to get back to universal movement: eternity. Bury invites to contemplation rather than to action. His kinetic constructions in addition often use sound, his volumes as they move bumping against stretched cords–like those of violins–that resonate inside the frame of the sculpture.

The Greek sculptor Takis was also to give sound an all-important place. For him sound was one of the constituent parts of space, that meeting ground of all possible worlds. His sculptures present themselves as total works of art in which noise, light and movement become spectacle. A self-proclaimed experimenter, Takis had already recognized the possibilities of magnetic fields before 1960. They enabled him to furnish space by the energy of forces and radiations to show paradoxically that there is nothing more active than the void: a fact made abundantly clear, moreover, by present-day physics. But for Takis, using the power of an electromagnet was only a primitive technological approach: "I don't use advanced technology, and I believe that only children born today will be capable of using it," he declared. He contented himself with exploiting the resources of electrical energy by giving them a poetic dimension. How astonished was the spectator who found himself able to make an abstract painting by tossing handfuls of nails onto a magnetized surface! How frightened he was to encounter masses suspended in space by magnetism! Takis' basic vocabulary has not changed, but the discovery and exploitation of sound have widened its signification. The cathode-ray tube, like the electromagnet, produces sound waves which he has amplified; he has also directly utilized collisions between masses in programming electric circuits. His monumental gong is universally remembered. Placing all the senses on the alert, Takis' environments vitalize and poeticize space.

Electricity has also tempted numerous sculptors by its potential for light and colour, but it was the invention of the laser that offered them unexpected possibilities. The first laser show was held at the Cincinnati Museum in 1969. Xenakis, Reuterswärd, Karavan, Merkado and Kowalski found in using the laser the chance of getting out of the museum and extending its environment to that of the city. Making energy visible, the laser permits the drawing of unlimited forms in space. Under supervision it enables effects of pure colour to be obtained; concentrated and orientated it makes possible the division of space according to perfectly manageable forms and directions.

With the laser, sculpture is on the verge of attaining a size-scale heretofore impossible at the same time as it becomes totally dematerialized.

THE UTOPIA OF THE MACHINE

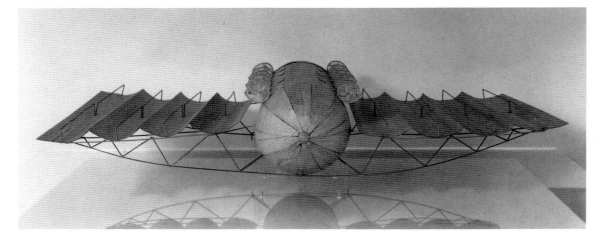

▷ Alice Aycock (1946):
From the series entitled
How to Catch and Manufacture
Ghosts: Collected Ghost
Stories from the Workhouse,
1980.
Project executed for the
University of South Florida,
Tampa, Florida.

◁ Panamarenko:
Object: General Spinaxis, 1968.
Length 36½".

The relations between art and technique are both complicated and contradictory. They form an ambiguous yet inseparable pair. Philosophical theories have arbitrarily attempted to dissociate the fields of application of intelligence and intuition although they have never ceased to renew and question themselves.

For more than a century now, specialization has given the sciences an autonomy that encouraged their development, but made them more difficult for non-specialists to understand. Techniques left no place for human potentialities by using fields of energy which might well have been anathema to artists, if they had not had a hand in the renewal of the awareness of space-time which is central to contemporary expression. And when technology is ubiquitous (it conditions our existence and behaviour at the same time that it modifies communication and knowl-

Rebecca Horn (1944):
Peacock Machine, 1982.
Installation at Documenta 7, Kassel, 1982.

edge), it has to be interrogated because of what it is. This interrogation becomes increasingly urgent when the actual development of machine or factory takes them far away from the mechanical reproduction of human gestures, and so changes their external appearance and actions that their actual functions are concealed.

This theorizing about technique is often pioneered by creative artists who began with Performance Art, i.e. by actual physical experimentation with space and time. It may even go as far as provoking a metaphorical reflection on the process of creation, if we are to believe the American Dennis Oppenheim: "It seems that no matter how brilliant the person who objectifies the thought, the result is never as powerful as the original idea. As if the mind, like a blast furnace, seems determined to hang on to its 'core' of the work of art at all costs. The reductive process used in the quest for form has always been a problem for the sculptor and ultimately asks outright if power is not lost during the transition from ideas to form. Why not reverse the process and allow the thought to take its place after the form has been achieved? The aim would then be to objectify the mind, to render it in terms of constructions which would be almost visual. Then those constructions would receive an energy, a force which would itself be similar to that of the thought."

In the construction of his factories, ludic presentations of the machine and the energy it employs, Oppenheim is looking for the visual and perceptional structures that will "reflect the thought that produced them, thus allowing the external form to function on the same plane of heightened energy as that of the thought which goes through the mind."

The aim of Alice Aycock, an American sculptress, is to endow the constructions which surround us and produce our consumer goods with meaning and expressiveness. Her creations seek to encourage each one of us to identify with the apparatus and architecture of our everyday life. Turning away from functionalism, she puts dreams and poetry in its place. All her projects develop according to a logic enabling them to qualify aesthetically and symbolically elements which have ceased to exist visually because they are overshadowed by the importance of their ultimate purpose. Awareness of duration, menace, procreation, cruelty and death thus reappear in objects usually

regarded solely in terms of their usefulness or productivity.

Fascinated by nature and its rhythm, by animal life and the dance, the German sculptress Rebecca Horn presents movement. Passing from Performance to Environment, she evokes time in the fleeting and the infinite. She transfers the art she had expressed with her body in her first actions to mechanical constructions which she situates and isolates in space to renew our consciousness of the inexorable and brutal elements of time.

Like Leonardo da Vinci, the Belgian Panamarenko refuses to separate art and science. A traveller in the realms of imagination, he constructs metaphors of the conquest of the interstellar universe which situate our terror of the void in abysmal space. Finding that "space shuttles" cannot give material form to all the concepts which motivate them, Panamarenko makes simulacra that can also include the dream. As Oppenheim says: "It is no longer the object as form, but the functioning of the apparatus which can suggest that something is going to or can happen."

Dennis Oppenheim (1938):
Launching Structure No. 3. An Armature
for Projection (from The Fireworks Series), 1982.

THE SPACE OF REPRESENTATION
FIGURATION AND DEFIGURATION

Jean Fautrier (1898-1964):
Nude, 1928.
Bronze, 25½″ high.

The nineteenth century had struggled desperately to invent a new image of man, but it rarely got beyond the craze for anecdote, gesture having lost all collective meaning. When the subject's attitude did not refer to any symbolic explication and was reduced to the time and purpose of the action justifying it, representation lost much of its significance, all the more so since the illusionist demands on artistic creation had dwindled after the invention of photography, a cheaper and more efficient technique for descriptive purposes.

Now the avant-garde was more interested in experimentation with that recently discovered fourth dimension, space, than in the expression of the human figure. History, however, had shown that man could not long escape the need to give himself an image: to reconsider his presence in real space. The individual who had survived the last world conflict was deeply bruised: that was what was expressed in existentialist philosophy, which gained wide acceptance and built itself upon nothingness and incommunicability. The threat of an atomic apocalypse weighed so heavily that it could not even accommodate the irony and sarcasms used by the Dadaists to exorcise the absurdity of the 1914-1918 war.

As the shattering and probing works of Alberto Giacometti testify, it was only in creations by a few widely scattered individuals that figurative representation survived. It did so on an intimist scale and through individualized expressions. And it would be less from the representation of gesture than from the traces left by it that a new conquest of the world by man could be elaborated.

The artist was thereby led to reconsider the potency of primitive archetypes, since he could find no other truth but in the experience of the most existential gestures. If the act is common to all, it also expresses the particular nature of each; it is at once singular and anonymous.

This *behavioural art* is situated beyond Surrealism while remaining saturated with its conquests. It does not aim at freedom from subjectivity through automatic writing, but rather seeks the unalterable through contact with the accidental and uncertain.

Interest no longer lay in the representation of gesture, but in its trace or imprint, allowing access to duration while at the same time signifying a state of consciousness.

When aesthetic canons are outworn and the main concern is less to express one's reasons for living than to seek those for surviving, reality is no longer in the image but in the shaping of matter or in elaborating the "found."

In these illuminations of human agency making it possible to repossess the world, painters were to play a decisive role. Fautrier turned his hand to sculpture during only two periods, but they were crucial: on the eve of the thirties and at the beginning of the *Hostages* series.

Now the *Hostages* were close to the modelling Fautrier had already done in 1928, and which enabled him to ex-

Jean Dubuffet (1901-1985):

The Duke, 1954.
Sponge, 24½″ high.

The Dancer, 1954.
Sponge and tow, 23½″ high.

press the simplest emotions, going beyond traditions and the fugacity of feelings to reach that reality that must subsist in the modelling of raw material, "the *live work* beneath the form that supports it and makes it live." "Sculpted in earth" like some Matisses, Fautrier's modelling gets down to the essential through direct contact with the pliable beyond all aesthetic effect.

Dubuffet first took up sculpture between March and December 1954. The *Little Statues of Precarious Life* were born after form in painting had been given new life by matter. By the assemblage of driftwood, furnace slag, sponges or stumps, Dubuffet called on the material to "cut a figure" by allowing it to express itself in the rough. Like Fautrier, Dubuffet rediscovered in this confrontation with volume the mystery emanating from primitive statuary; his figures have the same signifying potency as archaic fetishes, without owing anything to them aesthetically.

In the work on volume of the 1960s, Lucio Fontana, who already had great experience in ceramics, also experimented with gestural traces. The spatial concept worked out in painting from the crack and the hole found a more active presence in the third dimension, making it possible to achieve what he had announced in his *Technical Manifesto of Spatialism*: "a synthesis integrating all the physical elements: colour, sound, movement, space, into a unity at once ideal and material that would abolish the boundaries between art and nature."

We receive something of an archaeological and at the same time a modern impression before the work of Do-deigne. A stone-carver by training, he achieved in the direct carving of Soignie granite a cyclopean monumentality. The marks left by the working tool strengthen the drama staged by the assemblage of violent figures, standing up in space to defy time while seeming to submit to the force of natural elements. Dodeigne's figures, although hieratic, nevertheless depart from archaic models in their dynamism springing from an asymmetry of volumes that renders their fate more provisional.

A trained sculptor, trusting his gesture and his instinct, Etienne-Martin went a step further in transforming the object into a "wrapping." In 1958 he took up the "Dwelling" theme, nevermore to abandon it. Each of his constructions appeared as a polymorphic space to live in, figuratively or physically. Both a memory and a place, each "dwelling" resembles an archaeological matrix. Working from a ductile material, the direct plaster cast, Etienne-Martin, for whom the working process was more important than the end result, binds the imaginary to the real. Letting himself be guided by what can be assembled or torn apart, like the Postman Cheval or Schwitters in his Merzbaus, he devised mazes in which physical experience revives a previous memory and man rediscovers his scale at the same time as his spiritual measure.

The empty here becomes active, forms the heart of the work. But Etienne-Martin's experience, like that of the other creators discussed here, remains of the individualistic sort, more intimist than social. For all of them, touching is more fundamental than seeing.

Lucio Fontana (1899-1968):
Nature, undated.
Five bronze balls, diameters: 38″, 36″, 36″, 40″, 43″.

Eugène Dodeigne (1923):
Group, 1964–1970.
Massangis stone from Burgundy, 13′2″ high.

Etienne-Martin (1913):
Dwelling No. 3, 1960.
Plaster, 16′4″ × 7′4½″ × 8′2″.

NEW IMAGES OF MAN

Roel D'Haese (1921):
To Lumumba, 1961.
Bronze, 56″ high.

Kenneth Armitage (1916):
Diarchy, 1957.
Bronze, 68½″ high.

In painting, the years that followed the war saw the quarrel between figuration and abstraction exacerbated to its extreme. This antagonism did not stir the same passions in the field of sculpture, where, the context being different, positions were less sharply defined. On one hand, those who remained attached to figurative expression, led by Giacometti, Richier and Marini, attained an expression so individualized that it could not be imitated; and as for Picasso, he had explored so many possibilities of metaphor and metamorphosis that he could not found a school, even if he became accepted as the inevitable reference for all invention. Elsewhere, exclusively abstract investigation had already reached its limits, and those who carried on with Constructivism were reduced to being integrated into architecture, where their creation soon had no other purpose than that of an aestheticizing and ornamental "capital appreciation" in a milieu dehumanized by the necessities of economy and prefabrication.

On the level of sculptural representation a third way was still to be found, starting from archaic examples to which this generation was always more sensitive and which showed that no form could live in space without being charged with a *content*.

To build a real form *without a model* was nonetheless no easy task. Scarred by the recent conflicts–mutilations, massacres and genocides had never been carried so far, whether in the Nazi and Soviet death camps or in the atomic blasts–mankind knew that its image had been devalued forever. Even the most far-fetched distortions of Expressionism fell short of the horror that had been lived through. The individual had to build himself a new image, but that image was especially blurred since he was doomed by the renouncement of all religious and idealist reference to recognize as authentic only the evidence of his subjectivity and intuition. If he could trust only the truth of his own experience, the mystery of life remained entire. The gesture had lost all meaning, but the act remained productive.

Fascinated by the disturbing exemplariness of the most archaic achievements, the modern sculptor went in search of a new archetype. By definition it would be anonymous, monolithic. It was less a matter of reproducing life than of discovering the hope of survival. If the horrors of war had debased the cultural values that underpinned anthropocentrism, even the springs of modern art were dried up, for they continued to be fed from the same depths. To wipe the slate clean of history so as to go back to archaeological origins came to be seen as the only way out of such confusion.

Roel D'Haese and Kenneth Armitage display the alternatives justified by this new attitude. Both construct anonymous figures, but they attain the timeless by opposing means. D'Haese, with a grating and sarcastic humour recalling that of his ancestors Bosch and Bruegel, picked up refuse scraps which he embedded in "lost wax" before transmuting them into bronze; in making use of chance

and the freedom of instinct he encounters a magic life. Armitage, on the contrary, built walls, where there soon sprouted a life that was fragile and precarious. His frontal vision, his hieratic gesture, produced emblematic stelae; they marked the dawn of another world. We sense this revelation of a new humanity, too, before the works of Lynn Chadwick, who did not come to sculpture until late, after studying to be an architect. Starting in 1950, he constructed anthropomorphic images from bristling and aggressive skeletons, frameworks offering dynamic and subjective geometries. It is interesting to note that the English–in the field of painting as well, with Bacon and Sutherland–are the only ones to preserve so direct a relation with man and nature; to give them such emotional force and dynamism.

Among the sculptors of the next generation the image of man was to have a less subjective, more symbolic character. Often it would result from a more direct confrontation with the possibilities of the material. Coming from ceramics, Mario Ceroli discovered the possibilities of wood assemblages in 1958, and soon sought to bend them to his representational requirements. This violent and ag-

◁ Mario Ceroli (1938):
Imbalance, 1967.
Wood, diameter 13'.

▽ Lynn Chadwick (1914):
The Watchers, 1960.
Bronze, 7'8" high.

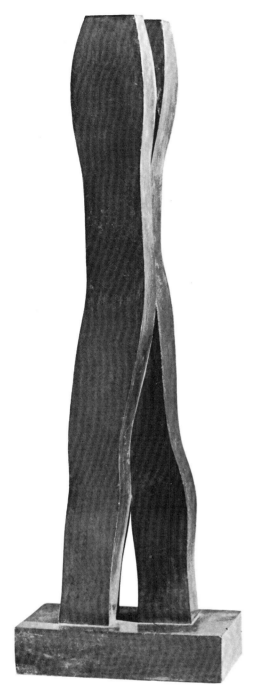

Joannis Avramidis (1922):
Walking Man, 1966.
Aluminium, 67¼″ high.

gressive relationship to the material enabled him to escape from tradition and reintroduce a mythical image by superimposing and juxtaposing silhouettes linked to their background. Playing on antinomies (inside-outside, filled-empty), Ceroli went as far as to confirm the ideal man of Leonardo da Vinci; but symbolically the circles that defined the harmony of his proportions are transformed here into a cage.

Greek by origin but Austrian by nationality, a pupil of Wotruba, Joannis Avramidis was still more uncompromising in his search for an image of man, which he set out to construct from a geometric formula requiring redefinition. Starting from the coherence between framework and form, from the coinciding of inner and outer, he returned to closed shapes identified with our time only by a slight dynamism.

"My work," he said, "demonstrates the constitution of an objective form, that is to say, a form totally comprehensible. This form is the first condition of the creation of a work of art. That is why it is so important for me to keep all personal stylistic influences out of my work."

Seeking the foundation of man, his essence and spirituality, Avramidis rediscovered the vertical: that of the column or stela; his image of the "walking man" is at the opposite pole from the subjective one of Giacometti. Solitary and absolute, it becomes like the column of a temple built by the individual to his own measure.

That same drive towards a spiritual affirmation of human potential through coherence and the absolute value of form is again seen in the approach of Henri Presset. His objective conquest of the external world through the experience of self led him to perceive that "the more a form is interior the more it is abstract."

Preoccupied with the position of man in space, Presset worked on the light which linked them together. The organic reality of forms, their purity and duration, like their cracks or undulations, would catch the light and make it shine, producing a timeless and physical, indeed a sexual presence. To work in the third dimension is to keep one's distance from the fugacity of the real in order to give it duration.

Henri Presset (1928):
Figure X, 1973.
Iron, 41¾″ high.

METAMORPHOSIS OF THE ASSEMBLAGE

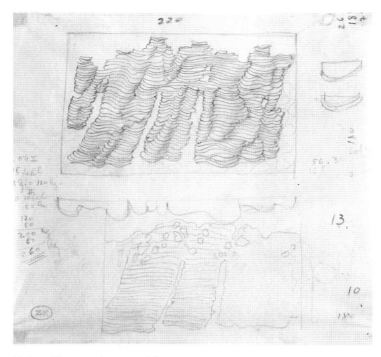

Zoltan Kemeny (1907-1965):
Drawings for Pacific, 1963.

With the advent of the assemblage the line dividing painting from sculpture became blurred. The freedom of the painters opened so many unexpected possibilities to practitioners of traditional sculpture that the problematics of contemporary sculpture were at last seen to have followed the lead of painting. From the fifties onward, however, that primacy of painting over sculpture tended to be reversed, as the involvement of the third dimension became the most fertile field of experimentation with reality. The direct use of material, space and light made for a new experience of the world and of life in a universe increasingly drained of the real by the power of the mass media.

If the invention of the assemblage had shown sculptors the importance of space and emptiness, it had also worked at the level of the image: as a Cubist, Picasso had used it to match up signifier and signified before going on to explore its metaphorical possibilities; the Surrealists had exploited it as another possibility of psychic automatism; the Constructivists and Dadaists (in particular Arp and Schwitters) were alone in perceiving its constructive potentialities; another way to make images—abstract, yet real.

The experiments of Kemeny and Nevelson acquire their full meaning when these artists are considered as painters doing sculpture in order to arrive at the creation of real objects after denying the origin, history and sentimental value of the refuse-elements entering into their constructions.

Zoltan Kemeny (1907-1965):
Pacific, undated.
Brass high relief, 64½″ × 95¼″.

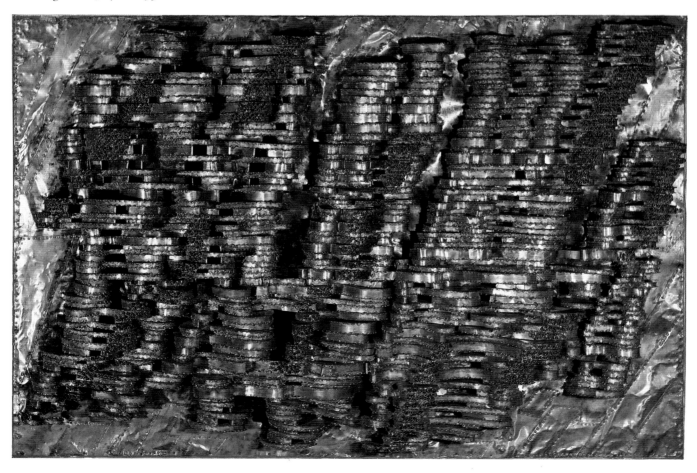

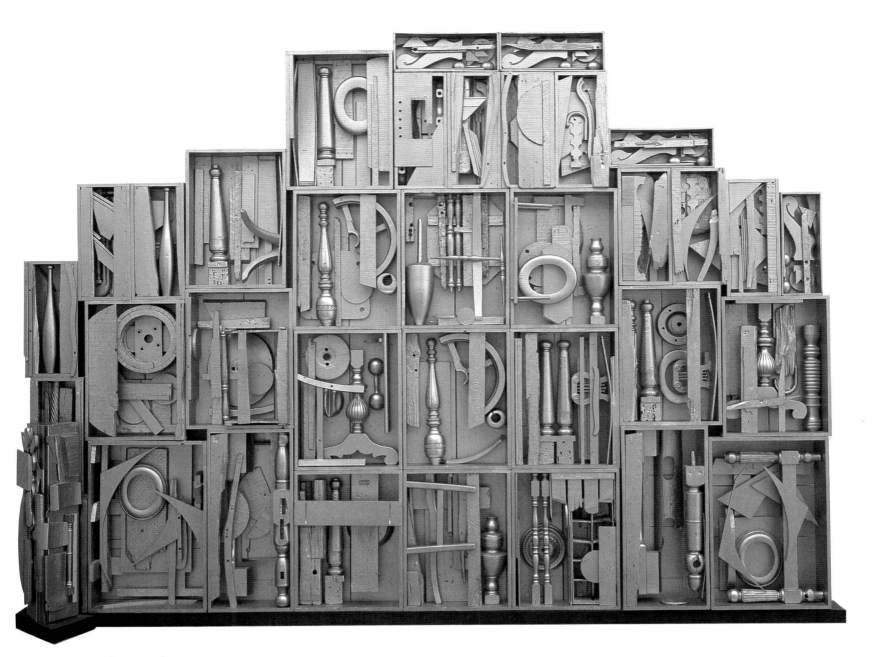

Louise Nevelson (1900):
Royal Tide IV, 1960.
Wood, 11′ × 14′.

At first a painter, then a fashion designer, the Hungarian Zoltan Kemeny did not come back to painting until the end of the forties. His first metal reliefs date from 1954. Welding, bending, hammering and the oxidizing of copper or iron and its derivatives removed him from the virtuality and illusionism of painting methods. The passage from paintbrush to blowtorch, achieved naturally as it were, imparted a different presence to his works by directly recording the life of light in the reality of matter.

"The sculpture-image is also a creation in which the human imagination can make a journey", he found, but the reality of the constituent elements of that sculpto-painting gave painting a new effectiveness, for "iron possesses heart and nerves. The respiratory system of a plant may be the same as the molecular system of steel. There are strange resemblances between molecules of metal and a jar of microbes."

This abstraction, obtained with real elements, acted on the spectator physically; gave new expressive efficacy to drawings and volumes based on the solid substance of the work, which no longer owed anything to the "abstractions" that had hitherto governed painting: the plane of the canvas, line, colour and value. The picture was a work

in relief, to which metal and its fashioning had imparted as many rhythmically coloured possibilities as those given to traditional painting.

More monumental and organic, the works of Louise Nevelson perform the same function on another scale and with another material. Assembling elements of wood, which she "holds in place like a tightrope-walker on a high wire," she inscribes them in frontal and rectangular structures which she afterwards modifies by covering the whole with monochrome painting.

"I wanted," she said, "simply to give structure to shadow; now I want to give structure and permanence to reflection."

Those words sum up the road she has travelled since her first constructions of the forties, which led her in 1953 to the use of wood assemblage for the first time, down to the present day. Nevelson makes play with the pieces of wood she finds, limiting herself to a few homogeneous elements; she articulates depths like the Cubists, but on a scale that transforms the object into an environment. These clusters of objects, evolved into organic wholes radically removed from their original use by a coating of paint, allow Nevelson to keep her distance from Surrealism, so as less to

John Chamberlain (1927):
Johnny Bird, 1959.
Enamelled steel, 59″ × 53″ × 45½″.

sculptures starting from concrete suggestions. An omnivorous collector–stone, scrap-iron, tree-stumps, etc.–, he heaps up in his studio the rejects of nature and industrial civilization. His daydreams enabled him to give a new value to things, to turn common sense aside.

"In a field where passage of time becomes a criterion of quality," he wrote, "what the work bears within it is the unremitting effort to include habit only insofar as it may resist the critique of creative reason."

Indeed, his works are not so much searched for as found: they possessed him intimately at first through the recognition of far-fetched associations which, in the work of composing them, acquired a deep meaning. Eggenschwiler reduces everything to essentials, to fundamentals; for, to him, artistic expression and its liberty remains the last sphere in which man can recapture his roots and his originality. What to us he appears always to have seen, he makes new by use and time to give it denser meaning. Fetishism is no longer reserved for the use of a cult; it must restore to man the sense of the mystery of life, the possibility for wonder.

The circle is closed. The discovery of tribal art has promoted the freedom of representation and awakened a new aesthetic sensibility. In its latest incarnations it questions man directly about his origins and evolution; about his reasons for living.

suggest her particular problems than to tend towards a general and collective meaning, the one we sense behind the stelae and totems of archaic civilizations. Shadow enables her to work in physical and spiritual depth.

The temptation to make painting more effective by constructing it in real space with real materials, with volumes and colours taken directly from life–yet so as to give them an essentially plastic dimension–is seen again to be at the root of John Chamberlain's development, even if it evolves here in a more typically sculptural style. From the end of the fifties Chamberlain employed fragments of used cars as his sole material. He chose his pieces according to their shapes and colours, and assembled them in an abstract manner, which made him appear as an Abstract Expressionist or non-figurative artist. Gradually he came to use the suggestions contained in those compressed and buckled plates, those twisted mudguards or crushed mechanical parts, so as to return to a dramatic and hallucinatory figuration in which the ironically mocking nature of the refuse is counteracted by the use of a luxuriant polychromy.

Franz Eggenschwiler, a Swiss artist, only made his name as a creator of objects after 1970. He, too, constructs his

Franz Eggenschwiler (1930):
Ovulation Object, 1976-1978.
Iron, wood, bronze, stone, 13⅜″ × 14½″ × 22⅞″.

NEW REALISM...

Niki de Saint-Phalle (1930):
Pink Childbirth, 1964.
Painted relief, 86¼" high.

Around 1960 there began to be much talk of a New Figuration. After the successive waves of Abstract Expressionism and lyrical abstraction, the pendulum of taste swung back to the need for an image of the visible world. The New Figuration soon found its ultimate expression in Pop Art and the New Realism, which based it not so much on a reassessment of concepts of nature and representation as on a new attitude vis-à-vis the real: *appropriation, taking over*. Its way having been paved by the aesthetic use of the found and the used object, this figuration was characterized by the recognition of everyday reality in its immediate and sociological relation.

According to its founder and theorist, Pierre Restany, "The New Realism undoubtedly marked a historic turning point by showing (through action and deed) that the 'objective reality which forms the normal milieu of our life' had been profoundly affected in its essence by technical progress and human relationships: it was up to us to see modern nature in its true light. It had to be accepted that the New Realists were evolving an organic and coherent body of work out of their fundamental expressive gestures: the colour saturation of Yves Klein, the mechanical animation of assemblage structures by Tinguely, the accumulation or smashing of objects by Arman, the 'trapping' of Spoerri."

In the violence of the urban and economic scene, faced with the rising tide of advertising and the aggressiveness of the machine, man can no longer be content to portray himself. "To express oneself is to take possession of the world," said the New Realists, who responded less to nature than to the phenomena of mass civilization and production. The appropriation achieved by Marcel Duchamp and his Readymades was diverted here by the search for quantitative thresholds that changed the relationship between the sculpture-object and its components; that relationship became unresolvable if not conflicting. *Pink Childbirth* by Niki de Saint-Phalle, for instance, presents a totemic and narratory figure of the feminine condition trivialized by the found elements (toys, tissues, trimmings) that compose it.

In contenting himself with displaying the leftovers of a meal on a vertical tabletop after having glued them in place, Daniel Spoerri, on the contrary, set up as being "the topographer of objective chance." But he warns: "Don't mistake my *trap-pictures* for works of art. It is a news flash, a provocation, a prompting of the eye to look at things it isn't used to look at. Nothing else... And besides, what is art? Perhaps a way and a chance to live."

This neo-Dadaist attitude, preferring life to art, took on more sculptural and monumental dimensions with Arman. Accumulating real objects, he discovered in the phenomenon of quantity the possibility of transcending the commonplace: excessive repetition lifted the curse of submission to consumption. By ransacking trashcans, he replaced art with reality.

Daniel Spoerri (1930):
Not to be, 1961.
Assemblage, 35½" × 29½" × 9".

matter and colour. By reducing sculpture to the original block, César's *Compressions* reverse its direction, since they make it the end product of the life of an object: "At the beginning," César admitted, "I believed that sculpture was a purely physical act. I believed that it was above all skill, virtuosity, technique. I didn't know that it was technique serving the mind."

César had attained such a degree of virtuosity that his iron assemblages might be mistaken for his modelling. The New Realist spirit led him to discover that art and performance cannot be combined. The press which produced the compressions revealed emptiness to him... an emptiness that had to be filled.

The interrogation of nature and its vitality could not take place without a re-evaluation of the products of culture, in this case, those of the consumer industry. During the twentieth century, the object enjoyed a special status in art and in its representation; in a civilization which produces for the sake of producing it becomes a secondary subject.

Arman (1928):
Nail Fetish, 1963.
Accumulation of revolvers, 22″ high.

César (1921):
Compression, 1962.

It was in the context of the New Realism as well that César's *Compressions* made their appearance, exhibited for the first time at the 1960 Salon de Mai in Paris. They created a special stir since César had gained recognition as one of the masters of metal sculpture. As early as 1947 he had hit upon its possibilities, then gradually built up an important body of work in which arc-welded metal elements were transformed into organic wholes of great plastic potency, often in the shape of a fantastic animal or even of a woman.

In the New Realism, where the guiding ethic caused the idea to prevail over the doing, César abruptly tacked about by eliminating gesture in favour of seeing. His first *Compressions* were cars industrially pressed into blocks for salvage, but he was not so much interested in what they represented as in what they were: anti-assemblages, pure, abstract, compact volumes with hard edges. If the *past* of the object had been effaced, the external volume nevertheless directly reproduced what lay at the heart of the object, thereby making a compression the very antithesis of a traditional sculpture, where the sheath concealed what it contained. With César, by contrast, the pure volume is the direct result of what produces it, in internal capacity,

... AND NEW ENGLISH SCULPTURE

The object crystallizes all the contradictions and ambiguities of our age; it represents a necessity which denotes desire and connotes social standing. Publicity lures us to seek it more for its own sake than for its function, so condemning it to an ephemeral existence. The "coachwork" which surrounds and conceals its useful purpose asserts itself as the more important end product.

From Duchamp's readymades to Pop art, the object has always been prominent in the development of sculpture. In the early eighties, in what is known as the new English sculpture, it is once more behind a revival of interest in praxis. A structural element and the subject of metamorphoses, it is also the buttress of a social criticism encouraging an archaeology of everyday life.

Of the same generation as Gilbert and George, and Richard Long, Barry Flanagan stands apart, because he never shared the romantic relationship with nature and the material maintained by his compatriots. Even though he stimulated renewed interest in the metaphorical power of the assemblage, Flanagan was not so much concerned with the production of objects as with the associations for which they might be the pretext. Essentially, Flanagan belongs to the family of eccentrics and instigators, exploring the paradoxical relationships a form can maintain with the material of which it is composed. Springing from one experiment to another, from commonplace materials to

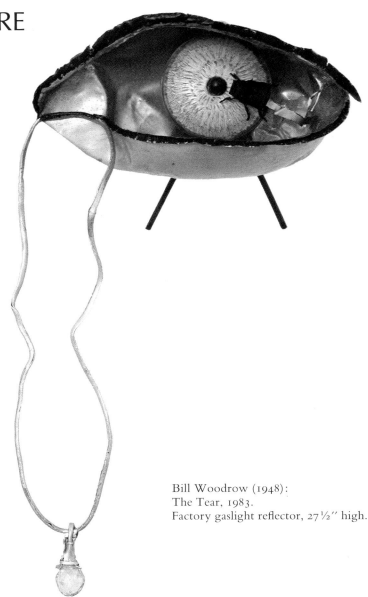

Bill Woodrow (1948):
The Tear, 1983.
Factory gaslight reflector, 27½" high.

Barry Flanagan (1941):
After Bell, 1982.
Polychrome bronze, 28¾" high.

sophisticated creations he never lingers, but is always opposed to predominant tendencies by rendering image and symbol with impish humour and irony. Nevertheless, all his constructions reflect the same impossible, paradoxical equilibrium. The amazed wondering look he turns on things, his nervous eager gestures, enable him to make everything his own. In search of the laws which govern exceptions, he distorts everything he touches–the anvil has no connection with the cast of the bell which supports it.

Tony Cragg and Bill Woodrow belong to an earlier generation and inherit its phantasy and freedom, but they express themselves with an economy of material and a theoretic concentration which makes their approach more coherent. Their reply to inundation by consumer goods is "recycling." Making use of everyday objects, they do not share the disinterested way in which Marcel Duchamp looked at similar material. They construct with what is readily to hand, but the waste products they exhibit comment on and criticize the consumer industry and society which produced them. They fossilize them by a drastic treatment which renews their meaning by producing new images, veritable facsimiles, which paradoxically began as objects whose origin is no longer recognizable. And in a society which no longer knows what to do with its waste, English sculptors reconstitute it as art. In Bill Woodrow's work the link between image and object is such that we can no longer tell which fathered the other.

ANOTHER MATERIAL: PLASTIC

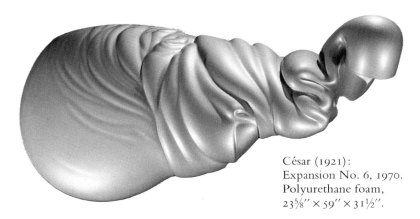

César (1921):
Expansion No. 6, 1970.
Polyurethane foam,
23⅝″ × 59″ × 31½″.

The first synthetic materials were discovered in 1838-1839, when Victor Regnault observed the formation of a solid substance in a recipient filled with vinyl chloride exposed to light, and Simon recorded the solidification of styrene. From the invention of vulcanization in 1839 to the production of the first synthetic fibre in 1939, plastic has assumed a thousand shapes and names: celluloid, plexiglass, Bakelite, until chemists discovered the colloidal particles which opened the way to polymerization and polycondensation giving rise to all contemporary products: polystyrene, polyamide, polyester, polyurethane, etc. From the object of everyday use to architecture, plastic is found everywhere in the form of fibres, plates, volumes, glues or colours.

Artists could not remain indifferent to this material. Gabo, Pevsner and Moholy-Nagy had already incorporated it in Constructivist creations, but it was especially after 1930 that plastic was able to change the practice of sculpture. That year the sculptor Saint-Maur created the first sculpture in polyester resin. In that form plastic could be moulded and be both resistant and transparent.

But it was expanded polystyrene that would especially open up new possibilities. Rigid, isothermic, it is the material found in most compact wrappings. Its substance easily shaped by knife or hot wire, its lightness, would tempt

The product of a chemical synthesis, plastic has invaded our era until it has become its commonest material. Its derivatives are so numerous as to make possible the replacement of almost all natural products, becoming, in the words of Roland Barthes, "the first magical substance to consent to be prosaic." Chameleon-like, it has adapted to all the necessities of mass production and consumption; it has been used and abused past the point of saturation, presenting today, as a synthetic, non-biodegradable substance, a serious pollution problem.

Jean Dubuffet (1901-1985):
Portable Landscape, 1968.
14 elements transferred to polyester, 31½″ × 51″ × 29½″.

Marta Pan (1923):
Floating Sculpture I, 1961.
White polyester, 89″×85″×72″.
Kröller-Müller Museum, Otterlo, Holland.

some to make it a substitute for stone. More generally, it became the ideal and rapid way to make full-scale maquettes for transfer to stone or bronze. It even gave an artist like Singer the possibility of inverting the practice of modelling by carving the mould directly for concrete or resin volumes which the sculptor would see for the first time only after casting.

This ease of handling of polystyrene counted heavily in the revival of carving or modelling, as we shall see in the cases of Pistoletto and Abakanowicz. Its lightness also enabled experimentation with other equilibriums, and it was in addition the ideal support for polychromy. It was in July 1966, after finishing the *Hourloupe* cycle, that Jean Dubuffet started work on polystyrene. Shaping it with heated iron he found the means of creating forms that broke completely with the traditional framework, and which he then went over with a marker and afterwards with vinyl paint. From the painted object he proceeded rapidly to environment sculptures, going as far as turning them into genuine landscapes. Working in polystyrene formed the basis for all his monumental works from the *Cabinet Logologique* (Word-Study Room) to the *Villa Falbala* at Périgny (1971), from the *Enamel Garden* (1972) to the *Summer Salon* (1974). Depending on their situation they were either left as they stood, or coated with epoxy resin or moulded in concrete; but the shaping and colouring possibilities of polystyrene directly oriented Dubuffet's entire output of monumental groups.

Because of its lightness, polyester can have the faculty of floating. That was masterfully demonstrated by Marta Pan in her sculpture for the Kröller-Müller Museum at Otterlo in 1961, which was also one of the first landscape sculptures. It was commissioned by the director of the museum, A.M. Hammacher. "I suggested a sculpture on the park pond," she said, "and he made me additionally responsible for the plan of the pond, lawns, alleys and clearing in which the other sculptures would stand."

The discovery by César in 1965 of polyurethane, an expanding foam that hardened on exposure to air, had a stunning impact on his development. There he found a substance allowing him to make the opposite of the *Compressions*: the *Expansions*. He first exploited its resources during Happenings. This worked and freely poured mass spread, swelled and increased its volume, changing until it hardened. At first it was cut into pieces and handed out to participants in the events. Then César looked for a way to turn it into *durable* expansions: forms that, by their dynamisms and folds, freeze instants of action and chance, which he rendered still more definitive by lacquer- and varnish-work. These colours, in their brilliant perfection, rendered the apparition of the object intentionally artificial. But at the same time, just as the *Expansions* ran counter to the *Compressions*, so they brought back the same separation between desired and perceived volumes; the same paradoxical relation between inside and outside. Because plastic was also present in the composition of most textiles, synthetic fibre played a part in the environment, which it could make flexible and enveloping; it provided the basis for a transformable *architecture*, malleable and transparent, which joined with that achieved by the pioneers of the new tapestry when they left the plane of the wall to project themselves outward in space. Soft Art was born.

POP SCULPTURE

Claes Oldenburg (1929):
Project for a Cemetery in the Shape of a Colossal Screw:
Skyscraper for São Paulo, Brazil, 1971.
Pencil and watercolour, 14½″ × 11½″.

Like the European New Realists, the American Pop artists rehabilitated figuration by integrating the object into their constructions, but they did so in a way that was less conceptual and sociological and more individualized and subjective.

Robert Rauschenberg played a pivotal role. Beginning in 1952, he foresaw the limits of Abstract Expressionism in which he had been schooled, and revitalized it through the

Jasper Johns (1930):
Painted bronze, 1960.
5½″ × 8″ × 4¾″.

assemblage, which gradually led him to leave painting for sculpture. His Combine Paintings, the name he invented in 1955 to designate this new form of expression, show Dadaist influence; but they nevertheless depart from it by allowing the origin of the component elements to become more and more exposed (even Schwitters had effaced them in the interest of the organic quality of the whole). Rauschenberg's assemblages, veritable patchworks composed of elements taken from mass consumption, reflect like a mirror everything that goes to make up everyday reality.

Rauschenberg was the first artist to show that twentieth-century man's reality is not so much *nature* as *industrial production*, the advertising of which stepped up consumption, and *information*, which an accelerated and invasive mediatization ended by distorting. In his sculptures Rauschenberg compelled a reappraisal of the *commonplace*; that is to say, of everything reduced to its utility or its function alone. His interventions fixed the eye on what no one took the time to see.

In his assemblages all the elements of urban folklore were integrated pell-mell: Coca-Cola bottles, neckties, automobile tires, stuffed animals, newspapers, wrappers, advertising matter. In them, Rauschenberg *stratified* chance discoveries by also questioning the hierarchy of the senses that had been elaborated by rationalist thought. That thought was no longer legal tender in the world of consumption, which simultaneously immersed and assaulted the individual on all perceptual levels. Displaying the real in its rough state, Rauschenberg turned sculpture into a piece of reporting.

During the fifties Rauschenberg was closely associated with his studio neighbour, Jasper Johns. The latter made only rare incursions into the sculptural domain, but those were decisive, for he dared to confront the real with its representation. As a matter of fact even when painting sets itself up as being ultra-illusionist, it remains abstract, since it obliges the painter to contrive a solution enabling him to express on the pictorial plane the depth that escapes him. On the other hand, sculpture—which is carried out in all three dimensions of reality—had always signed its own death-warrant when it had no other aim than the literal representation of the real. Johns put the question lucidly after having taken as subjects for his painting such *perspectively* simple objects as a flag or a target. The banality of such subjects taught him to recognize what distinguishes the object from its artistic transposition: the interposition of the artist. Confirming this experience in sculpture, he cast familiar objects in bronze (here two cans of Ballantine's, his favourite beer), but kept them at a distance by the way he *mounted* and painted them. On the borderline of exact reconstruction he emphasized in imperceptible details the gap between representation and reality.

Claes Oldenburg is the only Pop artist to practise pure sculpture. Working on the gap between the real and its representation, he proceeds by the true methods of the sculptor, that is to say, by exploiting materials and scale; and thereby manages to create a new relationship between the object and its milieu. He began with ironic trompe-l'œil figures in plaster: "fast food" displays which he distorted by exposure of the casting material and the expressionist colour with which he coated them. Using all these consumer society archetypes, Oldenburg increasingly focused on the creative, that is the *denaturalizing* possibilities of sculpture.

Robert Rauschenberg (1925):
Monogram, 1955-1959.
Combine, 48″ × 72″ × 72″.

◁ Claes Oldenburg (1929):
Soft Washstand, 1965.
Vinyl, plexiglass, kapok, 55″ × 36″ × 28″.

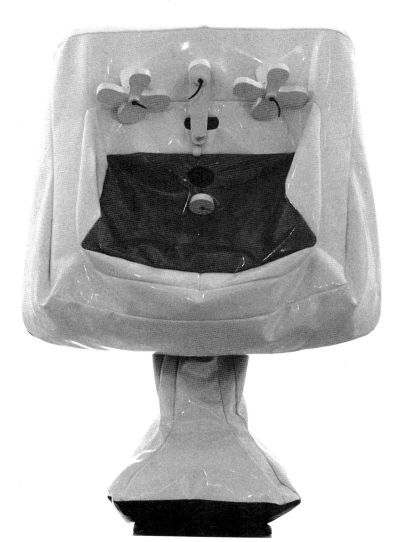

"I found," he said, "that by interpreting ordinarily hard surfaces as being soft I arrived at a new kind of sculpture and a stock of new symbols... The possibility of movement in soft sculpture, its resistance to any fixed position, its life, all stand in relation to the idea of time and change."

Having thus discovered that sculpture might depend on a simple decision–the substitution of one material for another being sufficient to produce an image quite different from the model–Oldenburg went on to exploit this possibility by carrying it to its furthest conclusions in the changes of scale that led him to conceive a series of monumental projects, some of which were completed. Making the commonplace object sacred by constructing it on the scale of the city brought out the formal symbolic content of the most humdrum accessories; blowing them up in size sufficed to focus the spectator's gaze on the aesthetic presence alone.

Oldenburg thereby replied to the question Rauschenberg had asked himself when leaving Abstract Expressionism: "I wanted to find out if an aesthetic presence survived beyond an object previously so necessary to art and that was now given another direction."

239

CASTS AND IMPRINTS

In 1943 Jean-Paul Sartre recorded in *Being and Nothingness*: "I exist in a situation which has *an outside* and which by virtue of that very fact possesses a dimension of alienation of which I can in no way divest it any more than I can act directly on that situation."

He thereby summed up the relation between subject and object which, from Cézanne to Giacometti, lay at the heart of *realistic* artistic experiences of the most passionate kind; those based on an experimentation with the real, bringing into play what philosophers were to call the phenomenology of perception. But Sartre also seemed to foresee the coming shift in the Pop art era in which the distance between the visible and the possible consciousness of it became a more important stake than the distance between observer and observed.

In fact, the situation was turned around in the 1960s, when the real itself gave way, being no longer but a mediatized reproduction or its industrialized caricature. Sartre's *outside* appears then as an artificial, conditioned, stereotyped *real*. And the artist who hitherto had only to project himself into his work suddenly felt so alien to the reality he had fabricated for himself that he no longer had any option but to become in his turn the object of an experience thrust upon him by an anonymous environment. The situation had reversed itself: it was the observed which made it possible to see the observer.

In such a context it was less a matter of providing something to see than of reappraising the presence of the onlooker. There was no longer time for speculations about the form and finality of the work; man, who had lost even the consciousness of what he was, needed—it was a question of survival—to examine his own existence by assessing its scale and the meaning of his actions. His self-questioning was particularly sharp and uncompromising in that he sentenced himself to a self-imposed anonymity by effacing all physical resemblance and blotting out all affective and sentimental reactions so as to make the individual more indistinguishable from the genus, for it was to humanity as a whole that the question was once more addressed: *What are we?*

This sculpture, which once again became *realist*, indeed hyperrealist, took its place at the opposite pole from the figurative representations of the nineteenth century. Its function was not to glorify but to examine. By questioning the human presence in its scale and through its gesture—and by the process of casting that excluded any interpretation—it started from the point that had marked the uttermost limit of the sculptural, down through the ages: *the perfect likeness*. But it was able to transcend that likeness and give it new meaning by a fresh use of the space surrounding the figure, till then always arbitrarily isolated. The space into which the cast penetrated was no longer illusionist but authentic environment, constructed from real objects that enabled it to be dated independently of the artist's work by its *historical* identification with the taste and technique of a moment in time. When all of the real is present except for the life that gave it a meaning and a

George Segal (1924):
Rush Hour, 1983.
Bronze with blue-black patina
on concrete base, 6 casts,
72″ × 96″ × 96″.

240

John De Andrea (1941):
Couple, 1971.
Acrylic on polyester and hair,
man 5′8″ high, woman 5′2″ high.

temporary and accurate material–polyester–and by combining the printing of copies from life with acrylic painting. The illusionism they achieved was even more convincing than those of waxwork figures, for they started with an integral mould and took the paintwork to the limits of perfection.

John De Andrea and Duane Hanson gained celebrity at the start of the seventies. Andrea was interested in the nude; he was fascinated by everything that went on inside and beneath the skin, and his integral verism dramatically highlighted immobility. In his attachment to the expression of commonplace situations, Hanson met with the pathetically ludicrous. "The subject matter that I like best," he said, "deals with the familiar lower and middle-class American types of today. To me, the resignation, emptiness and loneliness of their existence captures the true reality of life for these people. Consequently, although I am a realist, I am not interested in the ideal human form... but in the face or the body that has suffered, like a landscape in which the eroding effect of time shows through."

Hanson suggests time in a dual way: not only do his subjects carry in their flesh the scars of their own experience, but their clothes and appurtenances tie them to the prevailing taste of a moment in history. Traditional sculpture had made it possible to escape from time; with Hanson, sculpture became the means of focusing attention on time at all levels.

The uncompromising gaze of the hyperrealists brought out the hardness of appearances; it especially placed in the limelight the fragility and littleness of man. Deprived of life, he seemed much smaller than in reality.

function, the interpretation of the real by its telltale signs rests on a critical distancing.

Struck by the loneliness of cities in which each is imprisoned in the gestures of his function, George Segal carried out his first plaster casts in 1958. But he did not use a negative impression that would enable him to recover the original, as in traditional casting. Instead, he reconstructed his model by sticking together again piece by piece the light plaster shells with which he had covered it. The gesture and attitude were identical, but his figures became anonymous, for the resemblance remained within. Segal increasingly placed his subjects in the real situation accounting for their gesture. "For me," he says, "there is no feeling as long as the figure, which is the form of a certain gesture, is not combined with the 'gest' (overall attitude) of the accessory." Segal's works appear, then, as frozen happenings; the artist having acted as a photographer immortalizing instantaneous movement. His compositions, in which the figures have a phantom-like whiteness due to the use of plaster, become like mirrors of a world where objects are more real than men, who end by existing only as a function of them. Starting from these *commonplaces* Segal refers back to the collective experience of living.

Even more influenced by the potency of the photograph and the questions posed by resemblance, the hyperrealists looked for a casting technique that would enable them to make things appear more real than they did in nature. They found a way of doing so by exploiting a more con-

Duane Hanson (1925):
The Tourists, 1970.
Polyester resin, polychrome glass fibre.

PLACING IN SITUATION

Turning the spotlight on the real also made story-telling possible. That was demonstrated in the development of Kienholz, who transformed Pop art environments into a dramatic placing in situation through introducing narration, that is, by tying the elements of the real together subjectively. While everyone else in the sixties was trying to be light, decorative, ironic, Kienholz narrated snatches of life with violence and pathos. He told of his anxieties and failures, exposed lies and injustices. Against the rose-water of advertising and magazines he set, life-size, the sordidness of the everyday world, the violence of struggles for basic liberties: racial, sexual, political.

His installations were ruthless "genre scenes" in which he immersed the beholder. They were not assemblages of found objects, but slices of life recomposed in dramatic shortcuts, dominated by the dread of death. Kienholz turns the spectator into a voyeur, forcing him to live through what he prefers to ignore or forget.

This narrative necessity is again found in the Spanish artist Lopez-Garcia, who used it as a means of giving the academic tradition a different meaning: here precisionism emphasizes the discrepancy. With Ipoustéguy it is expressed more traditionally by placing in a situation fragments of bodies, bodies torn between death and desire, devoured by time. Attracted at first by abstraction, Ipoustéguy dis-

Jean Ipoustéguy (1920):
Man Pushing the Door, 1966.
Bronze, 78¾″ × 50⅜″.

Edward Kienholz (1927):
Portable War Memorial, 1968.
Environment with objects.

Raymond Mason (1922):
Illuminated Crowd, 1979.
Epoxy resin, acrylic, gouache, plexiglass, 15¾″ × 45″ × 20″.

covered the expressive potential of matter and its tactile potency. But it was when he once more felt the need for portrayal that he succeeded in exploiting what it offered, for the space in which he set up his figures then acquired its meaning. Aggressive and voluptuous, fecund and at the same time fragmented, his works became symbolically meaningful.

Pausing a long while on the borders of painting and sculpture, Raymond Mason was equally obsessed by the necessity to narrate. He expressed his attention to everyday events with an emotion that did not rule out humour. The crowd, with its disparate and conflicting movements, fascinated him. It was the desire to breathe new life into painting which led him to volume–but he could not rest content with relief that lacked the "distance" of colour. Such was the lesson he drew from the observation of creators of the past: "The sculptors of antiquity, the Middle Ages, the Renaissance and in general the Baroque period did not conceive their art in terms of 'sculpture' but rather in terms of what they desired to represent. The proof is that they painted their refined forms with loud colours, forcefully applied. They spared no effort to make those forms live. A sculpture in colour is more human than one in marble or bronze."

That colour which came in to give life and feeling to inert volume is also found in the three-dimensional production of the painters who revived Expressionism.

Antonio Lopez-Garcia (1936):
The Burned Woman, 1964.
Wood relief, 32″ × 36¼″.

THEATRE OF ACTION

Gilbert and George did this by turning themselves into living sculptures and exhibiting the phenomena of distance and memory. Traditional statuary captured movement and art represented life. By immobilizing themselves, Gilbert and George simultaneously suggested sculpture and brought life into the museum. They called the whole past of sculpture in question by their performance in which true and false are confused.

In spite of their external similarity, the environments of Joseph Beuys and Wolf Vostell have little in common with those of the Arte Povera or post-minimalist artists. To the latter environments were settings for space and material, whereas to the Germans they were the result or consequence of a Happening, as Beuys admitted: "They are documents left by my actions and sometimes they may illustrate the character of my actions. But that is not the most important thing. They are the necessary remains of all the activities, documents and tools which make possible the reconstitution of those actions." Consequently the traditional critical approach is overturned, because the spectator can no longer find the justification for the work in the work itself, he has to read the "happening script" that gave birth to it to grasp its meaning. Indeed, the Germans of this generation look on sculpture as a social and political act taking place during a performance which is unique and limited in time and of which only film and photography can preserve a record even more essential than the objects composing the environment.

The German art scene in the early sixties was stirred up by the Fluxus movement which made an impact on all fields of expression. Directly inspired by Dada and Duchamp, Fluxus won over everyone who wanted to escape

Gilbert and George (1943 and 1942):
Underneath the Arches, Singing Sculpture, 1970.

After the appearance of collages and assemblages in 1912, the traditional distinction between the world of ideas and the world of things became blurred. The gap between the signifier and the signified was finally wiped out in the avant-garde experiments of the sixties which tried to make art out of life itself.

Joseph Beuys (1921-1986):
Coyote: I like America and America likes me, 1974.
Performance, Rene Block Gallery, New York, 1974.

Wolf Vostell (1932):
E.d.H.R., 1968.
Electronic Happening Room.

from political and economic constraints to rediscover their freedom, everyone who no longer had a share in guilt for the Nazi past. Violence and derision are the most effective weapons for wiping out the norms of the order of civilization which has removed from them the meaning of a life whose sole inexorable reality remains the appointed time of death. Conscious of being dispossessed by a dehumanized environment and a pragmatic philosophy reducing everyone to the status of slave of the consumer industry and the State, the members of Fluxus find in the world of art the last stronghold in which to stage a total revolt against a culture which acts as a screen, concealing life and justifying the enslavement of the individual.

Vostell's Fluxus Happenings, whose decor is the museum, consisting "of facts of real life consecrated as works of art," are an attempt to demonstrate that every man is a work of art, because Art = Life. "To proceed," he says "so that man is not confined to a single path, but remains open to all the forms of life offered to him, to make life a work of art and have that constantly in mind, that is my present and future position vis-à-vis the aesthetic problem."

All Vostell's actions denounce those threats to life, hostility and violence. Spectators are invited to take part in Happenings, but they are equally immersed in environments.

Joseph Beuys began to make a name in 1961, the year in which he was appointed Professor of Sculpture at the Düsseldorf Academy of Fine Arts. The Kassel Documenta IV of 1968 was to establish his international reputation. His environments preserve more mystery, but his real fame came from his skilful exploitation of the media. He gave his actions and lectures a directly social and political dimension based on the concept of "expanded art": a therapy of the social body intended to transcend ideologies and constraints working from the subjective reactions of the individual. In his Happenings, Beuys presents concepts which confront art by refusing to dissociate it from life. Each artistic action is a means of subversion and reflection leading to a changed awareness of nature and human potentialities. In a world where everything is programmed by a "phony happiness," Beuys imagines actions or multiplies his own image to give evidence of his own experience of unhappiness and distress. *Coyote* was a Happening that lasted a month. Shut up in a tiny room with a coyote Beuys, with only a cane and a felt cloak to protect himself, finally mastered its savage instincts. In this action, which reverses the course of history by taking us back to the dawn of time, Beuys tries to efface the social and a-social divorce between man and nature to which civilization has led us. By renewing contact with the primitive chaos, a starting point from which everything becomes possible again, the artist proves the need of the creative act as a means of escaping from the alienation produced by civilization.

245

RENEWAL OF EXPRESSIONISM

Lucio Fontana (1899-1968):
Mask, 1948.
Coloured ceramic, 35¼″ high.

Cheap, light, easy to handle, painting was throughout the development of modern art the privileged field for experimentation in new problematics, with rare but determinant exceptions where painters felt obliged to invent the third dimension to verify the *reality* of their findings. On each occasion these raids on the third dimension were fraught with consequences.

The same phenomenon recurred around 1980, centring on what might aesthetically be termed the *renovation* of Expressionism, and which was the doing of artists previously recognized as painters. Looked at more closely, that is, beyond the vehemence of the forms, this neo-primitivism was very different from that which dominated the years around 1910. Beyond some analogies—bringing out of gesture, direct carving of wood, polychromy, etc.–, differences materialized around problems of scale, gesture and fragment. They revealed a radical change of attitude. Expressionism had been based on the desire for a renaissance, on faith in life and its elemental force; this neo-Expressionism, more than its aggressive side, presents us with a more conceptual inquiry into the image and its meanings.

In fact, it is as if art, emerging from avant-garde problematics, could survive only by immersing itself in the whole history of culture, and especially its most ancient forms, to rediscover its own necessity, as if culture–always the interpreted *double* of reality–had wound up substituting itself for that reality, and the real could once more be found only by confronting those signs to which culture had imparted a sacred character.

The return to primitive, narrative, symbolic images has its roots in the impulse towards a critical distancing of signs devalued by a surfeit of communication. This going back towards prehistory expressed a rebellion against language and writing. And sculpture, even more than painting, would make it possible to imagine, in the phrase of Michel Thévoz, the *mythology of visibility*; to rediscover the reality of signs distorted by the excesses of information and mass consumption. This reference to Art Brut was not gratuitous. The communications explosion, after having condemned our whole society to incommunicability, would now oblige it in consequence to verify the existing relationships between form and content, signified and signifier. The return to the prelingual, initiated by Dubuffet, became a necessity.

It was during his pictorial invention of puncturing and tearing that Fontana created those pathetic figures, as if they enabled him to completely void that subjectivity which no longer had a place in so abstract a pictorial approach. Formed solely by the imprint of the gesture in the earth, they are not unrelated to those carried out by de Kooning.

The latter's encounter with modelling came by chance. In Rome, during the autumn of 1969, at the home of a sculptor-friend, de Kooning suddenly put his talent to the test on earth, on a material he handled like a blind man, as

Willem de Kooning (1904):
Digger, 1972.
Bronze, 29½″ high.

if to get a clearer view of gesture, the possibilities of the hand and the imprint of his fingers. He acted as if he were making his self-portrait *automatically* by directly imprinting in the malleable earth his innermost drives. Before long he was asked to increase the size of these amulets. Changing scale, de Kooning's figures make references to those of Matisse by stressing the outline and the sensitive surface of the flesh. The elementary act of kneading takes on monumental dimensions by the energy it releases; surrendered to the gaze it is as fragile as it is brutal.

Baselitz was to find these sculptures "highly irritating because they do not correspond to the form of the sculptures we know... They have neither muscles, nor skeleton, nor skin. They have only a surface with no content."

Georg Baselitz in point of fact was one of the first neo-expressionist painters to come back to sculpture. He did so on the occasion of the 1980 Venice Biennale, where the *Man With Raised Arm* caused a genuine shock. Stressing the gesture and its meaning, he turned the whole modernist tradition inside out. Baselitz, who had already turned

painting topsy-turvy, came to sculpture because he found in it a more radical ground for breaking with convention: "When I took up a piece of wood, it was not to go with the grain but against it. It is working with disharmony, and that work must extend to all fields."

That same possibility of attaining through sculpted figures a communication that is immediate, elementary and universal in scope is again to be found in the evolution of A.R. Penck. By magnifying body fragments he gives mystery and meaning to the most devalued of signs. Penck reached the third dimension after long adventures in graffiti which led him to develop a theory on the production of information.

The works of Markus Lüpertz, harshly carved and coloured fragments that take us back to the pre-figurative, grew out of the same needs. The example of primitive art no longer acted as a liberating aesthetic model; it served as a confrontation in a combat waged by the creator to recover his existential and spiritual reality in a world where nothing any longer made sense.

A.R. Penck (1939):
The Ghost of L., 1981.
Wood, 6′10″ high.

Markus Lüpertz (1941):
Bearing Leg, Free Leg, 1982.
Painted bronze, 10½′ high.

Georg Baselitz (1938):
Untitled, 1984.
Painted lindenwood, 8′4″ high.

REVIVAL OF STATUARY

▷ Magdalena Abakanowicz (1930):
Catharsis, 1985.
Thirty-three bronze sculptures, 8½' high.
Fattoria di Celle, Santomato di Pistoia.

George Segal (1924):
The Restaurant, 1976.
Bronze, bricks, cement, steel, aluminium,
hardened glass and lamps, 10' × 16' × 8'.
Federal Office Building, Buffalo, N.Y.

Michelangelo Pistoletto (1933):
Marble Giant, 1981-1983.
Polyurethane, 19'7'' high.

All the figurative suggestions previously examined were in general put forward at the level of the museum or private collection, but some creators were not slow to reintroduce human representation into the space of the city or of nature.

So it is with the compositions of Segal. Everyday gestures find a different expression frozen in the banality of a real setting than they do in a museum. Appearances are identical, but the fragility and littleness of man are further enhanced when small chance happenings are at a double remove; the futility of action is even more blatant in the reality of the landscape.

Michelangelo Pistoletto came to sculpture in the round after having attempted to *trap* the real in mirrors which gave back to the spectator his very image in an artificial perspective. When he left trompe-l'œil for volume, he did so to materialize that "cloud of smoke which Aladdin let out of his magic lantern." From the polished surfaces he has rubbed, Pistoletto suddenly makes figures emerge that look down upon us from above, seeming to ask us what we want and what we are doing.

For Pistoletto, there exists in the whole tradition of statuary–from Easter Island to Michelangelo–the incarnation of a metaphysical consciousness, the presence of a soul that has detached itself from life but which becomes the everlasting reference for all feelings. Sculpture is the material representation of the spirit. It passes from the mirror to the volume so as to give from the body a physical reality *to the smoke* of its imagination. Playing on the ambivalence of past and present, positive and negative–for energy is always the product of the clash of opposing elements–it creates works that interrogate us, like the questioning image of someone who looks at his reflection in the bottom of a well. Here the past becomes present, like a scrap of memory from which the dream of the future again becomes possible.

It was after long experience with fibre and thread that Magdalena Abakanowicz felt once more the necessity *to portray*. Weaving forms of which the skin was the direct image of what composed them, she discovered, around 1970, the spirit and materiality of new biomorphic forms.

From the image of the head she could go on to experiment with the body, finding again intuitively those fibre knots that lay the groundwork of the form while acting as a vehicle of life. These denuded figures acquire a presence rendered especially dramatic by the fact that they are often multiplied. Putting them into a situation expresses the threats suspended over their destinies by human follies.

Strong in this experience, she was able in 1983 to take up casting. In polystyrene blocks she carved an inextricable maze of canals and vessels in which flowed bronze, producing a simultaneous image of inside and outside, of front and back. Planted dramatically in a field, like trees that might have grown there, her monumental figures make their statement. Pathetic, without gesture because without limbs, her bodies stand up heroically, bearing witness to an ever renewed struggle to survive. But their metal flesh, furrowed by scars, irrigated by a relentless throbbing, interrogates today's humanity by sending out to it the image of nature's part in the eternal: life.

THE REDEFINITION OF AMERICAN SCULPTURE:
FROM MINIMALISM TO EARTHWORKS

Claes Oldenburg (1929):
Lingerie Counter, 1962.
Mixed media, 7′1″ high.

Walter De Maria
(1935):
Walk Around
the Box, 1961.
Wood,
box 15″ high;
painting 49½″ × 24″.

The grounds for the revolutionary redefinition of sculpture that took place in America in the Sixties are to be found in the post-Dada Happenings and environments of the Fifties. Inspired by the photographs and texts published by painter Robert Motherwell in his 1951 book *The Dada Painters and Poets*, artists like Allan Kaprow, Lucas Samaras and Robert Whitman, all of whom studied art history with Meyer Schapiro and hence were particularly sensitive to historical precedent, examined the tradition of Cubist and Constructivist sculpture with a critical eye. Along with Yale graduate Claes Oldenburg, all became involved in Happenings, which were known as "the theater of action." Taking the psychological and gestural content of Abstract Expressionist painting as a point of departure, avant-garde theater became a rallying point for many artists who would invent unprecedented forms of sculpture that implied a radical rupture with the past. Since much of the most celebrated American sculpture of the Sixties and early Seventies had its roots not in any earlier tradition of sculpture, but in theater and to some extent in painting, its novelty was assured.

Oldenburg's Happenings were originally held in a store he rented in 1962 on New York's Lower East Side. He, his wife Pat and Lucas Samaras were the principal performers. *The Store*, as Oldenburg termed the environment of plaster reliefs of consumer goods that he molded and painted, was combination gallery, private museum and theater. Among the misshapen parodies of manufactured objects Oldenburg ironically deformed and recreated by hand was *The Lingerie Counter*, where the "forbidden" goods of women's undergarments were displayed in informal, casual, apparently random relationships. Oldenburg designed over-sized stuffed props for his Happenings which Pat, an excellent seamstress, ran up on her sewing machine. These were the first "soft sculptures"; they provided Oldenburg with a rich new formal vocabulary and influenced a younger generation of artists looking for an alternative to the planar classical style and hardness of welded metal sculpture.

On the West Coast, avant-garde performance art flourished around 1960 at the California School of Fine Arts, now known as the San Francisco Art Institute. The monotone "drone" music of La Monte Young, who like the Happening artists had been deeply influenced by the Zen-cum-Dada esthetic of composer John Cage, and the dance theater of Ann Halprin, with its psychodrama overtones, affected young artists working in the Northern California Bay Area. In 1959-1960 Walter De Maria, like Mark Di Suvero a University of California Berkeley graduate, directed the Music-Theater-Events program at the California School of Fine Arts, where Robert Morris studied briefly. Morris, whose 1960 painting show at the Dilexi Gallery was hailed as the best show of the year by a young artist in *Artnews*, met De Maria, La Monte Young and Yvonne Rainer, who was also studying with Halprin at the time.

Morris and his wife, choreographer Simone Forti, moved to New York in early 1960; Walter De Maria moved to Manhattan in spring, 1960. He and Morris had adjacent studios at 49 Bond Street for a short time. De Maria was writing scenarios for *Artyard*, a trench-digging performance anticipating earthworks; he also made a series of box-like wood constructions resembling coffins at the time. Morris stopped painting after he was proclaimed a success, and began building wooden props for his wife's performances. Soon after, he would begin performing himself with Yvonne Rainer in the influential theater events held at the Judson Memorial Church. Thus, one may locate the origins of the art of Oldenburg, Morris and De Maria, three of the most innovative and influential American sculptors after Abstract Expressionism, not in sculpture, but in theatrical performance.

Allan Kaprow (1923):
An Apple Shrine, 1960.
Environment.

ORGANIC FORMS

▷ David Weinrib:
Three Aerial Forms.
Plastic, 13′ × 7′ × 8½′.

George Sugarman (1912):
Bardana, 1962–1963.
Polychromed wood, 8′ × 12″ × 5′2″.

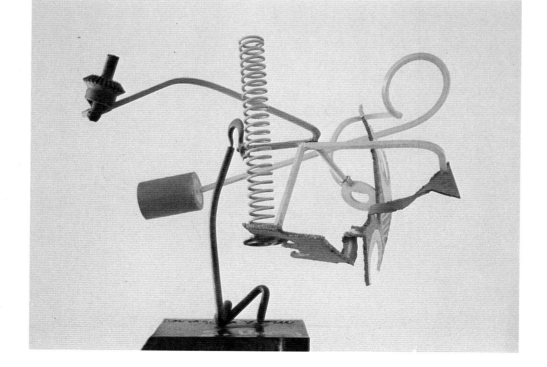

▷ Mark Di Suvero (1933):
Homage to Stuart Davis, 1965.
Painted metal.

▷▷ Peter Agostini (1913):
Summer Clouds III, 1963–1964.
Plaster, 10″ high.

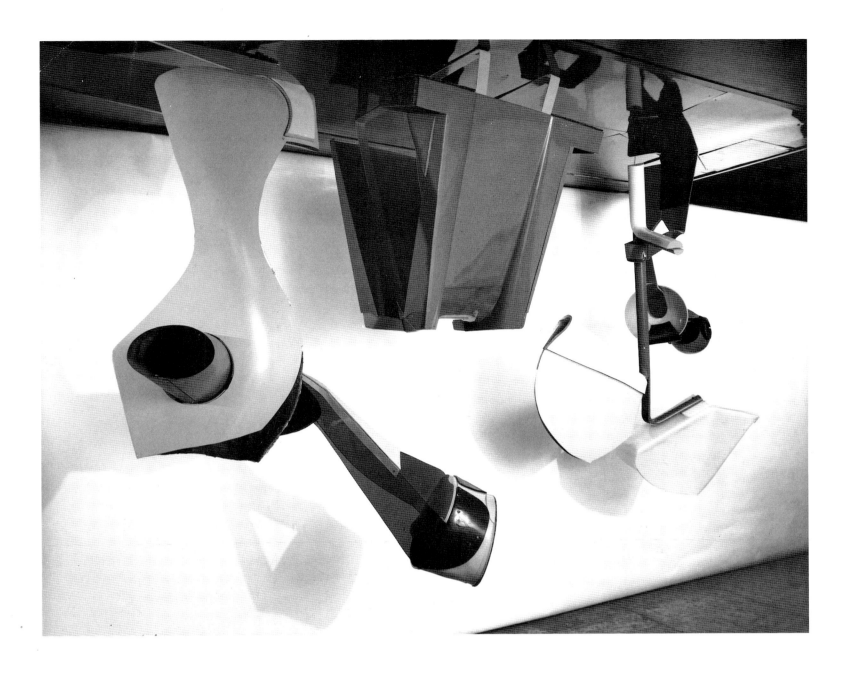

Other sculptors, however, like George Sugarman, David Weinrib, Peter Agostini and Mark Di Suvero, were finding fresh ways to expand the tradition of sculpture, criticizing from within its discipline rather than attacking it from an ironic Dada viewpoint that was at least initially negative and hostile to a bourgeois public. Sugarman's polychromed wood constructions were a three-dimensional homage to the American Cubist painter Stuart Davis, who based his bouncy rhythms on jazz. The painted kinetic metal assemblages by Mark Di Suvero were the heir to David Smith's vision of "drawing in air" on a scale larger than Cubism.

Working in cut and bent colored plastic, David Weinrib was among the original environmental sculptors of the Sixties. By suspending his constructions from the ceiling, Weinrib redirected the eye to novel perspectives while relating his forms to the bulbous shapes of nature and anatomy. These references humanized the artificiality of plastic and its industrial associations.

The first New York School artist to attempt to freeze the ephemeral in a concrete object, Peter Agostini cast objects in plaster because bronze was too expensive. A member of the same artistic generation as David Smith, Agostini had the experimental attitude toward materials and techniques of the younger generation like George Segal who came of age in the Sixties.

METAMORPHOSIS/METAPHOR

Louise Bourgeois (1911):
Spring, 1946–1948/1983.
Cast bronze, white patina, 61½″ high.

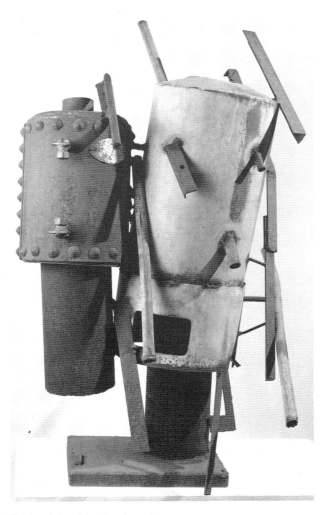

Sculpture was bound to be perceived in relationship to the human body, no matter how abstract its forms, because unlike painting, its scale and volumes were actual and existed in the same space as the spectator. This became an increasingly important concern. Louise Bourgeois, who emigrated to New York from her native Paris in 1948, still managed to shock a jaded art public with her phallic forms that were aggressively suggestive in shape, but often gracefully sensuous when carved in marble or cast in bronze. Wood was the material she usually used in her early works, once again for reasons of economy as well as for the opportunity to polychrome her works.

Assemblage artist Richard Stankiewicz, who was decisively influenced early in his career by Jean Follet, an artist whose delicate assembled metal reliefs have regrettably been forgotten, used scrap metal welded into configurations that suggested obvious analogies with the human figure.

In an early construction, the *"I" Box*, Robert Morris displayed a photograph of himself, wearing nothing but a grin, which anticipated the nudity of Body Art. Both Morris and H.C. Westermann were decisively affected by Dada precedents, such as Marcel Duchamp's found objects and Joseph Cornell's witty and poetic boxes. Westermann's *A Human Condition* also invites participation, asking, like Morris's *"I" Box*, to be opened and inspected. Lucas Samaras also used boxes containing autobiographical and erotic material during the early Sixties. Later, in his nude auto-polaroids, his involvement with Body Art as a psychological expression became more evident.

△ Richard Stankiewicz (1922):
Untitled, 1963.
Welded steel and found objects, 50″ × 31″ × 24″.

▽ H.C. Westermann (1922):
A Human Condition, 1949.
Pine, 38″ high.

◁ Robert Morris (1931):
"I" Box (open), 1963.
Wood and photograph.

255

△ Barnett Newman (1905-1970):
Broken Obelisk, 1966.
Cor-Ten steel, 25′5″ high.
Rothko Chapel, Houston, Texas.

▷△ David von Schlegell (1920):
Classical Study, 1965.
Aluminum, 4′ high.

▷ Ronald Bladen (1918):
The X, 1968.
Painted wood, 22′ × 24′ × 14′.

256

ARCHITECTURE/SCULPTURE

During the Sixties, as public consciousness of art increased in America, the possibilities of making sculpture, including monumental sculpture, proliferated. Industrial fabrication techniques were used to create large-scale works that could compete visually and even physically with architecture as autonomous spatial experiences. Artists like Kenneth Snelson, Will Insley and David von Schlegell made maquettes of oversize outdoor sculpture, some of which were ultimately fabricated. Von Schlegell specialized in a quirky use of geometry and bent and warped shapes that did not resemble Cubist or Constructivist sculpture; his obviously hollow volumes appeared conceived as a single curving form as opposed to a sequence of forms that rhymed formally, echoing parts.

The wholistic approach to art was pioneered by Barnett Newman in the single-image color-field paintings he began doing in the late Forties. Newman's radical approach to pictorial structure was opposed to the Cubist principle of part-to-part relationships of shapes depicted within a field. His idea of identifying the whole image with the field became the point of departure for minimal art. Dividing space into zones of color which related the image to its framing edge, Newman challenged the fundamental principles of composition. Younger artists like Frank Stella and Donald Judd identified as a distinctively American approach to composition the elimination of any hierarchy of elements or internal relationships.

Newman called his compositions "non-relational." When in the Sixties he produced several bronze sculptures,

they, too, were single "wholistic" forms that opposed the entire concept of fragmented assemblage. His Cor-Ten steel *Broken Obelisk* stands in solemn grandeur near the chapel containing Rothko's paintings in Houston, Texas. Cor-Ten, a brand of steel that rusted naturally, was a preferred material of sculptors who wished color to be intrinsic. The entire drama of the work is focussed on the diminishing point where the columnar volume meets its upward pointing triangular base. The visual detail of the serrated top of the inverted "obelisk" may be interpreted as a metaphor for the partially ruined state of ancient columns as Americans inherited them, and the symbolic connection between this space-age sculpture and antique precedents.

A close friend of Newman's, Tony Smith was a trained architect who also painted and engaged in polemics against the academicism of Cubism. Although his art has been associated with Minimalism because it deals with simple, geometric volumes, Smith was more involved with creating outdoor sculpture on an architectural scale, which could be experienced by the viewer from within as well as without in a variety of configurations, changing in relationship to the spectator's position.

Simplifying Tony Smith's volumetric forms even further, Ronald Bladen suggested metaphorical analogies with the human figure rather than with architectural enclosures in a series of monumental volumetric works. Intended for metal fabrication, these huge hollow pieces were initially made in wood and painted.

Tony Smith (1922):
The Snake Is Out, 1962.
Steel, 15′1½″ × 23′2″ × 18′10″.

Donald Judd (1928):
Untitled, 1971.
Anodized aluminum, each cube 4′ × 4′.

MINIMAL OBJECTS

Ellsworth Kelly (1923):
Blue Red Rocker, 1963.
Painted aluminum,
72″ × 66½″ × 37½″.

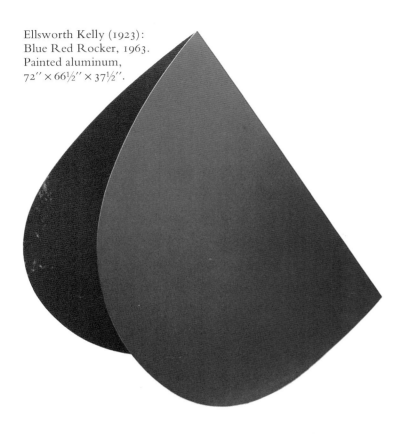

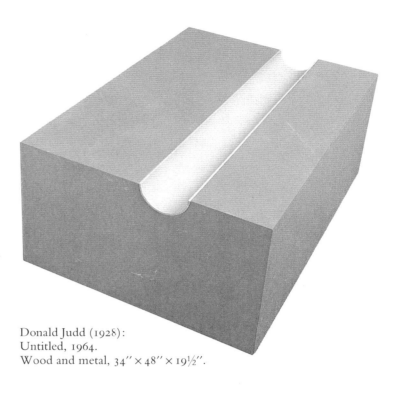

Donald Judd (1928):
Untitled, 1964.
Wood and metal, 34″ × 48″ × 19½″.

Donald Judd (1928):
Untitled, 1970.
Anodized aluminum, blue plexiglass, each box 9″ × 40″ × 31½″.

Among the first to use pared down geometric shapes and eliminate the pedestal or base from sculpture, Ellsworth Kelly provided a precedent for deriving a sculptural vocabulary from painting. Using cut-out, bright colored shapes similar to those employed in his geometric paintings, Kelly exacted maximum tension from minimal means by setting a curved form, easily rocked into motion, directly on the ground. This sense of a precarious balance, which one finds in the work of Di Suvero and Serra as well, may be interpreted as an abstract metaphor for the human condition.

Donald Judd, a leading exponent of and polemicist for minimal art, which he labelled "specific objects" in an influential article by that name he published in *Arts* magazine in 1965, was outspoken regarding his debt to Barnett Newman's art. Originally a painter as well as an art historian, Judd had studied with Meyer Schapiro at Columbia University, where he also came into contact with the pragmatic philosophy of John Dewey. Judd's attacks against illusionism as an outworn relic of a distant European tradition and his insistence that shape, structure, color and material be inseparable qualities were impressive in their straightforward conviction. As soon as the means were available, he had his metal and plastic boxes and stacks industrially fabricated, so that color and reflectiveness were intrinsic to his materials rather than applied. Judd's aim was to make the various qualities, both spatial and material, literally "real." This literalist, anti–illusionist attitude was shared by other minimal artists like Carl Andre, Dan Flavin and Sol Lewitt. Like Judd, they, too, used serial repetition as a compositional principle permitting non-hierarchical arrangements that did not suggest past sculpture and consequently looked very new in the context of sculpture.

Barry Le Va (1941):
Standard Tasks/Observation, Examination, Isolation, 1983.
Wood, hydrocal, metal.

MINIMAL ENVIRONMENTS

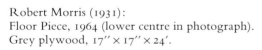

Robert Morris (1931):
Floor Piece, 1964 (lower centre in photograph).
Grey plywood, 17″ × 17″ × 24′.

Robert Morris (1931):
Grey Plywood, 1965.
Two pieces, 8′ × 8′ × 2′ each.

That the space of the gallery or museum could be used like the canvas field as an area to be divided was quickly seized upon by Robert Morris, Carl Andre and Dan Flavin who made the abstract equivalents of Oldenburg's Pop environments. In his 1964 Green Gallery exhibition, in New York, Morris impressed critics with his inert, neutral gray volumes that heightened one's physical awareness of actual space as well as of the space displaced by Morris's chunky, passive-aggressive forms. Exploring the possible permutations of a single, simple "L" shape, Morris revealed how even the most rudimentary forms implied potential reconsideration and rearrangement.

Like many of the leading Sixties' sculptors, Morris had a background in philosophy, psychology and art history. His M.A. thesis on the role of the base in Brancusi's sculpture surely heightened his awareness of Brancusi's closed monolithic forms as an alternative to the open, assembled "drawing-in-air" shapes of sculpture derived from Picasso and Gonzalez. Searching for a means to make sculpture more immediate, Morris used familiar *gestalts* that could be instantaneously perceived because the whole could be mentally projected from knowledge of one part of a regular geometric form.

As part of their rejection of traditional sculpture, minimal artists eliminated conventional bases that separated the art object from the viewer's space. The most radical rejection of the base, however, came from Carl Andre, who set identical square plates directly on the ground. Both Andre and Dan Flavin used standard identical industrial elements in their work. Andre's contention that an art work was not permanently assembled, but contingent on its specific installation, posited a radical new premise, as did the notion of looking down on as opposed to at or up to a sculpture. When Barry Le Va began in 1967 to scatter pieces of felt and ball-bearings in random arrangements on the floor in his "distributional" sculptures, he, too, emphasized the ephemeral as opposed to the permanence normally associated with sculpture.

These arrangements of scattered materials recalled Hans Namuth's film of Jackson Pollock painting, using a variety of materials dropped on the canvas, which was shown in art schools across America.

Carl Andre (1935):
Steel Magnesium Plain, 1969.
36-unit square,
each square 12″ × 12″ and overall 72″ × 72″.

MODULAR STRUCTURES

Eva Hesse (1936-1970):
Aught, 1968.
Double sheets of latex rubber, polyethylene plastic inside.
Four units, each 78″ high.

Sol Lewitt and Dan Flavin, leading minimalists, used standard modules to create a sense of rhythmic repetition. Lewitt's transparent cubes and grids had an elegant pictorial linearity, whereas his open boxes often looked like useless objects. Dan Flavin's configurations of fluorescent tubing rendered color and light literal. They were, in that sense, like three-dimensional versions of Newman's banded paintings. His corner pieces were derived from Russian Constructivist Vladimir Tatlin's experiments with environmental form as well as from Mark Rothko's luminous paintings. They flooded interior areas framed by the fluorescent tubing with colored light. The fluorescent tubes were now art materials anyone could cheaply and easily acquire. Flavin thus echoed Ad Reinhardt's democratic demystification of art, when Reinhardt proclaimed of his radically reductive paintings "This is your painting if you make it."

Among the first to rebel against the cold, industrial look of minimal art, Eva Hesse began by using soft materials like latex which nevertheless initially continued the serial imagery of minimalism. Soon, however, her art became increasingly subjective and expressive. Her tragic death of a brain tumor in 1970 at the age of thirty-three robbed the art world of one of its finest and most original talents.

Working in the all male world of minimalism, Hesse's brilliance and ability to innovate new forms which, like Oldenburg's soft sculpture, were subject to gravity and

Sol Lewitt (1928):
Modular Piece, Steps, 1971.
White painted wood, $24\frac{1}{4}'' \times 24\frac{1}{4}'' \times 24\frac{1}{4}''$.

Dan Flavin (1931):
Untitled (to Donna) 6, 1971.
Yellow, pink, blue fluorescent light,
8′ square across corner.

took on variable positions, catapulted her to a place of pre-eminence in American sculpture which her art retains many years after her death.

A number of important sculptors remained on the West Coast working in Los Angeles. Both Robert Irwin and Larry Bell stopped painting in the Sixties and began creating immaterial environments. Irwin used transparent theatrical scrim and hidden lighting to evoke an atmosphere of mysterious revelation. Bell progressed from precious mirrored boxes to environments of fragile optically coated glass that also reflected the viewer's image. Both artists were affected by the blinding form-dissolving sunlight of Los Angeles.

L.A. sculptor Bruce Nauman used colored neon script to ironically comment on the status of the object. Following Duchamp and Johns, he cast parts of his own body in enigmatic works which presaged Body Art. He was also a pioneer of mixed media environments using electronic feedback.

Ken Price's ceramic sculptures of the Sixties often had erotic overtones associated with California hedonism. In San Francisco, "funk" art with its bulbous organic forms was the indigenous sculptural style which also hinted at metaphors for anatomy and eroticism.

Larry Bell (1939):
Garst's Mind No. Two, 1971. Environment, coated plate glass.

Robert Irwin (1928):
No title, 1971.
Environment, fluorescent light and scrim.

CALIFORNIA STYLE

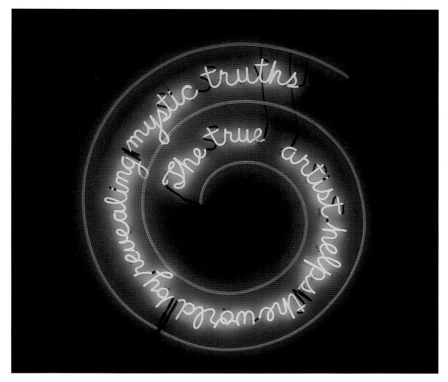

Bruce Nauman (1941):

Window or Wall Sign, 1967.
Blue-peach neon, glass tubing, 59″ × 55″ × 2″.

◁ From Hand to Mouth, 1967.
Wax over cloth, 30″ × 10″ × 4″.

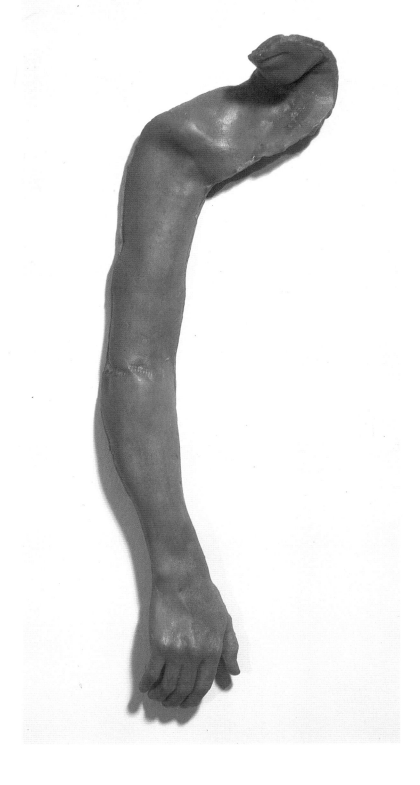

Ken Price (1935):
S.L. Green, 1963.
Fired and painted clay, height 10″, diameter 11″.

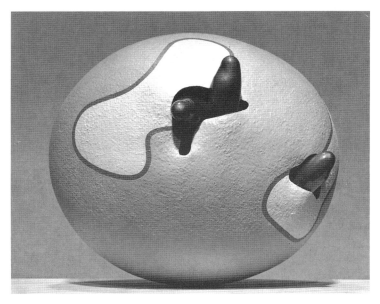

POST-MINIMALISM

John Duff (1943):
Tie Piece, 1969.
Wood and cloth, 41⅛" × 83½" × 76⅜".

In many ways, the art catalogued as "post-minimalist"–for want of a better inclusive term–which emerged in both New York and Los Angeles in the mid-Sixties, represented a more radical rupture with the preceding styles than had either Pop or Minimal, whose attitudes of belligerent aggression were built on the success and assurance of the New York School. As Robert Rauschenberg pointed out, the reason he and his contemporaries turned away from Abstract Expressionism was not out of disenchantment with its accomplishments but because they admired "action painting" too much to be merely imitators of the style that made New York the center of world art for the first time in history. Rauschenberg transmitted to the next generation the possibility of picking up certain Abstract Expressionist themes, such as process and gesture, which post-minimalists interpreted literally. Rauschenberg's unexpected juxtapositions and assemblages of images and materials, especially used, soiled, discarded materials that seemed to have a prior history, were also important to post-minimalists like John Duff and Keith Sonnier.

The task of Abstract Expressionism, exaggerated into a kind of cultural holy war by pop and minimal artists, was to demonstrate the originality and autonomy from European precedent of an independent American art. That this idea was mainly idle propaganda masking the continuing bond of American art to its European antecedents did not much bother either artists or critics, eager to forget how much America still owed to Cubism, Dada and Constructivism, no matter how thoroughly "post-Cubist" the new styles were. By the mid-Sixties, Europe had recovered sufficiently to sponsor lavish international exhibitions. Of special importance were the Venice Biennale and the encyclopedic Documenta exhibitions, held every four or five years in Kassel, West Germany. Subsidized by the Italian and German governments respectively, the two omnibus, trend-setting blockbusters gave those countries an edge in launching new styles promulgated by their own artists which were attractive to younger American artists as well. These artists, unlike the Abstract Expressionists, travelled widely and made comparisons that caused them to be critical of their own culture. Opportunities to work abroad turned a generation into art nomads; it changed their ideas about the permanence of art and its significance both to themselves and to their society. In the meantime, the political alienation created by an unacceptable war had eroded America's sense of itself as a unique and privileged nation obligated to impose its morality and political system internationally in order to realize its mission of a "manifest destiny."

If post-minimalist art has been characterized as "anti-illusionistic" because of the reluctance of its practitioners to disguise the nature of their materials or how they are put together, the reason may be that artists became intent on "demystifying" what they perceived as hypnotizing propaganda. Their project was the intentional disillusionment of an art that left traces of the creative process and emphasized the literal properties of "poor" materials.

Thus commonplace pieces of cloth or scrap metal are deliberately left raw and untransformed by the artist's manipulations. Of course there is much more to post-minimalism than social or political protest. However, we cannot avoid the issue of the overt intention to make impermanent works and art that could not be housed within an official museum or gallery context. In these antagonistic actions there is an implicit negative critique of the political situation and of officially endorsed art. Pop, minimal and color-field painting, by contrast, appear in apparent neutrality, to endorse the status quo. Until recently, the dominance of the formalist approach to criticism has caused many, although certainly not all, critics to refute any connection between art and economic, social and political structures because such a connection would not be "verifiable." However, it is virtually impossible to deal with post-minimal developments in strictly formal terms since that is not how the artists conceived their work. For example, such developments as "anti-formal" or "dematerialized" art, i.e. unstable structures built without permanent connective joining, are hard to understand except as a metaphor for the unpredictability and instability of the social structure itself.

By the mid-Sixties, current events had contradicted any form of optimistic idealism and Utopian notions of order to the extent that "reality" had to be located elsewhere—outside the museum–gallery institutional framework that neutralized any critical dimension.

Keith Sonnier (1941):
Neon and Flocked Glass,
No. 2, 1969.
Neon, flocking, latex,
glass, 72″ × 48″ × 33″.

The primary focus of minimal art was on the specific intrinsic qualities of materials, as subject to gravity, stress and deterioration. This focus, which was not formal but material, permitted art to be isolated from history, or at least from the tradition of art as something beautiful, pleasing, decorative or escapist. Although poverty of means and "found" material suggest the austerity of minimal art, the focus of post-minimal art was quite different. After 1966, the intent on the part of younger artists was to emphasize the fragile, vulnerable, human and transient—all of which are opposed to the values of minimal art. There is a definite degree of poetic and metaphorical allusion in the best post-minimalist art: anatomy and landscape, the body and nature, are both frequently evoked. However, the reaction called forth is not empathy, but brutal confrontation with mortality, decay, contingency, and flux.

In the case of Eva Hesse, terminally ill for the last blazing years of her exemplary creative life, the association with pain, with bandaging, confinement, internal organs, intravenous tubing and traumatic shock is unavoidable once the artist courageously decided to make an intimate, autobiographical art. Bruce Nauman also used himself as material; like Johns, he cast body parts. He also videotaped pointless repetitions of studio behavior such as walking around or bouncing his testicles up and down, which is less shocking than it is a depressing commentary on the vacuity and spiritual emptiness of the moment.

As cultural historian Leo Marx has persuasively written in *The Machine in the Garden*, there is a distinctively antiprogressive streak running throughout the history of American art and literature. In the Sixties, at the height of the proposed marriage between art and technology, the idea of progress, negated by world events, began to seem more questionable than ever to American artists. The lack of any kind of industrial fabrication, even if the material were in fact industrial surplus, in post-minimalism, can be seen as a general critique of the idea of progress through technology. A refusal to create commodities for consumption, the use of dirty, prickly, physically repellent materials and the ironic way technology is used augment such a negative critique. Even when television, sound equipment or neon are included in a work, they are used ironically. The post-minimalist stance is definitively antiprogressive and fundamentally sceptical of any forms of permanence, stability or closure. It is critical as well of the interpretation of "art" as a privileged and value-free way of ordering experience. Although structuralist concepts play a large role in post-minimalist art, the art itself seems to lack that internal scaffolding or external joining that defines a "structure."

Eva Hesse (1936-1970):
Contingent, 1969.
Rubberized cheesecloth, fiberglass,
8 units, each c. 14′ × 3′.

Richard Serra (1939):
Right Angle Prop (Prop Series), 1969.
Lead antimony, plate 72″ × 72″, angle 36″.

For example, the structure of serial imagery in Robert Smithson's or Eva Hesse's repeated modules is compromised by the ephemeral quality of their works. Hesse's fiberglass cylinders collapse in gestures that strike one as metaphors for human exhaustion; Smithson's accumulations of rocks translate the dumping activities of excavations into gallery environments in all their mindless randomness. In their cases, as well as in those of the other artists associated with post-minimalism, the gallery or museum is conceived of as an "environment" with specific characteristics. It is not a neutral container. That the environment either acts on or is acted upon by the art work is central to the post-minimal contextual attitude. For one cannot speak of post-minimalism as either a style or even a sensibility; rather it is an *attitude* toward art as a kind of activity or exercise, accentuating the process of form creation as intentional but not necessarily stable. It is also an attitude toward the world: a relativistic world-view in which art interacts with man and nature rather than existing apart from everyday experience in a static, immortal, unchanging Ivory Tower that is the assumption of any art-for-art's-sake formalist movement.

Minimal and post-minimal art were only ostensibly abstract. Because Carl Andre's "carpets" were made of square plates of common metals obviously not attached to each other, the viewer in whose space such a visual event took place was highly conscious of the fugitive, provisional nature of the work of art. Emphasis on the ephemeral, the changeable and the impermanent reflected the general feeling that in the late Sixties, the unstable social fabric was held together only conditionally or arbitrarily. Richard Serra's lead plate "prop" pieces, made of a material that was visibly heavy, and his constructions of flat or tubular rolled sheets of lead were implicitly dangerous. Their precarious balance suggested imminent collapse, adding an element of danger to the notion of potentiality. That lead is a soft vulnerable metal, responsive to stress to the point of collapsing, can again be seen as a metaphor for the social stress Americans were experiencing as the war and its impact at home strained individuals and institutions.

PERFORMANCE/BODY ART

Lucas Samaras (1936):
Corridor, 1970.
Mirror on woodframe, 7½′ × 50′ × 3½′.

There is some disagreement regarding the exact moment when American art underwent a radical transformation, ceasing to express the optimism, boldness and impact of the styles connected to the international success of Abstract Expressionism, or the sense of a triumphant, economically superior and psychologically self-confident (even self-righteous) post-war America. However, it is clear that some time during the mid-Sixties unmistakable signs of a new aesthetic, one diametrically opposed to Pop

and Minimal art—the two officially reigning Sixties styles—began to manifest themselves. Instead of the glamorous and deliberately blatant images of Pop, the alluring hedonism of color-field painting, or the aggressive toughness of minimal art, a new sensibility, which stressed such qualities as vulnerability, fragility and the ephemeral nature of art, as well as of life, started to emerge. This new work posed questions, rather than providing solutions to the problematic relationships between art and reality, art and other kinds of objects, and art and its physical context. It attempted to deal with time and space, change and mutability in a manner relevant to the moment. Challenging the role of the art object as a tradeable commodity in the late capitalist economic system, art was sometimes conceived more as a kind of "framed" behavior rather than as an unchanging static object. The artist assumed the role of the Stoic philosopher Diogenes, seeking to expose the truth regarding the various social, economic and political structures with which art interacted, and to illuminate hidden contradictions and challenge received ideas. In exposing the elements of the various institutional, critical and aesthetic structures and processes involved with art, post-minimalism effectively deconstructed the meaning of art before this system of analysis was officially announced as dogma in France.

During this questioning period, some artists gave up making anything at all. They turned their attention to analyzing the "language" of art discourse in a variety of conceptual manifestations. The scene was also set to interpret art in a behavioristic manner as a certain kind of activity. Artists like Lucas Samaras demanded viewer participation and disoriented the senses in his mirrored cube. Once entered, the mirrors on all four sides split and fragmented the reflected images of the spectator. In his auto-polaroids, Samaras photographed himself nude as a subject to be manipulated like any other material.

Joan Jonas (1936):
Mirage: The Moon, 1978.
Performance.

Hannah Wilke (1940):
Starification Object Series, 1974.
28 photographs from S.O.S. Mastication Box,
each photo: 6¾″ × 4¼″.

Yvonne Rainer (1934):
This is the story of a woman who...,
1973. Performance.
Yvonne Rainer and John Erdman.

The tradition of Happenings continued throughout the Sixties and Seventies in multi-media performances by artists like Yvonne Rainer and Joan Jonas, who used projected images and sound as well as their own bodies in theater pieces closely related to sculpture. Rainer had been an influential force in shaping the esthetic of both minimal and post-minimal sculpture, which paralleled developments in her performances. As a film-maker, she extended these concerns in a series of heavily textured psychodramas aware of film space as a container or envelope. Sculptor Hannah Wilke used photographs of her own nude body. Emphasizing the vulnerability of female nudity in her feminist performances, she implied a devastating critique of male domination of female creativity and sexuality.

Vito Acconci, Dennis Oppenheim and Chris Burden also made critical, anti-social statements in their performances, which were often calculated to alienate or shock the audience. Acconci attacked taboo themes, masturbating in public and using the American flag as a prop in one of his pieces made in the hostile climate of the last years of the unpopular Vietnam war.

After the public revealed its attraction to sensationalistic exposure, serious artists found more oblique and less titillating forms of protest art.

Vito Acconci (1940):
FOLLOWING PIECE
Activity
'Street Works IV,' Architectural League of New York; October 1-31, 1969.

The terms of the exhibition were: do a piece involving New York streets. My piece, then, was designed with this specific place in mind: on New York streets, I could see myself as a *receiver* of another agent's activity (elsewhere the piece would have had different intentions–in a less populated place, I would have had to consider myself more of an intruder).
Each day, during the month allotted for the show, a person is chosen, at random, in the street, any location.
Each day I follow a different person, as long as I can, until that person enters a private place–his/her home, office, etc. (The following episodes range from two or three minutes–when a person might get into a car, and I'm unable to follow–to six or seven hours–when a person might go to a restaurant, a movie...)
(The next month, there's a follow-up to the FOLLOWING PIECE. Each day a letter is sent to a different person: the letter describes that day's following episode of the previous month. This–and rumor of the general scheme–constitute the reportage (or the aura) of the piece.)

SPACE DIVIDED: THE VOID AND THE FIELD

Sylvia Stone (1928):
Crystal Palace, 1971-1972.
Plexiglass, 78″ × 14′ × 16′.

Richard Serra (1939):
Untitled, 1972.
One hot roll steel plate measuring the distance
of the bisected rectangle (42′); plate then
cut into two equal triangles and placed in opposite
corners.

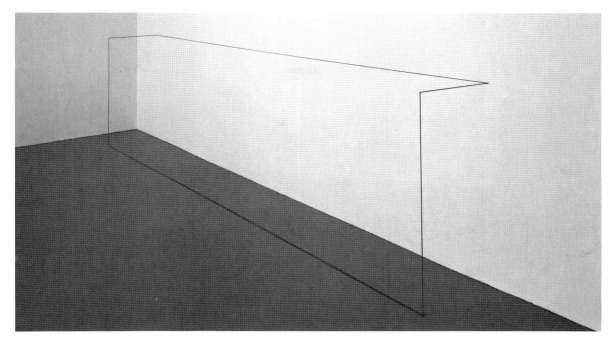

Frederick Sandback (1943):
Untitled 17, 1967.
Horizon grey, elastic cord and steel rod, 35½″ × 16⅜″ × 11′8″.

In the sixties, artists threw into question virtually all certainties regarding the function and identity of the art object. As we have seen, they also questioned its relationship to the context within which their work was exhibited. The museum or gallery was now seen as a "space," the "site" of the work only temporally installed. In a series of influential articles published in *Artforum* in 1976 titled "Inside the White Cube," Brian O'Doherty, who began making performance pieces and environmental works under the name Patrick Ireland, essentially deconstructed the complex interrelationships existing between art and its social, cultural, economic and political context. No more could the museum or gallery be seen as neutral: it had become a specific physical as well as social-cultural "frame" that operated on the perception of the art work with the potential to alter its significance or be altered by it. Floor, ceiling, walls, corners, etc. were considered interactive with the work of art, which no longer was necessarily an object, but could be an environment just as well.

Space could be divided or filled, excluding the spectator entirely from entering the gallery or museum exhibition. Sylvia Stone's fragile glass sculptures were physical presences, yet close to dematerialized form in their transparency. Fred Sandback's string pieces, which simply delineated an absence of solid structure, eluded classification as objects altogether. To change the status of art as object into art as environment was, as we have remarked, one strategy to outwit growing speculation in art as a consumer commodity. Richard Serra's steel plate pieces dividing the gallery space were "site specific," i.e. they were made exclusively for a specific temporary installation and would have little meaning elsewhere.

Among the most daring anti-form projects was Walter De Maria's earth-filled dirt room which entirely excluded the viewer from entering its space. A pioneer of earthworks, De Maria mixed hostility and surprise in a series of environments that ultimately brought him to work outdoors, outside the gallery-museum context entirely.

Walter De Maria (1935):
The New York Earth Room, 1977.
250 cubic yards of earth and earth mix (peat and bark) weighing 280,000 pounds; covering an area of 3,600 square feet of floor space to a depth of 22 inches.

EARTHWORKS AND LAND ART

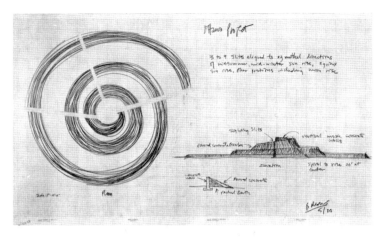

Robert Morris (1931):
Ottawa Project, May 1970.

The ongoing debate of nature vs. culture was carried on in Europe as well as America, as the land itself was threatened, along with whole species, by the advances of technology. If "advanced" was the dominant encomium of the early Sixties, then "entropy" was the favored expression of many artists associated with post-minimalism. Introduced by Robert Smithson in his article "Entropy and the New Monuments," published in the June 1966

issue of *Artforum*, the idea that matter tends toward increasing disintegration and disorganization or "entropy," a concept borrowed from nuclear physics, provided artists with a rationale for altering the procedures and goals of art. Among the favored art world texts of the moment was Morse Peckham's *Man's Rage for Chaos*. Peckham held that man is naturally attracted to create chaos rather than order.

Minimal art and Pop art had been clean, orderly styles, in keeping with the indigenous American Puritan-Protestant ethic. The "well-built" was intrinsic to its esthetic. Post-minimalism, on the other hand, was an assault on good housekeeping: it was literally a mess, spilled, poured, dropped, splashed, draped, melted and crumpled. It was uncontrolled or deliberately uncontrollable as well as apparently uncollectable. Above all it was *dirty*–like the dirty war being fought in Indochina, for example. Indeed, it could be argued that earthworks, in which artists use the soil itself as their material, began with Walter De Maria, Robert Smithson and Robert Morris literally filling galleries up with dirt. These provocative and psychologically regressive acts once again paralleled high-level official behavior that was transparently infantile. Such actions were converted to more productive ends in earthworks, pioneered by Smithson. Originally designed as land reclamation projects, they must also be seen as part of the international ecology movement.

Robert Smithson (1938-1973):
Spiral Jetty, Great Salt Lake, Utah, April 1970.

Robert Smithson (1938-1973):
Closed Mirror Square, 1969.
Rock salt, mirrors and glass.

Richard Serra's pessimism regarding industrial society and the potential of technology not for progress but for destruction is summed up in his statement for the 1970 catalogue of the *Art and Technology* exhibition held at the Los Angeles County Museum of Art: "Technology is a form of toolmaking, body extension. Technology is not art and not invention. It does not concern itself with the undefined, the inexplicable. It deals with the affirmation of its own making. Technology is what we do to the Black Panthers and the Vietnamese under the guise of advancement in a materialistic theology."

The constant shadow of the war, ecological catastrophes and the apocalyptic images they generated fell over those years in a way that seems hard to recreate now that television has succeeded in making catastrophe entertaining and saleable. Serra himself prophesied this in his video experiments involved with the function of advertising, his 1973 video piece "Television Delivers People." Sonnier and Nauman both incorporated video into their works, but more as behavioristic feedback than as anti-propaganda, throwing the viewer back on his own perceptions and frustrating attempts to escape the present moment. The spirit of the time was perhaps most succinctly summed up

by Philip Leider, then editor of *Artforum*, in an article in the September 1970 issue of that magazine, archly titled "How I Spent my Summer Vacation or Art and Politics in Nevada, Berkeley, San Francisco and Utah." In the piece, Leider describes his visit to the sites of earthworks by Michael Heizer and Robert Smithson and reproduces a conversation he had with Serra:

"What, we argued, was the most revolutionary thing to do? Serra was wondering whether the times were not forcing us to a completely new set of ideas about what an artist was and what an artist did. Revolution was the most often used word I ran into this summer. Nobody used it to mean the transfer of political powers from one class to another. Most of the time it seemed to refer to those activities which would most expeditiously bring America to her senses and force her to stop the war, end racism and begin to take the lead among nations in rescuing the planet from the certain destruction toward which it is heading.

"Smithson said: 'All those sins. And here's 2000 coming so near. Sin everywhere. The dead river, with its black oil slime. The crucified river instead of the crucified man. When do you think they'll start burning polluters at the stake?'"

LAND ART AND SITE SCULPTURE

Once Michael Heizer and Walter De Maria found the means to realize their immense outdoor projects which altered nature, land art and site sculpture became a major avant-garde development. As Robert Smithson, who died in a plane crash while completing an earthwork in Amarillo, Texas, in 1973, wrote: "Nature is never finished. When a finished work of twentieth-century sculpture is placed in an eighteenth-century garden, it is absorbed by the ideal representation of the past, thus reinforcing political and social values that are no longer with us. Many parks and gardens are re-creations of the lost paradise or Eden, and not the dialectical sites of the present. Parks and gardens are pictorial in their origin—landscapes created with natural materials rather than paint. The scenic ideals that surround even our national parks are carriers of a nostalgia for heavenly bliss and eternal calmness.

"Apart from the ideal gardens of the past, and their modern counterparts—national and large urban parks, there are the more infernal regions—slag heaps, strip mines,

Michael Heizer (1944):

Compression Line, 1968 (dismantled).
Wood in playa surface, 16′ × 2′ × 2′.
El Mirage Dry Lake, Mojave Desert, California.

Complex One/City, 1972-1974.
Concrete, steel and compacted earth, 23′6″ × 140′ × 110′.
Garden Valley, Nevada.

Walter De Maria (1935):
The Lightning Field, 1971-1977.
Quemado, New Mexico.

Michael Heizer (1944):
Rift, 1968 (deteriorated).
No. 1 of Nine Nevada Depressions
1 ½ ton displacement on playa surface, 52′ × 1′6″ × 1′.
Jean Dry Lake, Nevada.

and polluted rivers. Because of the great tendency toward idealism, both pure and abstract, society is confused as to what to do with such places. Nobody wants to go on a vacation to a garbage dump."

Despite Smithson's pronouncements, "site-seeing" has become a chic pastime for the art world elite. Collectors as well as critics and scholars visit De Maria's remote *Lightning Field* in New Mexico and Heizer's concrete complex *The City* in the Nevada desert, a project he has been working on since 1971, which remains to be completed. At the *Lightning Field*, apocalyptic overtones of potential destruction are implied in attracting bolts of lightning to metal rods; such an act may presage meteorological catastrophe, as the weather becomes as sinister and unpredictable as the possibility of nuclear war. It is against such unpredictability that Heizer's bunker-like *The City* appears to be a refuge. Thus, ambiguity, irony, and the confrontation with man-made or natural destruction has become the central concern of avant-garde artists, whom André Gide once described as "the antenna of the race."

THE AFFIRMATION OF SCULPTURE
ARTE POVERA

CIRCLE IN ALASKA.
BERING STRAIT DRIFTWOOD ON THE ARCTIC CIRCLE – 1977.

Richard Long (1945):
Circle in Alaska. Bering Strait
Driftwood on the Arctic Circle, 1977.

Behavioural art, ephemeral by definition, can only have access to communication when memorized by photography. Actions that were confined to the time and place of their staging would have no effect if the simultaneous publication of photographs did not spread them throughout the world. Paradoxically, just at the moment when art is trying to escape from the museum by rejecting the form of the work of art, artists most need the platform of museums to pass on the concepts motivating their change of attitude.

The link formed by photography is equally important for those artists who act directly on nature herself, creating what is known as Land Art. Their creations can only be perceived by the memory of the photograph. That is true of Richard Long, part of whose art consists in punctuating his cross-country journeys by marking them with primary signs made with materials found on the spot. They consist of signs of stay (circle, cross, square) and signs of movement (line, spiral, zigzag). He photographs all his works and publishes them in albums in which the photographic evidence becomes "art per se" for the spectator.

The exhibition "When Attitudes Become Form" inaugurated at the Kunsthalle in Berne in March 1969 caused an unprecedented scandal. By uniting the extreme avant-garde of the United States and Europe, Harald Szee-mann proved that antagonism between the creative artists of the two continents no longer existed and that above all art was changing fundamentally, concept and praxis becoming more important than the aesthetics of the resultant "object." Side by side with minimalists and post-minimalists, Joseph Beuys and the main Italian representatives of Arte Povera made a spectacular appearance.

This change of attitude was the consequence of the political revolution which shook the universities in 1967 and 1968. Originating from a radical criticism of our highly industrialized society, they opposed to it an extremist operational model, based mainly on the "values" which that society had demoted or rejected–liberty, consciousness that the unexpected may happen, pleasure... Henceforth artists could no longer separate the product of the aesthetic act from awareness and understanding of its technical constraints. Definition of the object would count for less than demonstration of the energy used in creating it.

In the fifties and sixties, Italy, with the help of the United States, experienced a vast financial and industrial miracle. Arte Povera appeared as a reaction to the phantasms of wealth, calling for a new political and aesthetic commitment to rejected and waste materials, responding to the images of Utopia by concrete experimentation with the real.

Manzoni, who died in 1963, opened the way by effacing, often ironically, the artist's intentions and sensitiveness behind the creative process, so that taking hold of reality became a poetic fact in itself. This "aestheticizing" of the real and the rediscovery of the value of experience was taken up by the Turin artists led by Merz, Kounellis and Zorio. The critic Germano Celant became the movement's propagandist and theoretician. He grouped their individual approaches under the generic title Arte Povera, which he defined at Bologna in 1968 as the desire to substitute for representation the rule governing its presentation: "The *poor* artist is an alchemist. He reveals the magic (of chemical reactions and compositions), the inexorableness (of vegetable growth), the precariousness (of material), the falsehood (of the senses), the realness (of a natural desert, a forgotten lake, the sea, the snow, the forest), the instability (of a bio-physical reaction). Arte Povera is at the same time a latent possibility in the material and a way of living in art."

In these "sculptures" the essence of the material should engender the logic of the development of the work, which is to be achieved in its actual presentation. The creation no longer emanates from the idea, but from the artist's direct engagement with the actual materials. The products of Arte Povera are not represented in a stylized manner, but presented in their immediate practical character to rediscover the primary reality of nature and man. Thus they imply a new union between art and life for both artist and spectator.

Mario Merz built his first igloos in 1968. He thinks that the igloo represents the ideal organic form. It is at once world and house. The fragility of its structure and of the elements which cover it place outside and inside in a dialectical relationship which restores a social dimension to man:

Gilberto Zorio (1944):
Piombi, 1968.
Lead plates, acids, copper tubing,
3′1½″ × 8′2½″ × 5′4½″.

"When I made the igloo," said Merz, "I acted with the power of the imagination, because the igloo is not only its elementary form, it is also a prop for the imagination. The igloo is a synthesis, a complicated image, because I torment the elementary imagined idea of the igloo (the one I have inside me). I believe that the igloo has two facets, one concrete, the other more mental."

As for Gilberto Zorio, he is essentially attracted by demonstrating energy through tension. As he put it in 1972: "The theme of my work is energy in both the physical and mental sense. My works are energy in themselves, because they are always works which live, works in action or works which time is going to modify. In my first works, this energy is expressed in a very physical form, at the level of chemical reaction, as a result of which the work is not completed, but continues to live by itself, while I become the spectator of its own reactions and those of the public. And that is the signification of the concept of process in my works."

For the Arte Povera artists, space is not to be taken as something in itself, but as a reality putting different people in touch with each other.

Mario Merz (1925):
Igloo of Giap, 1968.
Assemblage, height 3′11″, diameter 6′7″.

279

WORKING OF MATERIALS FOR THEIR OWN SAKE

Bernar Venet (1941):
Indeterminate Line, 1985.
Steel, 8'2" × 12'6" × 6'6".

Now that we have reached the early 1970s–a past still too close to be interpreted with historical detachment–we shall have to modify our method of approach. Instead of critical analysis, we shall adopt a more experimental, less exhaustive approach, based essentially on examples bringing out the new fields of exploration open to sculpture. Understanding the fundamental ideas in question becomes all the more necessary because they will indicate the predominance of sculpture over other fields of expression, such as painting and architecture, to which critics have often been tempted to give pride of place.

When it becomes the locus of a direct physical experience of matter and space, sculpture actually exhibits a new function. Here is an extremely significant phenomenon, because in all ages the function assigned to a sculpture has directly determined the character of its forms, its space and its material. This state of affairs is now simply reversed; after a century of experimentation, it is the sculpture itself which reveals its contemporary purpose.

Going beyond minimalism and Arte Povera, the next step was to experiment with a sculpture which would be sculpture and nothing else, the results of a direct confrontation between the artist and the material he is presenting. In this new approach the object would exist solely in the way it was worked and in its relationship with space, discarding any attempt to express an ideological or emotional content. By reducing creation to praxis, appearance is effaced in being and the work is seen as a present demonstrating the intrinsic and physical qualities of the real that is worked on. But by refusing to be the model of a representation, this work (as Carl Andre and Richard Serra had already sensed) becomes the field of a new experience involving a total renewal of perception.

This staging or presentation of work is a direct reaction to the dematerialization of a certain kind of conceptual art and the random components resulting from Happenings. Owing to its resistance and permanence, metal (especially in its most recent form, Cor-Ten, which integrates colour directly with form, oxydation acting as a vital protective element against corrosion by the air) is indispensable as a favourite experimental material for the creation of forms meant to interrogate rather than convince. Forging, twisting, cutting out means emphasizing the nuclear energy of the material, its centripetal or centrifugal dynamism, it means going to meet the reality of its weight, its resistance, its possibilities of equilibrium.

Bernar Venet only began to work with metal and space after a lengthy period of experimentation with a sign-form reduced to its mathematical definition in which he gave proof of his "aim to exhibit a figure that was monosemic and hence not subject to interpretation." Such an approach, allied to a desire to eliminate all subjective components, would have condemned him to systematization, had not the discovery of the plasticity of cut out forms revealed to him the possibilities of the line in space, an indeterminate line which opened up to him a new field of action: sculpture. "Since my first indeterminate line in 1979, anyone can see that a body of work has developed on this theme and that I have extended my activity to the field of mural sculpture and more recently to that of monumental sculpture... For me these developments meet a need to attack new terrains, to keep perpetually on the move. Sticking to an idea, shutting oneself up in a style, means believing that you have found a truth at last and thinking you have got it right, but it actually means you have understood nothing, because truth exists nowhere, except perhaps in the constant search for it."

This need for experimentation based on a rigorous critical analysis of the constituents also dominates the painting of the seventies, but it has more decisive consequences in sculpture in which it allows a reappropriation of the real in its most elementary, direct and fundamental form. Henceforth, sculptors started to make fewer references to the past of their art; instead they re-embarked on the adventurous voyage of construction from its very beginnings. Such sculptures may sometimes look like fragments or ruins to us and in fact they are inspired more by the desire to re-live history than to quote it.

Recognized in the context of the French Support/ Surface movement, Bernard Pagès explores fundamentals based on stone and concrete constructions. In 1979, after a whole series of environments on the ground, Pagès tackled the theme of the column. In the agglomerations of stones,

Bernard Pagès (1940):
Column, 1982.
Unworked and sawn stone, coloured and carved concrete.
Height 8'7" high.

Ulrich Rückriem (1938):
Untitled, 1983-1984.
Granite of Normandy, 8'2½" high, 5'11" square.

bricks and cement, he rediscovers the instinct of the first constructors. "A column," he said, "is only a component, it is a fragment of something to come. It invites us to imagine something else, a threshold, a lintel." The column is based on verticality, but Pagès turns it upside down by deliberately confronting base and capital. This possibility of inversion enabled him to emphasize simultaneously its relationship with the ground, its unfinished state or the possibility of a continuation.

The German Ulrich Rückriem shows himself even more radical by bringing out the natural, using raw, cracked, broken and polished material. His artistic venture began in 1968. Since then, "the theme of dividing a block of stone in a certain way and restoring it to its original form is still full of surprises for me and keeps me on the alert. In one way or another, all the subsequent themes have a link with this experiment which is the most essential for me." Rückriem reduces sculpture to no more than a base in search of a unity and a lost function, but in which coherence and division into elementary forms are opposed. As he says "geometric shapes such as square, circle, etc., had, have and will continue to have the symbolic power which man conferred on them and they will never lose it."

281

PLACES OF MEMORY

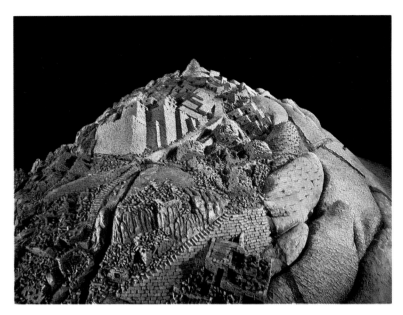

Charles Simonds (1945):
Age, detail, 1982-1983.
Clay, wood, plastic, 9'10" high.

Once the problematics which had made the avant-gardes between 1910 and 1960 so dynamic were exhausted, they left a vacuum which called for a revaluation of history. When a civilization loses its vital force, it is threatened with extinction if it lacks the strength to go back to its origins. Public acceptance of the "it goes without saying" attitude propagated by the media which reinforce conformism by their oppressive power, gradually caused a sense of uneasiness entailing a voyage back through history to rediscover the mysteries of existence. From the end of the sixties, Performances, Land Art, Body Art and Arte Povera reflect the need to escape from the inexorable development of technology, as well as the need

Robert Morris (1931):
Observatory, 1971, reconstructed 1977.
Earth, grass, wood, steel, granite, diameter c. 300'.
Oostelijk Flevoland, Holland.

to encourage the generative potentialities of the act as opposed to its virtuosity, opposing the real to its representations and meaning to habits.

The next step was to interrogate the actual course of history to escape from the consequences to which its development condemns us. To break rational postulates and strip the "true" of its cultural trappings, artists analysed the past, emphasizing the faults and setbacks they noticed in the course of an inflexible development. Inspired by scientific techniques taken from archaeology and anthropology, driven by their intuition, they rediscovered the demands of social life, interrogated the myths which determined essential choices by confronting the traces present in ruins or the remains of human activities.

There is nothing ultra-conservative about this approach, because it seeks to renew the perspective of history, to vitalize mythological thought and revive the potentialities discarded by reason or opportunity. This reconsideration of the present opens up new perspectives by reminding man of the limits of his autonomy. Such an interrogation of the past also encourages the reconsideration of the means of making and the return of spiritual renewal.

This approach also includes a revaluation of the functions of memory, because history is not total recall so much as an interpretation that is often artificial, biassed or fragmentary. To relive what has been distorted, to work on less or absence, to confront the product and its reproduction, are so many experiences renewing our awareness of the permanent. This return to an archetypal memory takes us away from the notion of progress where art and civilization are concerned, at the same time that it restores the dimensions of experience, of thought, of the physical and the spiritual.

Faced with the Greco-Roman dream, the French artists Anne and Patrick Poirier calculate the threats which weigh on the present; they seek their identity in an apocalyptic context. But studying the ruins of buried metropolises also enables them to rediscover the social sense in which all existence is illusory. Their reconstruction of ancient sites is "an excuse, a way of escaping from time or rather from the present," they say. "We take an interest in certain archetypes of thought and behaviour which are inevitably found in the past and are often hidden by the present. But who is to say that they will not also recur in the future?... What really interests us is not the past, but the timeless: the archetypal that is permanent yet ephemeral in us and in different cultures, and the 'why and wherefore' of this permanence and this fragility."

Distancing oneself, as the American Charles Simonds shows, is also a question of scale, of perspective. In his painstaking miniaturized reconstructions of imaginary archaeological sites (for "imaginary tiny people"), he presents the foundations of urban and communal life by working in public places to stimulate a direct reaction by the spectator. A builder of ruins, he restores a presence to the death that the modern town attempts to stifle, because forgetting death marks the end of a civilization, whereas the meaning we give it is at the origin of all social life. Simonds is not trying to objectify the history of humanity, but rather to underline the discontinuity of time which leaves man confronting the same eternal mysteries. But our environment has been so disfigured by over-exploitation that it became a matter of urgency to rediscover the reality of life, its rhythms and the transformations it under-

Anne and Patrick Poirier (1942 and 1942):
Hall of Black Architectures: Ausée, 1975-1976.
Charcoal, 33′ × 16½′ × 19¾″.

goes. A newly acquired ecological conscience directly inspired a reaction against the way in which industry and technology over-exploit life for utilitarian ends, proving that the worst danger is "denaturing."

American law makes it obligatory for the owners of quarries and mines to restore the sites they have ravaged. Bob Morris takes advantage of this to obtain subsidies for enormous Land Art projects. His construction of new landscapes is intended to bring vegetation back to places where it had been destroyed. In other works he confronts the natural landscape with "cultural elements" by interventions which interrogate the signs left by the history of human thought. The recreation of an "archaeological" observatory enables each one of us to rediscover the relationship between the life of nature and cosmic infinity.

In the past the sculptor had nearly always worked against nature. His work consisted basically in extracting from a block a form relating to an imagined model which conceptualized the consciousness that his period gave him of himself and of the cosmos. Then, in the twentieth century, the real slowly and imperceptibly infiltrated sculpture in the form of objects and through the use of space. Here taking possession of nature undergoes a radical change, the real presenting itself as the locus of the lived experience of the immanent.

The Provençal sculptor Jean Amado was stimulated to rediscover history after a period of complicated technical experiments. Taking ceramics as his point of departure, the study of working and firing clay soon led him to an original use of concrete. Working it by hand, piece by piece, he covers the whole history of architecture and social life. In his sculptures which are made of hundreds of assembled fragments, the means of internal communication (galleries, passages) is closely related to the openings on the outsides, which often resemble troglodyte dwellings or desert metropolises, the most natural forms invented by human communities. Amado's constructions may equally well recall prehistoric archaeological sites or the remains that researchers might find of our present-day civilization in a thousand years or so. An internal circuit exists in the mysterious depths opened up by the articulations of volume in which human communication is renewed by being at a historical and material remove. In increasingly monumental dimensions, Amado creates architecture which reverses the Utopias of eighteenth-century architects by emphasizing the essential qualities of space and material, and of the elementary and vital in their own reality, completely transcending symbolism or ideology.

Jean Amado (1922):
Doubt and Stone, 1984.
Basalt cement, 6′6″ × 11′ × 3′11″.

SPACE AS REALITY

Jean-Pierre Raynaud (1939):
The Artist's House at La Celle-Saint-Cloud, near Paris.

One of the objectives of creative artists has always been to give material form and meaning to something which was still on the unconscious plane until they started work. Already implicated by their confrontation with handling their materials, sculptors still had to adopt a position vis-à-vis space itself, the constituent dimension of their art and an essential one since the invention of the assemblage. Qualifying space aesthetically, giving an opportunity to confront the uncapturable so as to show its poetic side amounted to leading man to assess his presence and potentialities. It meant realizing materially what Merleau-Ponty formulated as an axiom in his *Phénoménologie de la perception*: "I experience myself in experiencing the world."

We all use space throughout the day: urban space, the space of nature or our own private space, but always in circumstances which obliterate its reality by transforming it into distance, work-place, dwelling-place, and so on. To explore space properly the artist must isolate it by making it non-functional and transforming it into an environment, so that when the spectator is immersed in that environment he rediscovers the possibility of experiencing himself mentally and physically through the qualities of volume, materials and light and through a different experience of space-time.

Experiencing oneself by experiencing the world is what the French sculptor Jean-Pierre Raynaud proposes. His most famous work is still the house he built for himself, an edifice which functions by breaking all the rules. It does not comply with any traditional criterion, but forces the inhabitants to move, live and breathe in a different way. Originally a painter, Raynaud transposes into the third dimension a concept already exemplified in Mondrian's work, especially in his "squares on the point." They were the first pictures not to present themselves as spaces concentrating what is external to them, but rather as points of energy, balance and tension radiating an order which would control all the surrounding space.

After his 6-inch square tiles of gleaming white faience, of the commonest, cheapest type found in hospitals, lavatories and laboratories, Raynaud moved from painting to volume, invading and arranging his own space. "I invent nothing," he said. "I am a catalyst. I take objects on the outside and restore them with the least transformation possible. I simply try to show their poetic side." Thus Raynaud creates spaces of meditation, order, purity and silence in which light, by its sources and in its reflections, finds a radiation that is both real and unexpected. Repeated ad infinitum, the geometry of the white tile outlined in black enables him to create "a maximum of tension with a minimum of elements to achieve extreme complexity with simplicity, the irrational by the rational, gentleness by power," as Georges Duby has written.

A landscape artist by training, Raynaud does not create nature, but allows a new vision of it through the openings he creates, the spaces he opens up for it and his settings.

Klaus Rinke (1939):
Project for a Sculpture in Homage to Bachelard, 1984.
Photomontage.

Christo (1935):
Running Fence, 1972-1976.
Steel poles, steel cables, woven nylon.
Height 18 ft., overall length 24 ½ miles.
Sonoma and Marin counties, California (dismantled).

These go from the dead tree burning in a hearth to his focussing on the growth of a tree through a window, by way of a fountain which nurtures an oasis of greenery. Here the absence of earth becomes a hymn to life.

This need for the experience of place is also the stimulus behind Christo's work, as well as giving it colossal dimensions (his *Running Fence* is 25 miles long). But he works indirectly, concealing features (of landscapes, etc.) the better to show them off. Christo Javacheff, a Bulgarian by birth, interrogates our knowledge and the usages of culture by provisional ephemeral transformations of what our vision and our existence have made commonplace. In the last century, the monument represented the image that power sought to give of itself. Christo's monuments look like unanchored flotsam underlining our inability to conceive of man and the world. All his works tend to a mnemonic praxis which restores the reality of things, as well as their form and function, to their rightful place. Christo's works may resemble the products of Land Art superficially, but they are not the same. They have a more precise social connotation, because they are not sited in the desert, but precisely where they disturb, i.e. where they have political implications, at the intersection of the urban fabric, on sites threatened by technological planning.

Christo began with packaging (wrapped landscapes, etc.). As an immigrant, he is marked by the ominous presence of frontiers, those political barriers which artificially dismember the reality of physical geography. Concealment and veiling means both exorcising fear and showing how image and function obliterate nature. Christo is an archaeologist working the wrong way round. He does not dig up the past, but hides the present to restore a value to situations which the consequence of his actions allows to him reappropriate, with absence emphasizing the importance and quality of presence.

The German Klaus Rinke first came to landscape after a series of actions involving water and only recently could he execute the sculptures of his dreams, enabling him to "group" the results of his work, "to meditate with and by it." Rinke rapidly abandoned abstraction for action: "When you said abstraction, you saw a bottle on a table with some sort of liquid in it. The bottle did not represent the bottle but what was inside it. In this dialectic, the bottle was the liquid. Without liquid, the bottle did not exist. It became a surrogate for reality." And so he became a water sculptor, because it is a vital product, now under so many ecological threats. "I often acted as the celebrant of enormous ceremonies at exhibitions and museums, filling buckets from a tap, emptying and filling things..." And today these ceremonies assume monumental form, homage to a grandiose natural phenomenon fixed in space and time.

SCULPTING WITH THE REAL

Herbert Bayer (1900-1985):
Mill Creek Canyon Earthworks, 1979-1982.
2½ acres, Kent, Washington.

Isamu Noguchi (1904):
Water Source, California Scenario, detail.
Sandstone.
Costa Mesa, California.

We must stand at a distance to evaluate the causes and consequences of the crises which shake society. We have already made several references to the revolts which shook the West at the end of the sixties and were to entail a radical change of attitude by creative artists. Nevertheless, we must re-examine more analytically these events and their economic origins to assess the decisive effects they were to have on the evolution of sculpture, effects which were indeed to make it the dominant artistic expression of our time.

The extraordinary financial and industrial expansion which followed the Second World War rapidly created a capitalist, materialist Utopia which the dramas of decolonization and the revolts of the satellite countries could not shake. However that Utopia could not avoid a bad attack of guilty conscience, made worse by the threat to world fuel supplies. 1968 was the year which saw the tragic public demonstration of doubt and revolt against the privileges of technology and the economy which were now solely at their own service. Distrust of the reigning system suddenly discredited functionalism and planning—the best agents of scientism. The West had to reassess its values and art did not emerge from the shock unscathed. Artistic practices, which had fallen prey to exaltation of the object and the formalist ideology of progress, were

reversed. Artists felt the need to manifest their disenchantment by proposing creation as the privileged place of the criticism of behaviour, the space of other perspectives, the object of relativity or the environment of communication. The new forms of expression which resulted, Performances, Environments, Land Art, were so utterly different that they were categorized under the generic title of non-art. The latter resulted in artists taking in hand the essential cultural problems which the previous ideological structure and traditional means could only include marginally and episodically. By its experimentation with the real, putting place and time on stage, favouring the present, non-art turned away from the memory preserved by museums at the same time that it helped us to rediscover man and nature. But this rejection of conventional artistic forms also coincided with a new form of primitivism.

We know how much the development of contemporary art owes to *Japonisme*, and the influences of Negro and Oceanic art. To renew the relation between art and nature, the artists of the sixties, who protested against the way in which culture had travestied nature until it threatened to wipe it out, returned to a prehistoric primitivism. Their move was parallel to that which was reflected on the political level by the appearance of ecological thinking that defended nature from its enslavement by science. The primitive references adopted by these new creators were Celtic in the case of the Europeans and Indian in the case of the Americans. They were often more important at the symbolic and spiritual than the formal level, because the idea was rather to rediscover the profound meaning of life than to renew aesthetics.

Anchoring oneself in a new awareness of nature and the real, appropriating space and time became all the more urgent because modernity, especially the town, had completely denaturalized society. In fact, under the restrictions of the economy and industrial planning in the name of false functional requirements (ordinances, rules, etc.), human space was gradually transformed into inhuman space. Architects, town planners, sociologists, and jurists became the servants of an administrative machine which crushed them and forced them to stifle individual aspirations instead of meeting them. And even the concepts of planning, functionalism and integration reveal their vanity when the town shows that it has lost its soul after the scientific mirage has faded. Each individual then recognizes that he has been driven into a sense of a loss of reality by an outrageous proliferation of the mass media, which has turned him into a consumer victim. The American Fleischner reintroduced nature to the town by making ironic travesties of the civic monuments intended to celebrate and honour the lives of great men on sites for observing natural phenomena that were threatened.

Realizing that their sick practice of homogenization was no longer able to contain the needs and contradictions of our society, some architects were quick to try to restore to their constructions their specificity and even a symbolic dimension.

But it was two formerly Constructivist artists, Herbert Bayer and Isamu Noguchi, who were among the first to assert in urban space the need and the possibilities of a new sculpture, bringing into play both nature and the physical and perceptive reactions of man. Trained in pre-war Germany at the Bauhaus, where he also taught, Bayer worked towards the definition of functional art. At the age of eighty, he finally had the opportunity to carry out a town

Robert Irwin (1928):
Nine Spaces, Nine Trees, 1983.
Mock purple plum trees, nylon coated fencing, concrete.
Public Safety Building Plaza, Seattle, Washington.

planning programme (for thirty years he had had a presentiment that this would happen, as the chronology of his projects attests). Laying out an area of land containing a system of reservoirs enabled him to construct a monumental space-itinerary and transform it into a poetic place, to substitute the sculpture *of* a park for a garden with sculpture in it.

As from 1950, but especially during recent years, Noguchi has been able to display his full abilities as a sculptor of space. He had already revived the Constructivist and Surrealist approaches by his knowledge of traditional Japanese art (its respect for materials and attention to the most secret and elemental qualities of life) but he seems genuinely revolutionary in his "sculpture" of places. Drawing directly on the spiritual Zen tradition of miniature landscapes, Noguchi works with the materials of nature and space itself to create spaces in the midst of contemporary American buildings which renew the potentialities and function of sculpture, something the inventors of Land Art were quick to copy when they were asked to work in public spaces. Instead of "an object to be looked at," sculpture became "a space to live in."

THE EXPERIENCE OF PERCEPTION

Mary Miss (1944):
Field Rotation, 1981.
Wood, steel, gravel, earth,
on 5 acre site.
Central well 60′ sq.
and 7′ deep.
Governors' University,
Park Forest South, Illinois.

The outcome of experimentation with raw materials or born in the desert (Land Art, etc.), present-day sculpture by transforming itself from an "object to be looked at" into "a space to live in" leaves the domain of culture to take its place in the reality of nature and the city. There it finds functions other than decorative or commemorative by demanding spectator participation after abandoning verticality to explore horizontality. Renouncing the visual conquest of space and the void for an experience valuing physical contact in situations that are flexible rather than definitive, this new sculpture asserts itself as the dominant sculpture of our time. Although architecture, sculp-

ture and painting were always closely associated, they never reached the summit of their possibilities at the same time. Whereas contemporary architecture and painting seem to have provisionally exhausted their problematics by electing to quote themselves (a Mannerist temptation found in the terms describing their most recent movements, which always start with the highly significant prefixes neo- or post-), sculpture finds a new impulse in its way of reinventing the real which simultaneously gives it another function–becoming the locus of a real experience of space. This experimentation is opposed to the illusionist space which painting no longer assumes since it has refused

Nancy Holt (1938): Sun Tunnels, 1973-1976.
View from the darkened interior of one of the tunnels, and general view.
Concrete, each pipe 18′ long, 9′ in diameter.
The Great Basin Desert, near Lucin, Utah.

to recognize itself as "a window open to the world." And when painting, which has held hegemony over the visual since the Renaissance, can no longer bring the world to the surface of the canvas, the role of sculpture becomes fundamental by putting itself forward as an experience different from nature, a physical, direct, immediate experience situated in a place and real time and making it possible to bring the world to the scale of our possibilities and our desires by giving us a different awareness. And was not that always the ultimate purpose of the most vital creations?

Thus this sculpture directs the spectator to a new way of living, to an immediate relationship with nature, enabling him to escape the division between mind and body imposed by culture. Abandoning self-enclosed volume, this sculpture (for better or worse we must still call it that) develops on the human scale, blends with the environment it competes with to renew the concept of it by sending us back directly to the understanding of life and its changes of rhythm. Meeting people where they live and work, the artist proposes above all a field of communication in which participation is given its true worth. The change in our consciousness of space and time effected by our civilization embraces the search for a different order in which rhythm and dynamism are as imperative as the free choice of the constituent materials. The individual must take the measure of his environment every time he modifies his own conception of himself.

Space may be either the frame for the work or the means of relating it to the nature whose mysteries it translates, the field of a phenomenal experience or the reservoir of materials meeting the tireless thirst for consumption of a society which denatures everything it touches. But because the artist expresses himself in real space—which also becomes the cultural space of creation and its consumption—it em-phasizes the complexity of the relationship between man and nature, thus questioning itself about the status of the real and the media that reflect it. The context of a representation cannot be separated from what lies outside the context. The experience of place is mainly that which helps us to see its way of seeing, to be "another way of being." And expression in and by the real still leaves room for the fortuitous, the imponderable and the unforeseen.

Nancy Holt, an American artist inspired by the remains of archaeological observatories, teaches us to reassess our dimensions when faced with the infinity of the universe by creating spaces where light shining through fissures allows us to evaluate the movement of sun and earth, and even grasp the "movement of the spheres" by pinpointing equinoxes and solstices, as was done at Abu Simbel, Stonehenge and pre-Columbian sites.

The environments of the American Mary Miss propose a physical and spiritual experimentation with elementary notions such as fullness, emptiness, depth, direction, in an arranged and deliberate structure, whereas Richard Serra interrogates our perceptual possibilities by presenting balance, weight and movement. Here, sculpture takes the place of architecture by suppressing its functionalism, because, as Serra says, "architecture is the only plastic language which offers the possibility of walking in, looking at and changing space." When architects no longer fulfil this essential function, sculptors revive it in works which abandon the object for space. *Clara-Clara*, made of two inverted conic segments, creates an area allowing us to apprehend the speed and mobility of the levels. Now that it has descended from its plinth, the new sculpture becomes an inhabited place with no other function but to suggest to the spectator the need to revaluate its potentialities and reality.

Richard Serra (1939):
Clara-Clara, 1983.
Cor-Ten steel.
Installation in the Jardin des Tuileries, Paris.

SCULPTURE REDISCOVERS A FUNCTION

This sculpture in and for "place" offers a social alternative to the cult of the object and this alternative once more poses the question of commissioning sculpture. Works on such a scale can only be carried out if they are financed by private patrons or public bodies. Incidentally, their value lies not so much in ownership as in a value expressed in terms of usage and communication. The very evolution of sculpture demands that these constructions become public and permanent because they are necessary. We have already seen how the commissioning of prestigious monumental works of art became imperative as from the fifties. It took some time before this sculpture-cum-landscape acquired a definitive form and the struggle has only begun. Since every great work of art has always aroused lively reactions by questioning accepted norms, how can social requirements and creativity be reconciled?

Encouraging contemporary creation, giving to the liberty of the artist the means to create it, is a political act which should be entirely unaffected by the "lottery" of election results even if such independence is all the more difficult because the gap between the creative artist and the public has widened over a century. We still expect beautiful objects from artists, whereas what they want is to renew our awareness of the universe by working directly on our everyday environment. For the hardest thing to accept

Dani Karavan (1930):
Main Axis: The Tower, 1985-1986.
Height 118'.
Cergy–Pontoise, France.

Gérard Singer (1929):
Le Canyoneaustrate, project for Paris-Bercy,
1982-1986. Two views.

Michael Heizer (1944):
180° Element of 45°90°180°, 1984.
8¼′ high, 18′ wide, 20′ deep.
Rice University, Houston, Texas.

is that certain special people can change our lives, that their artistic freedom can open up new horizons. Nevertheless, we must trust the artist. He is the only one to distrust the "it goes without saying" attitude because of the nature of his vocation. He is the only person bold enough to pass on his thought and his needs for quality before any other need. He is the only one who can perceive and experience a space that all the rest of us can only apprehend through the filters of the mass media. We should ask ourselves if our society is really qualified to distance itself from acquired or inherited culture in order to subsidize present-day creativity. Can we give the sculptors of today the right to expression, the chance to carry out projects which will only find their meaning and function in their construction? One thing is certain: public art has always supplied the essential documentation of a historical period. In all ages civilizations have left material traces and the evidence left by artists is irreplaceable. If we cannot encourage the free contribution of the artists of today, our age will deprive itself of an essential dimension for the future. For the moment, only one thing is clear: there will be no sculptural art in what remains of the twentieth century unless we can support the intuition of these creative artists, but we must also be convinced that public commissions cannot come before the exigencies of creation. At best, it can only encourage them by recognizing them. Such works might well have remained in the project stage, but for some years now in France (in the context of the New Towns) artists have been associated with town planning, with the architect and sociologist, from the start of the project. More recently they have also been associated with large public commissions. In the United States, for example, thanks to the National Endowment for the Arts (NEA) and the General Service Administration (GSA) and through the generosity of public and private patrons, such major works have been encouraged and able to assume definitive dimensions.

So now the Israeli artist Dani Karavan can at last begin to execute the major artery of Cergy-Pontoise, a stretch of several kilometres where man can rediscover his human dimension and renew his relationship with the elements: water, light and the infinity of space. Gérard Singer, working on the memory of nature, will restore their place to the rock, water and the reflection of the movement of the sky in a monumental fountain for Bercy (the Sports Ground of the city of Paris) which, unlike the nineteenth-century monuments that bristled with *jets d'eau*, will be a lake cascading into a canyon to restore to water its vital and nourishing significance.

All this has also meant that in the United States Michael Heizer has been able to show the violence of nature in the town and George Trakas to create poetic promenades which demand the spectators' participation at all levels of perception. This is the sculpture that our age is awaiting. It is also the sculpture that justifies the whole development of contemporary artistic endeavours.

George Trakas (1944):
Isle of View, 1985.
Steel, stone, wood.
University of Massachusetts, Amherst, Mass.

LIST OF ILLUSTRATIONS